NEW YORK: POEMS

EDITED BY HOWARD MOSS

 AVON
PUBLISHERS OF BARD, CAMELOT AND DISCUS BOOKS

For Chip, Dan, and Veronica

NEW YORK:POEMS is an original publication of Avon Books. This work has never before appeared in book form.

AVON BOOKS
A division of
The Hearst Corporation
959 Eighth Avenue
New York, New York 10019

Copyright © 1980 by Howard Moss
Cover photograph by M. Durrance
Cover design by Kenneth Hine
Published by arrangement with the author
Library of Congress Catalog Card Number: 80-66148
ISBN: 0-380-76067-3

First Avon Printing, September, 1980

AVON TRADEMARK REG. U.S. PAT. OFF. AND IN
OTHER COUNTRIES, MARCA REGISTRADA, HECHO EN
U.S.A.

Printed in the U.S.A.

ACKNOWLEDGMENTS

Conrad Aiken: "Doctors' Row" from COLLECTED POEMS by Conrad Aiken. Copyright © 1953, 1970 by Conrad Aiken. Reprinted by permission of Oxford University Press, Inc.

Grover Amen: "The Cot." Reprinted by permission; Copyright © 1962 The New Yorker Magazine, Inc.

A. R. Ammons: "The City Limits" is reprinted from BRIEFINGS: POEMS SMALL AND EASY, by A. R. Ammons, by permission of W. W. Norton & Company, Inc. Copyright © 1971 by A. R. Ammons.

Philip Appleman: "East Hampton: The Structure of Sound." Reprinted from OPEN DOORWAYS: POEMS by Philip Appleman, by permission of W. W. Norton & Company, Inc. Copyright © 1976 by W. W. Norton & Company, Inc.

John Ashbery: "The Wrong Kind of Insurance." From HOUSEBOAT DAYS by John Ashbery. Copyright © 1977 by John Ashbery. Originally appeared in *The New Yorker*. Reprinted by permission of Viking Penguin, Inc.

W. H. Auden: "City without Walls." Copyright © 1968 by W. H. Auden. Reprinted from W. H. AUDEN: COLLECTED POEMS, edited by Edward Mendelson, by permission of Random House, Inc.

Ben Belitt: "Battery Park, High Noon." Reprinted from THE ENEMY JOY by permission of Ben Belitt. Copyright © 1964 by Ben Belitt. "Xerox" reprinted by permission; Copyright © 1973 The New Yorker Magazine, Inc.

John Berryman: "The Statue" from SHORT POEMS by John Berryman. Copyright 1948 by John Berryman. Copyright renewed © 1976 by Kate Berryman. Reprinted with the permission of Farrar, Straus & Giroux, Inc.

Elizabeth Bishop: "From the Country to the City," "Letter to N. Y.," "Love Lies Sleeping," "The Man-Moth," "Varick Street," from THE COMPLETE POEMS by Elizabeth Bishop. Copyright © 1936, 1937, 1938, 1940, 1947, 1969 by Elizabeth Bishop. Copyright renewed © 1968, 1974 by Elizabeth Bishop. Reprinted with the permission of Farrar, Straus & Giroux, Inc.

Morris Bishop: "The Witch of East Seventy-Second Street." Reprinted by permission; Copyright © 1953 The New Yorker Magazine, Inc.

Paul Blackburn: "The Assassination of President McKinley," "Getting a Job," "In Winter," "Mother, in the 45¢ Bottle." From IN. ON. OR ABOUT THE PREMISES by Paul Blackburn. Copyright © 1968 by Paul Blackburn. Reprinted by permission of Viking Penguin, Inc. "The Stone." Reprinted by permission; Copyright © 1965 The New Yorker Magazine, Inc.

Robert Bly: "The Great Society" from THE LIGHT AROUND THE BODY by Robert Bly. Copyright © 1962 by Robert Bly. Reprinted by permission of Harper & Row, Publishers, Inc.

CONTENTS

INTRODUCTION

"Rapid transit"—the official designation of New York's subway system—serves as an apt description of the city's life as a whole. Even an ordinary day in New York is one of innumerable rapid transitions, none more astonishing than the lighting up, every night, of its skyline. A drab grid of perpendicular streets and avenues transmutes itself into a magic theater of electric images. The monumental becomes spectral, the commonplace romantic. Of all the cities in the world, New York is the most dramatic, and its transformations of movement and of light quicken the pulse rate, the blinking of an eye, the swing of a walker heading uptown.

That quickening (in a double sense of the word) occurs also in the poems collected here, transformations of another kind: moments of pure feeling, some of them; histories of desperation or hope; note-takings of the phenomenal; musings on loneliness, connection, isolation, joy. They are documentaries of the spirit, outcries of the body, commentaries of the intellect. Some poems have specific addresses or tell the reader what it's like to spend the night at a particular hotel. In others, the protagonists stand on corners, look down from windows, watch the river barges, wander through graveyards, or loll on rooftops. They are caught in traffic on the way to the country, or returning. They survive heatwaves and blizzards.

To catch the shifts of New York, the beholder, it seems, either has to be steeped in the city and approach it from inside out, or has to drop in on it occasionally, perhaps furtively, to see it in a manner outside the range of native observation. Anyone who knows New York and reads poetry for pleasure would see no disparity between the New York he finds in Frank O'Hara and the one he discovers in L. E. Sissman—the first freewheeling, rhapsodic, intimate; the second formal, cultivated, wide-angled. The close-up can be illuminating, the oblique view arresting.

From either vantage point, a version of nature emerges from these poems by default, as if some long-abandoned country were to be rediscovered, but only in bits and pieces. Elizabeth Bishop once said that if you listened closely to conversation in New York you would become aware of how frequently animals are mentioned, a kind of subtext to the dialogue one hears at dinner parties, chance meetings, lunches. And I think a case could be made for New York poems being by nature elegiac. Nature itself is being yearned for, mourned, or denied. The parks, rivers, trees, birds, flowers, and plants of New York are the last things to be associated with it, if at all; yet to New Yorkers they are significant connections to childhood, important backgrounds to events—they keep the scale human. There is, in these poems, an undercurrent, a running regret, perhaps, that sounds a small musical theme hardly heard in the large orchestration of subways, sirens, horns, voices (in English and Spanish), radios, TV sets, jet planes, and traffic. That regret can have a delicious undertone, the way nostalgia can be redeeming or the sadness of fall pleasurable. In the ruthlessness and indifference of a great city, whatever produces feeling has value, and in New York, the surprising facts of weather, the migration of birds, the trees coming alive each spring under the worst possible conditions have a testamentary quality. If someone—starting at Battery Park and ending up at Washington Heights—were to photograph the plants in the windows of apartments and offices, the pots of geraniums on fire escapes, the gardens, thriving rooftops, terraces, and window boxes of New York, he would end up with millions of photographs. And if dogs and cats were to carry ID cards, the files that contained their duplicates would have to be housed in something resembling a small Pentagon. At the end of subway rides of varying lengths, there is Central Park or Prospect Park, Coney Island and the aquarium, the Brooklyn Botanical Gardens, the Bronx zoo, the suburbs, and the country. Somewhere between a subway stop and a destination, one of the new hole-in-the-wall flower shops may be selling thin roses cupped in a cone of tissue paper or wrapped in yesterday's *Times*.

In putting this anthology together, I tried hard to find poems that would reflect the neighborhoods of New York and had to choose, sometimes, between geographical representation and my sense of what a poem should be. Though Brooklyn has had the good fortune to be represented by poets as accomplished and dissimilar as Walt Whitman, Hart Crane, and Marianne Moore, the Bronx, Staten Island, and Queens were not so lucky. Many poets I admire are absent; New York is not part of their emotional territory. There was more material than I could use, and less. Often, maddeningly, the same place—say, Trinity Church— would be the subject of three good poems, while Chinatown went begging.

Because it is perpetually changing, New York eludes crystallization. Its essential nature—made up of glimpses, contrasts, fleeting encounters—is most tellingly realized in the short story and the poem, forms congenial to their subject. Each keeps the welter of life, the threat of disorientation, just under control; each focuses, compresses, intensifies. Poems, in particular, present opportunities for quick changes of style, pace, and voice. When you turn a corner in New York, you're likely to see something quite different from what you saw a second before. Something similar happens, it is to be hoped, when you turn the pages of this book.

—HOWARD MOSS

NOTE: Several people led me to poems I didn't know and I want to thank Marilyn Hacker, Richard Howard, John Ashbery, John Brinnin, and Robert Phillips. I want also to thank Robert Wyatt, an ideal and patient editor, his assistant, Richard McCoy, for kindnesses beyond the call of duty, and Patrick Merla, whose gifts of organization are phenomenal.

HENRICUS SELYNS

[FIRST DOMINIE OF BROOKLYN]

Epitaph for Peter Stuyvesant

Stir not the *sand* too much, for there lies Stuyvesant,
Who erst commander was of all New Netherland.
Freely or no, unto the foe, the land did he give over.
   If grief and sorrow any hearts do smite, his heart
Did die a thousand deaths and undergo a smart
Insuff'rable. At first, too rich; at last, too *pauvre*.

CONRAD AIKEN

Doctors' Row

BROWNSTONE ECLOGUES

Snow falls on the cars in Doctors' Row and hoods the headlights;
snow piles on the brownstone steps, the basement deadlights;
fills up the letters and names and brass degrees
on the bright brass plates, and the bright brass holes for keys.

Snow hides, as if on purpose, the rows of bells
which open the doors to separate cells and hells:
to the waiting-rooms, where the famous prepare for headlines,
and humbler citizens for their humbler deadlines.

And in and out, and out and in, they go,
the lamentable devotees of Doctors' Row;
silent and circumspect—indeed, liturgical;
their cries and prayers prescribed, their penance surgical.

No one complains—no one presumes to shriek—
the walls are very thick, and the voices weak.
Or the cries are whisked away in noiseless cabs,
while nurse, in the alley, empties a pail of swabs.

Miserable street!—through which your sweetheart hurries,
lowers her chin, as the snow-cloud stings and flurries;
thinks of the flower-stall, by the church, where you
wait like a clock, for two, for half-past two;

thinks of the roses banked on the steps in snow,
of god in heaven, and the world above, below;
widens her vision beyond the storm, her sight
the infinite rings of an immense delight;

all to be lived and loved—O glorious All!
Eastward or westward, Plato's turning wall;
the sky's blue streets swept clean of silent birds
for an audience of gods, and superwords.

GROVER AMEN

The Cot

I stopped in a sidestreet surplus shop, just south of Yorkville,
a holy, antic basement where a butterfish in a bowl and a fierce
    Sahara cat,
a rarity in Manhattan, were guardians of wilderness relics:
    ancestral
buttons, bones of lizards, aggregations of driftwood and coral,
    remaindered
shells. More autumn museum than shop. Its gentle keeper—
in his time, I imagine, an explorer, hunting guide, or harbor
    tugboat captain—
kept for noon naps an outlandish cot in a corner, an antique of
    extinct
canvas and bandied wooden legs, quaint for terrace sleeping
and catching October faiths from the river winds.
                        Kind to young voyagers, the
                            keeper
decreed a just price, and, amidst uprisings of dust, the wild
    desert cat's protestations,
we dismantled the cot, which I carried home in a cab.
And I was warm enough on the cot, curled up like a pioneer,
like a mountain hunter, in a Western roll of blankets.
In the ambient winds were chances of change, scents of East
    River deities,
and there were more stars than usual for Manhattan, restless and
    cold,
as stars should be in October; but it was the windows I carefully
    wondered at,
their lights, by distance, quite warm and wicked, the dangerous
    shades
slightly drawn, to a wilderness watcher, on what promises of
    color

                                               NEW YORK:

and surprise. And although I knew well that, for a quick faith
before
sleep, the least stars are better, I kept to my choice of lights until
the last
windows went out, when, having little knowledge, for all my
pretensions, of dark,
I moved back to my own bed, leaving the wilderness prayer cot
(still good for naps at noon)
adrift in true night with the stars, the river winds and the abstract
faiths of October.

A. R. AMMONS

The City Limits

When you consider the radiance, that it does not withhold
itself but pours its abundance without selection into every
nook and cranny not overhung or hidden; when you consider

that birds' bones make no awful noise against the light but
lie low in the light as in a high testimony; when you consider
the radiance, that it will look into the guiltiest

swervings of the weaving heart and bear itself upon them,
not flinching into disguise or darkening; when you consider
the abundance of such resource as illuminates the glow-blue

bodies and gold-skeined wings of flies swarming the dumped
guts of a natural slaughter or the coil of shit and in no
way winces from its storms of generosity; when you consider

that air or vacuum, snow or shale, squid or wolf, rose or lichen,
each is accepted into as much light as it will take, then
the heart moves roomier, the man stands and looks about, the

leaf does not increase itself above the grass, and the dark
work of the deepest cells is of a tune with May bushes
and fear lit by the breadth of such calmly turns to praise.

PHILIP APPLEMAN

East Hampton: The Structure of Sound

Bedrooms ease their shingles
into the yawning gardens:
the silence sucks at my eardrums
and my skull flowers open like popcorn.
Perpetual Sunday morning:
the quiet spreads out like a meadow.
I loaf and invite my soul,
and it sprawls in the shade like a toadstool.

Mondays, Manhattan is shapely
in the perfect circles of sirens,
the shrill music of taxis
making symmetries, patterns, and bounds:
jackhammers chisel my brain
to correct community standards
as the dawn comes up like thunder
out of Brooklyn, the shaper of sunrise.

JOHN ASHBERY

The Wrong Kind of Insurance

I teach in a high school
And see the nurses in some of the hospitals,
And if all teachers are like that
Maybe I can give you a buzz some day,
Maybe we can get together for lunch or coffee or something.

The white marble statues in the auditorium
Are colder to the touch than the rain that falls
Past the post-office inscription about rain or snow
Or gloom of night. I think
About what these archaic meanings mean
That unfurl like a rope ladder down through history
To fall at our feet like crocuses.

All of our lives is a rebus
Of little wooden animals painted shy,
Terrific colors, magnificent and horrible,
Close together. The message is learned
The way light at the edge of a beach in autumn is learned.
The seasons are superimposed.
In New York we have winter in August
As they do in Argentina and Australia.
Spring is leafy and cold, autumn pale and dry.
And changes build up
Forever, like birds released into the light
Of an August sky, falling away forever
To define the handful of things we know for sure,
Followed by musical evenings.

Yes, friends, these clouds pulled along on invisible ropes
Are, as you have guessed, merely stage machinery,
And the funny thing is it knows we know
About it and still wants us to go on believing
In what it so unskillfully imitates, and wants
To be loved not for that but for itself:
The murky atmosphere of a park, tattered
Foliage, wise old tree trunks, rainbow tissue-paper-wadded
Clouds down near where the perspective
Intersects the sunset so we may know
We, too, are somehow impossible, formed of so many different
          things,
Too many to make sense to anybody.
We straggle on as quotients, hard-to-combine
Ingredients, and what continues
Does so with our participation and consent.

Try milk of tears, but it is not the same.
The dandelions will have to know why, and your comic
Dirge routine will be lost on the unfolding sheaves
Of the wind, a lucky one, though it will carry you
Too far, to some manageable, cold, open
Shore of sorrows you expected to reach,
Then leave behind.
                    Thus, friend, this distilled,
Dispersed musk of moving around, the product
Of leaf after transparent leaf, of too many
Comings and goings, visitors at all hours.
                              Each night
Is trifoliate, strange to the touch.

W. H. AUDEN

City without Walls

"Those fantastic forms, fang-sharp,
Bone-bare, that in Byzantine painting
Were a shorthand for the Unbounded
Beyond the Pale, unpoliced spaces
Where dragons dwelt and demons roamed,

"Colonized only by ex-worldlings,
Penitent sophists, and sodomites,
Are visual facts in the foreground now,
Real structures of steel and glass:
Hermits, perforce, are all today,

"With numbered caves in enormous jails,
Hotels designed to deteriorate
Their glum already corrupted guests,
Factories in which the functional
Hobbesian man is mass-produced.

"A key to the street each convict has,
But the Asphalt Lands are lawless marches
Where gangs clash and cops turn
Robber barons: reckless he
Who walks after dark in that wildnerness.

"But electric lamps allow nightly
Cell meetings where subcultures
May hold palaver, like-minded,
Their tongues tattooed by the tribal jargon
Of the vice or business that brothers them:

"And mean cafés to remain open
Where, in bad air, belly-talkers,
Weedy-looking, work-shy,
May spout unreason, some ruthless creed
To a dozen dupes till dawn break.

"Every workday Eve fares
Forth to the stores her foods to pluck,
While Adam hunts an easy dollar:
Unperspiring at eventide
Both eat their bread in boredom of spirit.

"The weekend comes that once was holy,
Free still but a feast no longer,
Just time out, idiorrhythmic,
When no one cares what his neighbor does:
Now newsprint and network are needed most.

"What they view may be vulgar rubbish,
What they listen to witless noise,
But it gives shelter, shields them from
Sunday's Bane, the basilisking
Glare of Nothing, our pernicious foe.

"For what to Nothing shall nobodies answer?
Still super-physiques are socially there,
Frequently photographed, feel at home,
But ordinary flesh is unwanted:
Engines do better what biceps did.

"And soon computers may expel from the world
All but the top intelligent few,
The egos they leisure be left to dig
Value, virtue from an invisible realm
Of hobbies, sex, consumption, vague

"Tussles with ghosts. Against Whom
Shall the Sons band to rebel there,
Where Troll-Father, Tusked-Mother
Are dream-monsters like dinosaurs
With a built-in obsolescence?

"A Gadgeted Age, yet as unworldly
As when faintly the light filtered down
On the first men in Mirkwood,
Waiting their turn at the water hole
With the magic beasts who made the paths.

"Small marvel, then, if many adopt
Cancer as the only offered career
Worth-while, if wards are full of
Gents who believe they are Jesus Christ
Or guilty of the Unforgivable Sin:

"If arcadian lawns where classic shoulders,
Baroque bottoms make beaux gestes
Is too tame a dream for the dislocated,
If their lewd fancies are of flesh debased
By damage, indignities, dirty words:

"If few now applaud a play that ends
With warmth and pardon the word to all
As, blessed, unbamboozled, the bridal pairs,
Rustic and oppidan, in a ring-dance
Image the stars at their stately bransels:

"If all has gone phut in the future we paint,
Where, vast and vacant, venomous areas
Surround the small sporadic patches
Of fen and forest that give food and shelter,
Such home as they have, to a human remnant,

"Stunted in stature, strangely deformed,
Numbering by fives, with no zero,
Worshipping a juju *General Mo*,
In groups ruled by grandmothers,
Hirsute witches who, on winter nights,

"Fable them stories of fair-haired elves
Whose magic made the mountain dam,
Of dwarves, cunning in craft, who smithied
The treasure hoards of tin cans
They flatten out for their hut roofs. . . .

"Still moneyed, immune, stands Megalopolis:
Happy he who hopes for better,
What awaits Her may well be worse."

Thus I was thinking at three A.M.
In mid-Manhattan till interrupted,
Cut short by a sharp voice:

"What fun and games you find it to play
Jeremiah-*cum*-Juvenal.
Shame on you for your *Schadenfreude!*"

"My!" I blustered. "How moral we're getting!
A pococurante? Suppose I were,
So what, if my words are true."

Thereupon, bored a third voice:
"Go to sleep now for God's sake!
You both will feel better by breakfast time."

BEN BELITT

Battery Park, High Noon

1
Suddenly the old fancy has me!
                    Suddenly,
Between flint and glitter, the leant leaf,
The formal blueness blooming over slate,

Struck into glass and plate,
The public tulips, treading meridian glare
In bronze and whalebone by the statue-bases
   Elude the Battery square,
      Turn, with a southern gesture, in remembered air,
        And claim a loved identity, like faces. . . .

2

Compute the season out of height and heat:
Cubes in the poised shaft dwindle; tackle moves;
Descending diners paddle into the grooves
And burst from bolts and belts upon the street.

Summer deploys upon the brims of hats;
Turns upon twill; affirms with colored drinks
A mimic solstice poised in flying inks
In Babylons of ribbons and cravats.

Here thoroughfares are blind upon the sea—
Enter the packed paths where the lanes converge
That drop the derelict stragglers by the surge,
Like targets in a shooting gallery.

In middle sleep, below the list of bells
That turn soft answers to a barge's brass,
These take their length in quarantines of grass,
Among the pigeons and the peanut shells.

Their capbrims crush out day. Fullfillments leap,
Sudden as bludgeons, in a vacuum:
They answer to the pricking of a thumb,
And serve him more than slumber, who would sleep.

(A stricter sleep I guess, with double dread,
Who waken now and dream these sleepers dead—
And yet, these are my dream that dream the lie,
And keep their sleep more deathfully than I.)

Bend then to seaward. The element you ask
Rarer than sea is, wantoner than time;
You bear it on you, strangely, like a mask,
And dream the sailing in a pantomime:

The element is blood; tired voyager, turn:
The reckoning you take is yet to learn.
Somber, at fullest flood, the continents ride,
And break their beaches in a sleeper's side.

3

Follow the loll of smoke, fallow over water,
The expense of power in retentive stone,
Where the barge takes the ripple with an organ tone—
Over water, over roof, over catchpenny green,
Into time-to-come and what-has-been:

    Into the wells of chimneys, into the smother of cisterns,
    Resin and amber shed on divided flame:
    Into the quick of the burning, combustion's vehement heart
    Flying the summery floor,
    Beating its pure pulse on the violet core—
    Into the million years' flowering . . . the ageless green . . .
    The sunken frond
    The charmed marine:
    Time's incorruptible, biding, through char and pulp
    The ceaseless diamond.

O lost and mythic scene,
Move yet within this frame!
This is that angel, whether gem or flower—
Leaven and gum and flint—
Recalled from carbon in explicit power,
Whose massive slumber wears the pure impress
Of old renewal and first fruitfulness,
Pledging the fern's shape in primordial tinder,
Sealing, in herb and mint,
The healing in the cinder.

Measure again the ruinous floor of the world,
Beyond the parkpath and the seaward paling,
The equal faces, stunned with light and void,
Tranced as in surmise, lost between myth and mood,
Derelict, decoyed,
In some astonished dream of sailing. . . .

BEN BELITT

Xerox

The original man lies down to be copied
face down on glass. He thinks what it is
to be other than he was, while the pilot light
goes garnet, a salamander's eye
blinks in the cave of the camera, green burns like the skin
of the water seen by a surfacing swimmer,
and the moving and shaking begin.

"What must be, to be many?" thinks the singular
man. Underneath, in the banked fluorescence, the rollers
are ready. A tarpaulin falls. A humming of flanges
arises, a sound like the meeting of rails
when power slams out of the fuses. A wick explodes
in the gasses—and under the whole of his length
the eye of the holocust passes.

And all that was lonely, essential, unique
as a fingerprint, is doubled. Substance and essence,
the mirror and the figure that printed the mirror,
the deluge that blackened creation and the hovering pigeon
with the taste of the leaf in his beak,
are joined. The indivisible sleeper is troubled;
"What does it mean to be legion?"

he cries in the hell of the copied. The rapists, the lovers,
the stealers of blessings, the corrupt and derivative
devils, whirl over the vacant emulsion.
The comedian peers from the brink and unsteadily copies
its laughter. The agonist prints its convulsion.
Like turns to like, while the seminal man on the glass
stares at his semblance and calls from the pit of the ink,

"Forgive our duplicity. We are human
and heterogeneous. Give us our imitations!
Heart copies heart with the arrow and lace
of a festival. The Athenian dream and the adulterers paired
in the storm tell us the mirrors are misted. The whole of our art
is to double our witness, and wait." And the original man on the
    plate
stands and steps down, unassisted.

JOHN BERRYMAN

The Statue

The statue, tolerant through years of weather,
Spares the untidy Sunday throng its look,
Spares shopgirls knowledge of the fatal pallor
Under their evening colour,
Spares homosexuals, the crippled, the alone,
Extravagant perception of their failure;
Looks only, cynical, across them all
To the delightful Avenue and its lights.

Where I sit, near the entrance to the Park,
The charming dangerous entrance to their need,
Dozens, a hundred men have lain till morning
And the preservative darkness waning,
Waking to want, to the day before, desire
For the ultimate good, Respect, to hunger waking;
Like the statue ruined but without its eyes;
Turned vaguely out at dawn for a new day.

Fountains I hear behind me on the left,
See green, see natural life springing in May
To spend its summer sheltering our lovers,
Those walks so shortly to be over.
The sound of water cannot startle them
Although their happiness runs out like water,
Of too much sweetness the expected drain.
They trust their Spring; they have not seen the statue.

Disfigurement is general. Nevertheless
Winters have not been able to alter its pride,
If that expression is a pride remaining,
Coriolanus, and Rome burning,
An aristocracy that is no more.
Scholars can keep their pity; from the ceiling
Watch blasted and superb inhabitants,
The wreck and justifying ruined stare.

Since graduating from its years of flesh
The name has faded in the public mind
Or doubled: which is this? The elder? Younger?
The statesman or the traveller?
Who first died, or who edited his works,
The lonely brother due to remain longer
By a quarter-century than the first born
Of that illustrious and lost family?

The lovers pass. Not one of them can know
Or care which Humboldt is immortalized.
If they glance up, they glance in passing,
An idle outcome of that pacing
Which never stops, and proves them animal;
These thighs, breasts, pointed eyes are not their choosing,
But blind insignia by which are known
Season, excitement loosed upon this city.

Turning: the brilliant Avenue, red, green,
The laws of passage; marvellous hotels;
Beyond, the dark apartment where one summer
Night an insignificant dreamer,
Defeated occupant, will close his eyes
Mercifully on the expensive drama
Wherein he wasted so much skill, such faith,
And salvaged less than the intolerable statue.

ELIZABETH BISHOP

From the Country to the City

The long, long legs,
league-boots of land, that carry the city nowhere,
nowhere; the lines
that we drive on (satin-stripes on harlequin's
trousers, tights);
his tough trunk dressed in tatters, scribbled over with
nonsensical signs;
his shadowy, tall dunce-cap; and, best of all his
shows and sights,

his brain appears, throned in "fantastic triumph,"
    and shines through his hat
with jeweled works at work at intermeshing crowns,
    lamé with lights.
As we approach, wickedest clown, your heart and head,
    we can see that
glittering arrangement of your brain consists, now,
    of mermaid-like,
seated, ravishing sirens, each waving her hand-mirror;
    and we start at
series of slight disturbances up in the telephone wires
    on the turnpike.
Flocks of short, shining wires seem to be flying sidewise.
    Are they birds?
They flash again. No. They are vibrations of the tuning-fork
    you hold and strike
against the mirror-frames, then draw for miles, your dreams,
    out countrywards.
We bring a message from the long black length of body:
    "Subside," it begs and begs.

ELIZABETH BISHOP

Letter to N.Y.

FOR LOUISE CRANE

In your next letter I wish you'd say
where you are going and what you are doing;
how are the plays, and after the plays
what other pleasures you're pursuing:

taking cabs in the middle of the night,
driving as if to save your soul
where the road goes round and round the park
and the meter glares like a moral owl,

and the trees look so queer and green
standing alone in big black caves
and suddenly you're in a different place
where everything seems to happen in waves,

and most of the jokes you just can't catch,
like dirty words rubbed off a slate,
and the songs are loud but somehow dim
and it gets so terribly late,

and coming out of the brownstone house
to the gray sidewalk, the watered street,
one side of the buildings rises with the sun
like a glistening field of wheat.

—Wheat, not oats, dear. I'm afraid
if it's wheat it's none of your sowing,
nevertheless I'd like to know
what you are doing and where you are going.

ELIZABETH BISHOP

Love Lies Sleeping

Earliest morning, switching all the tracks
that cross the sky from cinder star to star,
coupling the ends of streets
to trains of light,

NEW YORK:

now draw us into daylight in our beds;
and clear away what presses on the brain:
    put out the neon shapes
    that float and swell and glare

down the gray avenue between the eyes
in pinks and yellows, letters and twitching signs.
    Hang-over moons, wane, wane!
    From the window I see

an immense city, carefully revealed,
made delicate by over-workmanship,
    detail upon detail,
    cornice upon façade,

reaching so languidly up into
a weak white sky, it seems to waver there.
    (Where it has slowly grown
    in skies of water-glass

from fused beads of iron and copper crystals,
the little chemical "garden" in a jar
    trembles and stands again,
    pale blue, blue-green, and brick.)

The sparrows hurriedly begin their play.
Then, in the West, "Boom!" and a cloud of smoke.
    "Boom!" and the exploding ball
    of blossom blooms again.

(And all the employees who work in plants
where such a sound says "Danger," or once said "Death,"
    turn in their sleep and feel
    the short hairs bristling

on backs of necks.) The cloud of smoke moves off.
A shirt is taken off a threadlike clothes-line.
    Along the street below
    the water-wagon comes

throwing its hissing, snowy fan across
peelings and newspapers. The water dries
    light-dry, dark-wet, the pattern
    of the cool watermelon.

I hear the day-springs of the morning strike
from stony walls and halls and iron beds,
    scattered or grouped cascades,
    alarms for the expected:

queer cupids of all persons getting up,
whose evening meal they will prepare all day,
    you will dine well
    on his heart, on his, and his,

so send them about your business affectionately,
dragging in the streets their unique loves.
    Scourge them with roses only,
    be light as helium,

for always to one, or several, morning comes,
whose head has fallen over the edge of his bed,
    whose face is turned
    so that the image of

the city grows down into his open eyes
inverted and distorted. No. I mean
    distorted and revealed,
    if he sees it at all.

ELIZABETH BISHOP

The Man-Moth*

            Here, above,
cracks in the buildings are filled with battered moonlight.
The whole shadow of Man is only as big as his hat.
It lies at his feet like a circle for a doll to stand on,
and he makes an inverted pin, the point magnetized to the moon.
He does not see the moon; he observes only her vast properties,
feeling the queer light on his hands, neither warm nor cold,
of a temperature impossible to record in thermometers.

            But when the Man-Moth
pays his rare, although occasional, visits to the surface,
the moon looks rather different to him. He emerges
from an opening under the edge of one of the sidewalks
and nervously begins to scale the faces of the buildings.
He thinks the moon is a small hole at the top of the sky,
proving the sky quite useless for protection.
He trembles, but must investigate as high as he can climb.

            Up the façades,
his shadow dragging like a photographer's cloth behind him,
he climbs fearfully, thinking that this time he will manage
to push his small head through that round clean opening
and be forced through, as from a tube, in black scrolls on the
        light.
(Man, standing below him, has no such illusions.)
But what the Man-Moth fears most he must do, although
he fails, of course, and falls back scared but quite unhurt.

*Newspaper misprint for "mammoth."

Then he returns
to the pale subways of cement he calls his home. He flits,
he flutters, and cannot get aboard the silent trains
fast enough to suit him. The doors close swiftly.
The Man-Moth always seats himself facing the wrong way
and the train starts at once at its full, terrible speed,
without a shift in gears or a gradation of any sort.
He cannot tell the rate at which he travels backwards.

Each night he must
be carried through artificial tunnels and dream recurrent dreams.
Just as the ties recur beneath his train, these underlie
his rushing brain. He does not dare look out the window,
for the third rail, the unbroken draught of poison,
runs there beside him. He regards it as a disease
he has inherited the susceptibility to. He has to keep
his hands in his pockets, as others must wear mufflers.

If you catch him,
hold up a flashlight to his eye. It's all dark pupil,
an entire night itself, whose haired horizon tightens
as he stares back, and closes up the eye. Then from the lids
one tear, his only possession, like the bee's sting, slips.
Slyly he palms it, and if you're not paying attention
he'll swallow it. However, if you watch, he'll hand it over,
cool as from underground springs and pure enough to drink.

ELIZABETH BISHOP

Varick Street

At night the factories
struggle awake,
wretched uneasy buildings
veined with pipes
attempt their work.
Trying to breathe,
the elongated nostrils
haired with spikes
give off such stenches, too.
And I shall sell you sell you
sell you of course, my dear, and you'll sell me.

On certain floors
certain wonders.
Pale dirty light,
some captured iceberg
being prevented from melting.
See the mechanical moons,
sick, being made
to wax and wane
at somebody's instigation.
And I shall sell you sell you
sell you of course, my dear, and you'll sell me.

Lights music of love
work on. The presses
print calendars
I suppose; the moons
make medicine
or confectionery. Our bed
shrinks from the soot
and hapless odors
hold us close.
And I shall sell you sell you
sell you of course, my dear, and you'll sell me.

MORRIS BISHOP

The Witch of East Seventy-Second Street

"I will put upon you the Telephone Curse," said the witch.
"The telephone will call when you are standing on a chair with a
     Chinese vase in either hand,
And when you answer, you will hear only the derisive popping of
     corks."
But I was armed so strong in honesty
Her threats passed by me like the idle wind.

"And I will put upon you the Curse of Dropping," said the witch.
"The dropping of tiny tacks, the dropping of food gobbets,
The escape of wet dishes from the eager-grasping hand,
The dropping of spectacles, stitches, final consonants, the
     abdomen."
I sneered, jeered, fleered; I flouted, scouted; I
     pooh-pooh-poohed.

"I will put upon you the Curse of Forgetting!" screamed the
    witch.
"Names, numbers, faces, old songs, old joy,
Words that once were magic, love, upward ways, the way home."
"No doubt the forgotten is well forgotten," said I.

"And I will put upon you the Curse of Remembering," bubbled
    the witch.
Terror struck my eyes, knees, heart;
And I took her charred contract
And signed in triplicate.

PAUL BLACKBURN

The Assassination of President McKinley

Before Trinity Church
on lower Broadway
3:30—3:35 P.M.
while the casket was being lowered into
the grave at Canton, Ohio,

the portals of giant buildings draped in black,
flags flying at half-mast,
the street is jammed dead with people,
maybe half of the men in bowlers and caps
the other half with their heads bared . Some

twenty Lex & Columbus Ave. & Broadway trolleys
stopped as far back as the eye can see on a muggy day,
most everyone jamming the windows murmuring or silent
while the bells of Trinity tolled for 5 minutes .

At Jackson Bros., at 66,
   the first-floor windows equally draped, the drapers,

black, one of the brothers takes
advantage in the back of the store
of the dead stop, of
the new little typist in accounting, makes
her bend over the great rolls of fabric
in the stockroom, lifts the voluminous skirt, pulls
down the sad white bloomers,
      undoes his fly,
          spits on the end of his cock, &
            fucks her, the last rite
for the assassinated Mr. McKinley,
          September 19, 1901
Five minutes of hushed silence, the
bells booming and
schluk-schluk, the soppy petals of cunt, the groans, &
Tyley Jackson's yell of come is drowned, gone
under the final two strokes of Trinity's bell.

PAUL BLACKBURN

Getting a Job

How can we stand the soup?
How can we love the pope?
How can we put up with the cops?
         and we do . . .

But plenty
of Dante
destroys us,
that great light over us

And the light enters the asshole
and the asshole enters the office
and the office records it.

🌱

PAUL BLACKBURN

In Winter

All evidence
of birds is queer,   the

square (it is not
square, inter-
section of 9th & 10th Streets, Second Avenue, near

    (& within the grounds)
      of a church called St. Mark's in-the-Bouwerie
(it is off the Bowery
at least a block of the Bowery)   Bouwerie = -ing farmland
& in this case, the Pieter Stuyvesant farm, well, this square

        is
        filled
        with . young . trees
        which in this case on

a minus-20 morning in February, are filled

                with sparrows
                screaming
as tho this snow were a spring rain somehow

Another day (same month) another
occurrence is clearer : off the Battery
against an ice-blue sky, some gulls
so soundlessly, the
sound of their wings is all, they
glide above the backs of boats, stern,
up, crying, or surrealisticly quiet

And .
in the body of each bird . are . go —

SUMMER CLOUDS / HIGH AND

SWIFT AGAINST THE HORIZON

or else the snow .

PAUL BLACKBURN

Mother, in the 45¢ Bottle

SLOW LINES lay down the curve, curve
from Astor place & Cooper Square down,
center in the eye into
Third
Avenue, the
Bowery, the parallel lines
of light the cock lies limp inside of lines
that join at the top and bottom some old prick
lying curled drunk in the doorway
(the parallel
lines of sleep under the blue argon lights on his old face
down, join at the top and bottom, Cooper Square into Bowery
(parallel lines of

For better or worse,
lights, bars of light
in sickness & in periodic
imitation of death, the fierce
lust in sleep
stiffening of old men

PAUL BLACKBURN

The Stone

The stone found me in bright sunlight
around 9th and Stuyvesant Streets and
found, if not a friend, at
least a travelling companion.
Kicking, we crossed
Third Avenue, then Cooper Square, a-
voiding the traffic in our oblique and
random way, a cab almost got him, and I had
to wait a few seconds, crowding
in from the triangular portion edged about
with signs, safety island, crossed
Lafayette, him catching between the cobbles, then
with a judicious blow
from the toes of my foot (right), well, a
soccer kick aiming for height, we cleared
the curb and turned left down Lafayette,
that long block,
with a wide sidewalk and plenty of room to maneuver
in over metal cellar doorways or swinging
out toward the curb edge. The low worn
curb at 4th was a cinch to make, and

at Great Jones Street the driveway into a
gas station promised no impediment. But
then he rolled suddenly to the right
as though following an old gentleman in a long
coat, and at the same time I was addressed
by a painter I know and his girl on their way
to Washington Square, and as I looked up to
answer,
I heard the small sound. He had fallen
in his run, into water gathered in a sunken
plate which they lift to tighten or loosen
something to do with the city water supply I think,
and sank out of sight.
I spoke to Simeon and Dee
about a loft it turned out he hadn't gotten, but
felt so desolate at having lost him they didn't
stay long, I looked at the puddle, explained
we'd come all the way from beyond Cooper Square,
they hurried away.
I suppose I could have used my hands, picked him
out and continued, he'd have been dry by the time
we got home, but just as I decided to abandon him
the sun disappeared.
I continued on down Bleecker finally,
a warm front moving in from the west, the
cirrus clotting into alto-cumulus, sun seeping through
as the front thickened, but not shining, the air turned
cool, and there were pigeons
circling
over the buildings at
West Broadway, and over them a gull, a
young man with a beard and torn army jacket walked
a big mutt on a short leash teaching him to heel.
The mutt was fine, trotting alongside, nuzzling
lightly at his master's chino pants, the young

man smiled, the dog smiled too, and on they went.
They had each other.
I had left him there in the puddle, our game
over, no fair using hands I had told myself.
Not that he could have smiled.
The sun gone in.
He had been shaped like a drunken pyramid, ir-
regularly triangular.

ROBERT BLY

The Great Society

Dentists continue to water their lawns even in the rain;
Hands developed with terrible labor by apes
Hang from the sleeves of evangelists;
There are murdered kings in the light-bulbs outside movie
  theaters;
The coffins of the poor are hibernating in piles of new tires.

The janitor troubled by the boiler,
And the hotel keeper shuffles the cards of insanity.
The President dreams of invading Cuba.
Bushes are growing over the outdoor grills,
Vines over the yachts and the leather seats.

The city broods over ash cans and darkening mortar.
On the far shore, at Coney Island, dark children
Play on the chilling beach: a sprig of black seaweed,
Shells, a skyful of birds.
While the mayor sits with his head in his hands.

JOHN MALCOLM BRINNIN

Love in Particular

When the orchard that clings to the terrace is boxed for the
      winter
And birds take the sun deck and the first hieroglyph of snow
Sprawls on the darkening side street under crawling cars,
      There is much to be reconsidered
      About the nature of this place;
      Because of all doomed capitals
      Certainly none was less
      Love's climate or to its light more false.

In the encroaching blue of its twilight, the exciting
Approach of still another enormous evening, how many
Desolate figures watch the first lights of Radio City
      Burn for a little while—
      As those who in great harbors,
      Framed in a thousand portholes,
      Attend the huge maneuverings of liners
      And the infinitesimal farewells?

Each to his own fake fireplace, each to his hobby
Of glass elephants that trumpet in duplicate herds
Across twenty square inches of table-top mirror,
      While the modest leaf of love
      Fumes like a steaming orchid
      In the center of the room,
      Costly, rootless, and naked,
      And disappears like flame.

Ah, the swift matings and undernourished affections,
The pledge of troth as tidy as a business deal

Of unexpected advancement with a comfortable equity;
    In their profitless commerce at midnight,
    Pulverous shadows strive
    To gain their random image,
    While bartenders give them nerve
    And the bankers give homage.

To admit this is not an accident but an achievement
Is but to marry St. Patrick's to the Onyx Club
With dancing afterwards and mingling of the guests,
    For in the sacrifice of appetite,
    The angel of love hangs in the sky
    Like a corpse of warning.
    Many murders are in his eye
    Every blessed morning.

The lights and lives that stratify these avenues
Shine at the frayed nerve ends of a prodigious hunger
Not to be answered by a million appetites
    For love without identity
    Or burned to exhaustion in a night
    Of gaiety and anger;
    For the anarchies of appetite
    Are not the feasts of hunger.

Leave it, then, to an impromptu drift of snow,
Some falling, final, graciousness of snow
That brings its trophies and mistakes to burial;
    If to begin again
    Means other faces, other ambitions,
    Love is as long as time
    And as full of notions.
    Let the day perish, let the day come.

NICHOLAS CHRISTOPHER

Big City Glissando

A crowded balcony and she
In white, with a waist
That could fit through a bracelet,
Whispers, "Three dreams in one eye,
A dove bursting out of the other . . ."
Black pitchers of tequila,
Quick music from a corner,
Sallow women and raincoats
Slung over the railing,
Manhattan below, a mix
Of silver and yellow snakes.
Later she complains of the heat,
The winds trapped in white altitudes,
Of the heavy river and its evening jewels,
"Lost stars," she mumbles,
And disappears . . .
In a far room the leaning man
Blows dust off his sleeve,
Directs actors who paint
Words on their faces,
Slips me a note from her,
Yellow ink, an unsure hand:
"Up here the sun melts all of us
As if we had wings . . ."

NICHOLAS CHRISTOPHER

John Garfield

The heat's on, dead wind shoots up
9th Avenue, flutters the T-shirt
On the covertible's antenna, lulls
The stragglers into Billy's Pool Parlour.
The city's last tough guy
Sidles down 44th Street,
Bumming a smoke, feinting a punch—
Used to show a good left, they say . . .
Later, hat doffed, fingers drumming,
He watches East River tugs
Link the bridges with foam;
Whatever left Brooklyn Harbor
In the last war died, or
Maybe is still out at sea.
After Hollywood, the big money,
The girls with the roulette eyes,
He's blacklisted out of pictures
When he won't give names—
"A matinee socialist," McCarthy calls him.
His voice a hoarseness,
Health gone to hell,
The good looks rumpled into anonymity,
He holes up in West Side hotels
With ex-society girls and B-actresses,
In the end drinks
For nine months straight,
Blacks out regularly at dawn,
Dead at 39, journalists delighted
To report an English girl,
Under-aged and on junk,
In bed with him at the time.

Uptown in a Bronx trainyard
Three kids play blackjack
Under a bridge, blow dope
And belt cough medicine,
Tend a low fire—the fastest one,
In black, keeps losing,
Can't pay up, leans back
And watches rain come down
On a southbound express.

ALFRED CORN

Fifty-Seventh Street and Fifth

Hard-edged buildings; cloudless blue enamel;
Lapidary hours—and that numerous woman,
Put-together, in many a smashing
Suit or dress is somehow what it's, well,
All about. A city designed by *Halston*:
Clean lines, tans, grays, expense; no sentiment.
Off the mirrored boxes the afternoon
Glare fires an instant in her sunglasses
And reflects some of the armored ambition
Controlling deed here; plus the byword
That "only the best really counts." Awful
And awe-inspiring. How hard the task,
Keeping up to the mark: opinions, output,
Presentation—strong on every front. So?
Life is strife, the city says, a theory
That tastes of iron and demands assent.

A big lump of iron that's been magnetized.
All the faces I see are—Believers,

Pilgrims immigrated from fifty states
To discover, to surrender, themselves.
Success. Money. Fame. Insular dreams all,
Begotten of the dream of Manhattan, island
Of the possessed. When a man's tired of New York,
He's tired of life? Or just of possession?
A whirlpool animates the terrific
Streets, violence of our praise, blockbuster
Miracles down every vista, scored by
Accords and discords intrinsic to this air.
Concerted mind performs as the genius
Of place: competition, a trust in facts
And expense. Who loves or works here assumes
For better or worse, the ground rules. A fate.

✌

ALFRED CORN

Tokyo West

Eating out alone, one makes solitude
More remarkable. Better this, I suppose,
Than the day I've spent trying to feel actual
In the absence of a human echo. . . .
I sense a counterpart in the waitress,
In fact, each recognizes each from last year;
Sleeker, less urban then, less desperate,
Maybe, but the same person, one who has
Clearly been suffering the strain of exile.
Hypocrites both, we smile.
"Clear soup and sashimi."
Too bad the décor happens to include fish:
Goldf— calico, really; that don't mind being
On display and gambol like kittens in

The bright tank. Hooked over its edge, a tube
Injects a downward fountain of bubbles

That quickly fall back to a ceiling they
Flute. A westerner in barbaric diving
Costume surveys this world through the grilled
Eye of his helmet. Everybody looks
At everybody. And I wonder what
Detail of my appearance so rivets
His attention, that Japanese, whose hair,
Sheared down to teddy-bear fur, rivets my own.
Enough that I'm alone,
No doubt, or don't look away
Fast enough. Oh, here's the soup—clear as mud.
"I'm sorry, didn't you say bean?" "Never
Mind, I'll have this." So few things ever come
Clear anyway. For example, tonight
At my place I've left on the FM, *mf*;
With no one to hear, is there music or not?

What to make of things? Walking home in fog
And cold, full of beans, raw fish, tea, rubbing
Shoulders with so many of us, exiles
And at home—the fat girl in jeans and leather,
The black policeman, the streetwalkers with
High boots, hopes, and Pompadour hair—I feel
The misery that loves company; which may be
A worldwide motive for swarming in cities.
Assemblage of the homeless, on the move,
Apartment, job, lover, self, everything
Improvised, raw, temporary; and I
Discover how strange it is to work all day
Then dine—no, eat—alone,
Like so many others.
Anonymous, at loose ends, finally
I belong. They swim forward to greet me.

GREGORY CORSO

Eastside Incidents

Aside from ashcans & halljohns & pigeoncoops
there were the sad backyards
the hot July stoops
There were those mad Valenti kids who killed my cat
with an umbrella
There was Dirty Myra who screwed the Rabbi's son
in the cellar
And there was Vito & Tony & Robby & Rocco
I see them now
eating poisoned mushrooms and vomiting air
killing Mr. Bloom the storekeeper
and getting the chair
I see them now
but they aren't there

HART CRANE

To Brooklyn Bridge

THIS AND ALL FOLLOWING SELECTIONS
ARE FROM *THE BRIDGE*

How many dawns, chill from his rippling rest
The seagull's wings shall dip and pivot him,
Shedding white rings of tumult, building high
Over the chained bay waters Liberty—

Then, with inviolate curve, forsake our eyes
As apparitional as sails that cross
Some page of figures to be filed away:
—Till elevators drop us from our day . . .

I think of cinemas, panoramic sleights
With multitudes bent toward some flashing scene
Never disclosed, but hastened to again,
Foretold to other eyes on the same screen;

And Thee, across the harbor, silver-paced
As though the sun took step of thee, yet left
Some motion ever unspent in thy stride,—
Implicitly thy freedom staying thee!

Out of some subway scuttle, cell or loft
A bedlamite speeds to thy parapets,
Tilting there momently, shrill shirt ballooning,
A jest falls from the speechless caravan.

Down Wall, from girder into street noon leaks,
A rip-tooth of the sky's acetylene;
All afternoon the cloud-flown derricks turn . . .
Thy cables breathe the North Atlantic still.

And obscure as that heaven of the Jews,
Thy guerdon . . . Accolade thou dost bestow
Of anonymity time cannot raise:
Vibrant reprieve and pardon thou dost show.

O harp and altar, of the fury fused,
(How could mere toil align thy choiring strings!)
Terrific threshold of the prophet's pledge,
Prayer of pariah, and the lover's cry,—

Again the traffic lights that skim thy swift
Unfractioned idiom, immaculate sigh of stars,
Beading thy path—condense eternity:
And we have seen night lifted in thine arms.

Under thy shadow by the piers I waited;
Only in darkness is thy shadow clear.
The City's fiery parcels all undone,
Already snow submerges an iron year . . .

O Sleepless as the river under thee,
Vaulting the sea, the prairies' dreaming sod,
Unto us lowliest sometime sweep, descend
And of the curveship lend a myth to God.

HART CRANE

The Harbor Dawn

Insistently through sleep—a tide of voices—
They meet you listening midway in your dream,
The long, tired sounds, fog-insulated noises:
Gongs in white surplices, beshrouded wails,
Far strum of fog horns . . . signals dispersed in veils.

400 years and more . . . or is it from the soundless shore of sleep that time

And then a truck will lumber past the wharves
As winch engines begin throbbing on some deck;
Or a drunken stevedore's howl and thud below
Comes echoing alley-upward through dim snow.

And if they take your sleep away sometimes
They give it back again. Soft sleeves of sound
Attend the darkling harbor, the pillowed bay;
Somewhere out there in blankness steam

Spills into stream, and wanders, washed away
—Flurried by keen fifings, eddied
Among distant chiming buoys—adrift. The sky,
Cool feathery fold, suspends, distills
This wavering slumber. . . . Slowly—
Immemorially the window, the half-covered chair
Ask nothing but this sheath of pallid air.

And you beside me, blessèd now while sirens   *recalls you to*
Sing to us, stealthily weave us into day—   *your love,*
Serenely now, before day claims our eyes   *there in a*
Your cool arms murmurously about me lay.   *waking dream*
                                                      to merge
                                                      your seed

While myriad snowy hands are clustering at the panes—

> *your hands within my hands are deeds;*
> *my tongue upon your throat—singing*
> *arms close; eyes wide, undoubtful*
> > *dark*
> > > *drink the dawn—*
> *a forest shudders in your hair!*

The window goes blond slowly. Frostily clears.   *—with whom?*
From Cyclopean towers across Manhattan waters
—Two—three bright window-eyes aglitter, disk
The sun, released—aloft with cold gulls hither.

The fog leans one last moment on the sill.   *Who is the*
Under the mistletoe of dreams, a star—   *woman with*
As though to join us at some distant hill—   *us in the*
Turns in the waking west and goes to sleep.   *dawn? . . .*
                                                      whose is the
                                                      flesh our feet
                                                      have moved
                                                      upon?

HART CRANE

The Tunnel

*To Find the Western path
Right thro' the Gates of Wrath*
BLAKE

Performances, assortments, résumés—
Up Times Square to Columbus Circle lights
Channel the congresses, nightly sessions,
Refractions of the thousand theatres, faces—
Mysterious kitchens. . . . You shall search them all.
Someday by heart you'll learn each famous sight
And watch the curtain lift in hell's despite;
You'll find the garden in the third act dead,
Finger your knees—and wish yourself in bed
With tabloid crime-sheets perched in easy sight.

> Then let you reach your hat
> and go.
> As usual, let you—also
> walking down—exclaim
> to twelve upward leaving
> a subscription praise
> for what time slays.

Or can't you quite make up your mind to ride;
A walk is better underneath the L a brisk
Ten blocks or so before? But you find yourself
Preparing penguin flexions of the arms,—
As usual you will meet the scuttle yawn:
The subway yawns the quickest promise home.

Be minimum, then, to swim the hiving swarms
Out of the Square, the Circle burning bright—
Avoid the glass doors gyring at your right,
Where boxed alone a second, eyes take fright
—Quite unprepared rush naked back to light:
And down beside the turnstile press the coin
Into the slot. The gongs already rattle.

And so
of cities you bespeak
subways, rivered under streets
and rivers. . . . In the car
the overtone of motion
underground, the monotone
of motion is the sound
of other faces, also underground—

"Let's have a pencil Jimmy—living now
at Floral Park
Flatbush—on the fourth of July—
like a pigeon's muddy dream—potatoes
to dig in the field—travlin the town—too—
night after night—the Culver line—the
girls all shaping up—it used to be—"

Our tongues recant like beaten weather vanes.
This answer lives like verdigris, like hair
Beyond extinction, surcease of the bone;
And repetition freezes—"What

"what do you want? getting weak on the links?
fandaddle daddy don't ask for change—IS THIS
FOURTEENTH? it's half past six she said—if
you don't like my gate why did you
swing on it, why *didja*
swing on it
anyhow—"

And somehow anyhow swing—

The phonographs of hades in the brain
Are tunnels that re-wind themselves, and love
A burnt match skating in a urinal—
Somewhere above Fourteenth TAKE THE EXPRESS
To brush some new presentiment of pain—

"But I want service in this office SERVICE
I said—after
the show she cried a little afterwards but—"

Whose head is swinging from the swollen strap?
Whose body smokes along the bitten rails,
Bursts from a smoldering bundle far behind
In back forks of the chasms of the brain,—
Puffs from a riven stump far out behind
In interborough fissures of the mind . . . ?

And why do I often meet your visage here,
Your eyes like agate lanterns—on and on
Below the toothpaste and the dandruff ads?
—And did their riding eyes right through your side,
And did their eyes like unwashed platters ride?
And Death, aloft,—gigantically down
Probing through you—toward me, O evermore!
And when they dragged your retching flesh,
Your trembling hands that night through Baltimore—
That last night on the ballot rounds, did you
Shaking, did you deny the ticket, Poe?

For Gravesend Manor change at Chambers Street.
The platform hurries along to a dead stop.

The intent escalator lifts a serenade
Stilly
Of shoes, umbrellas, each eye attending its shoe, then
Bolting outright somewhere above where streets
Burst suddenly in rain. . . . The gongs recur:
Elbows and levers, guard and hissing door.
Thunder is galvothermic here below. . . . The car
Wheels off. The train rounds, bending to a scream,
Taking the final level for the dive
Under the river—
And somewhat emptier than before,
Demented, for a hitching second, humps; then
Lets go. . . . Toward corners of the floor
Newspapers wing, revolve and wing.
Blank windows gargle signals through the roar.

And does the Dæmon take you home, also,
Wop washerwoman, with the bandaged hair?
After the corridors are swept, the cuspidors—
The gaunt sky-barracks cleanly now, and bare,
O Genoese, do you bring mother eyes and hands
Back home to children and to golden hair?

Dæmon, demurring and eventful yawn!
Whose hideous laughter is a bellows mirth
—Or the muffled slaughter of a day in birth—
O cruelly to inoculate the brinking dawn
With antennae toward worlds that glow and sink;—
To spoon us out more liquid than the dim
Locution of the eldest star, and pack
The conscience navelled in the plunging wind,
Umbilical to call—and straightway die!

O caught like pennies beneath soot and steam,
Kiss of our agony thou gatherest;
Condensed, thou takest all—shrill ganglia
Impassioned with some song we fail to keep.
And yet, like Lazarus, to feel the slope,
The sod and billow breaking,—lifting ground,
—A sound of waters bending astride the sky
Unceasing with some Word that will not die . . . !

                    *   *   *

A tugboat, wheezing wreaths of steam,
Lunged past, with one galvanic blare stove up the River.
I counted the echoes assembling, one after one,
Searching, thumbing the midnight on the piers.
Lights, coasting, left the oily tympanum of waters;
The blackness somewhere gouged glass on a sky.
And this thy harbor, O my City, I have driven under,
Tossed from the coil of ticking towers. . . . Tomorrow,
And to be. . . . Here by the River that is East—
Here at the waters' edge the hands drop memory;
Shadowless in that abyss they unaccounting lie.
How far away the star has pooled the sea—
Or shall the hands be drawn away, to die?

Kiss of our agony Thou gatherest,
                    O Hand of Fire
                        gatherest—

HART CRANE

Atlantis

*Music is then the knowledge of that which
relates to love in harmony and system.*
PLATO

Through the bound cable strands, the arching path
Upward, veering with light, the flight of strings,—
Taut miles of shuttling moonlight syncopate
The whispered rush, telepathy of wires.
Up the index of night, granite and steel—
Transparent meshes—fleckless the gleaming staves—
Sibylline voices flicker, wavering stream
As though a god were issue of the strings. . . .

And through that cordage, threading with its call
One arc synoptic of all tides below—
Their labyrinthine mouths of history
Pouring reply as though all ships at sea
Complighted in one vibrant breath made cry,—
"Make thy love sure—to weave whose song we ply!"
—From black embankments, moveless soundings hailed,
So seven oceans answer from their dream.

And on, obliquely up bright carrier bars
New octaves trestle the twin monoliths
Beyond whose frosted capes the moon bequeaths
Two worlds of sleep (O arching strands of song!)—
Onward and up the crystal-flooded aisle
White tempest nets file upward, upward ring
With silver terraces the humming spars,
The loft of vision, palladium helm of stars.

Sheerly the eyes, like seagulls stung with rime—
Slit and propelled by glistening fins of light—
Pick biting way up towering looms that press
Sidelong with flight of blade on tendon blade
—Tomorrows into yesteryear—and link
What cipher-script of time no traveller reads
But who, through smoking pyres of love and death,
Searches the timeless laugh of mythic spears.

Like hails, farewells—up planet-sequined heights
Some trillion whispering hammers glimmer Tyre:
Serenely, sharply up the long anvil cry
Of inchling æons silence rivets Troy.
And you, aloft there—Jason! hesting Shout!
Still wrapping harness to the swarming air!
Silvery the rushing wake, surpassing call,
Beams yelling Æolus! splintered in the straits!

From gulfs unfolding, terrible of drums,
Tall Vision-of-the-Voyage, tensely spare—
Bridge, lifting night to cycloramic crest
Of deepest day—O Choir, translating time
Into what multitudinous Verb the suns
And synergy of waters ever fuse, recast
In myriad syllables,—Psalm of Cathay!
O Love, thy white, pervasive Paradigm . . . !

We left the haven hanging in the night—
Sheened harbor lanterns backward fled the keel.
Pacific here at time's end, bearing corn,—
Eyes stammer through the pangs of dust and steel.
And still the circular, indubitable frieze
Of heaven's meditation, yoking wave
To kneeling wave, one song devoutly binds—
The vernal strophe chimes from deathless strings!

O Thou steeled Cognizance whose leap commits
The agile precincts of the lark's return;
Within whose lariat sweep encinctured sing
In single chrysalis the many twain,—
Of stars Thou art the stitch and stallion glow
And like an organ, Thou, with sound of doom—
Sight, sound and flesh Thou leadest from time's realm
As love strikes clear direction for the helm.

Swift peal of secular light, intrinsic Myth
Whose fell unshadow is death's utter wound,—
O River-throated—iridescently upborne
Through the bright drench and fabric of our veins;
With white escarpments swinging into light,
Sustained in tears the cities are endowed
And justified conclamant with ripe fields
Revolving through their harvests in sweet torment.

Forever Deity's glittering Pledge, O Thou
Whose canticle fresh chemistry assigns
To wrapt inception and beatitude,—
Always through blinding cables, to our joy,
Of thy white seizure springs the prophecy:
Always through a spiring cordage, pyramids
Of silver sequel, Deity's young name
Kinetic of white choiring wings . . . ascends.

Migrations that must needs void memory,
Inventions that cobblestone the heart,—
Unspeakable Thou Bridge to Thee, O Love.
Thy pardon for this history, whitest Flower,
O Answerer of all,—Anemone,—
Now while thy pedals spend the suns about us, hold—
(O Thou whose radiance doth inherit me)
Atlantis,—hold thy floating singer late!

So to thine Everpresence, beyond time,
Like spears ensanguined of one tolling star
That bleeds infinity—the orphic strings,
Sidereal phalanxes, leap and converge:
—One Song, one Bridge of Fire! Is it Cathay,
Now pity steeps the grass and rainbows ring
The serpent with the eagle in the leaves . . . ?
Whispers antiphonal in azure swing.

VICTOR HERNANDEZ CRUZ

going uptown to visit miriam

on the train
old ladies playing football
going for empty seats

very funny persons

the train riders
are silly people
i am a train rider

but no one knows where i am
going to take this train

to take this train
to take this train

the ladies   read popular
paperbacks   because they
are popular   they get off
at 42 to change for the
westside line   or off
59 for the department store

the train pulls in & out
the white walls   dark-
ness   white walls   dark-
ness

ladies looking up i
wonder where they going
the dentist   pick up
husband pick up wife
pick up kids
pick up ?grass?
to library   to museum
to laundromat   to school

but no one knows where i am
going to take this train

to take this train

to visit miriam
to visit miriam

& to kiss her
on the cheek
& hope i don't
see sonia on the
street

but no one knows where i'm taking
this train
            taking this train
            to visit miriam.

NEW YORK:

E. E. CUMMINGS

plato told

plato told

him:he couldn't
believe it(jesus

told him;he
wouldn't believe
it)lao

tsze
certainly told
him,and general
(yes

mam)
sherman;
and even
(believe it
or

not)you
told him:i told
him;we told him
(he didn't believe it,no

sir)it took
a nipponized bit of
the old sixth

avenue
el;in the top of his head to tell

him

MADELINE DEFREES

In the Hellgate Wind

January ice drifts downriver
thirty years below the dizzy bridge. Careening traffic
past my narrow walk
tells me warm news of disaster. Sun lies
low, can't thaw my lips. I know
a hand's breadth farther down could freeze me solid
or dissolve me beyond reassembling.
Experts jostle my elbow.
They call my name.
My sleeves wear out from too much heart.

When I went back to pick up my life
the habit fit strangely. My hair escaped.
The frigidaire worked hard while I slept my night
before the cold trip home.
Roots of that passage go deeper than a razor
can reach. Dead lights
in the station end access by rail.
I could stand still to fail the danger,
freeze a slash at a time, altitude for anaesthetic.
Could follow my feet in the Hellgate wind
wherever the dance invites them.

The pure leap I cannot take stiffens downstream,
a millrace churned to murder.
The siren cries
at my wrist, flicks my throat, routine
as the river I cross over.

EDWIN DENBY

City without Smoke

Over Manhattan island when gales subside
Inhuman colors of ocean afternoons
Luminously livid, tear the sky so wide
The exposed city looks like deserted dunes.
Peering out to the street New Yorkers in saloons
Identify the smokeless moment outside
Like a subway stop where one no longer stirs. Soon
This oceanic gracefulness will have died.
For to city people the smudgy film of smoke
Is reassuring like an office, it's sociable
Like money, it gives the sky a furnished look
That makes disaster domestic, negotiable.
Nothing to help society in the sky's grace
Except that each looks at it with his mortal face.

REUEL DENNEY

A March with All Drums Muffled
FOR CAPTAIN FROST, EUROPEAN THEATER

A scrim of twilight, dropping on Manhattan,
Grows limestone shadow on our Customs House
Till Africa and Asia, sculptured there,
Show less of grime.

Their physical culture biceps
Are flexed at Bowling Green, a tarnished Ruysdael.
And walkers many, down on lower Broadway,
And many passers hear the pigeon whirr,
And many a person powerfully passes lilacs
That shed spring talc on a provincial grave
And make each walker dream of being born.

Then, to the slot of twilight, into Wall Street's
Pale river door comes on, as if on casters,
A captain, to the first commander's feet
—The Washington at the Treasury whose hand,
Palm down, outstretched, enacts a muted No,
No Money, to the lobbies there below.

Of those who crossed the sea and met with death,
Those Cadmuses with vitamin alphabets
And alternate cold feet in straw-stone squares,
He is the one who seems now to return
—Under the snow of Caesar he has been
This tenth return of our red maple wing,
Sleeping with that old bag who rode the bull,
Europa.

              Equivocal one, still posing as Minerva,
Known at the Public Library, she has taken
All the *placebos* of the pill of wisdom
And cannot get the lice out of her hair
And yet she is a true distraught Madonna
Who took them all as if they were her own.

Now he comes back alone when time is fluent
In double rivers slipping sparkle seaward,
To Broad Street, in its old Egyptian shade,
Where under the temple pent-house of the Banker's,
Commuters run, and crowding at the ferry,
Wave once to Pluto with their evening news.
Autonomous and unannounced he glides
And flickers up along an emptying street
To pause and wait, by an inhuman head,
Reporting to the long-cloaked general's feet.

What makes our guilt an overflowing innocence
Of love and dark grown on the selfsame ground,
As if our being here were childishness
Ashamed to shame what is a faulted dome?
The harvest in the midlands, subsidized,
Is fed by hungers of a Naples orphan
And feathers for many a farm the Eagle's nest
While officer and father, here and calm,
Exchange a glance that marshals all death's field.

❧

JAMES DICKEY

Coming Back to America

We descended the first night from Europe   riding the ship's
    sling
Into the basement. Forty floors of home weighed on us. We
    broke through
To a room, and fell to drinking madly with all those boozing,
    reading

The Gideon Bible in a dazzle of homecoming
        scripture   Assyrian armies
The scythes of chariots blazing like the windows of the city   all
        cast
Into our eyes in all-night squinting beams of unavoidable violent
        glory.
There were a "million dollars in ice cubes" outside our metal
        door;
The dead water clattered down hour after hour as we fought with
        salesmen
For the little blocks that would make whole our long savage
        drinks.
I took a swaying shower, and we packed the whole bathroom of
        towels into
Our dusty luggage, battling paid-for opulence with whatever
        weapon
Came to hand. We slept; I woke up early, knowing that I was
        suffering
But not why. My breath would not stir, nor the room's. I sweated
Ice in the closeness   my head hurt with the Sleep of a
        Thousand Lights
That the green baize drapes could not darken. I got up, bearing
Everything   found my sharp Roman shoes   went
        out   following signs
That said SWIMMING POOL. Flashing bulbs on a red-eyed panel, I
        passed
Through ceiling after ceiling of sleeping salesmen and whores,
        and came out

On the roof. The pool water trembled with the few in their rooms
Still making love. This was air. A skinny girl lifeguard worked
At her nails; the dawn shone on her right leg in a healthy, twisted
        flame.
It made me squint   slick and lacquered with scars   with
        the wild smoky city
Around it   the great breath to be drawn above sleepers
                the hazy

Morning towers. We sat and talked. She said a five-car wreck
Of taxis in Bensonhurst had knocked her out and taken her
    kneecap
But nothing else. I pondered this   the sun shook off a last
    heavy
Hotel   and she leapt and was in the fragile green pool as
    though
I were still sleeping it off eleven floors under her; she turned in a
    water
Ballet by herself   graceful   unredeemable   her tough
    face exactly
As beautiful and integral as the sun come out of the city.
    Vulnerable,

Hurt in my country's murderous speed, she moved   and I
    would have taken
Her in my arms in water throbbing with the passion of travelling
    men,
Unkillable, both of us, at forty stories in the morning   and
    could have
Flown with her   our weightlessness preserved by the magic
    pool drawn from
Under the streets   out of that pond   passing over the
    meaningless
Guardrail   feeling the whole air pulse like water sleepless
    with desperate
Lovemaking   lifting us out of sleep into the city summer dawn
Of hundreds of feet of gray space spinning with pigeons now
    under
Us   among new panels of sun in the buildings blasting light
    silently
Back and forth across streets between them: could have moved
    with her
In all this   over the floods of glare raised up in sheets   the
    gauze

Distances where warehouses strove to become   over the ship
    I had ridden
Home in riding gently   whitely   beneath. Ah, lift us,
    green
City water, as we turn the harbor around with our legs   lazily
    changing
The plan of the city with motions like thistles   like the
    majestic swirling
Of soot   the winged seed of pigeons   and so would have
    held her
As I held my head   a-stammer with light   defending it
    against the terrible
Morning sun of drinkers   in that pain, exalting in the blind
    notion
Of cradling her somewhere above ships and buses   in the air
    like a water
Ballet   dancing deep among the dawn buildings in a purely
    private
Embrace of impossibility   a love that could not have been
    guessed:
Woman   being   idea   temple dancer   tough girl
    from Bensonhurst
With a knee rebuilt out of sunlight   returned-to
    amazement   O claspable
Symbol   the unforeseen on home ground   the thing that
    sustains us forever
In other places!

NEW YORK:

JAMES DICKEY

For the Running of the New York City Marathon

If you would run

If you would quicken the city with your pelting,
Then line up, be counted, and change
Your body into time, and with me through the boxed maze
flee
On soft hooves, saying   all saying in flock-breath
Take me there.

I am against you
And with you: I am second
Wind and native muscle in the streets   my image lost and
discovered
Among yours: lost and found in the endless panes
Of a many-gestured bald-headed woman, caught between
One set of clothes and tomorrow's: naked, pleading in her
wax
For the right, silent words to praise
The herd-hammering pulse of our sneakers,
And the time gone by when we paced
River-sided, close-packed in our jostled beginning,
O my multitudes.   We are streaming from the many to
the one
At a time, our ghosts chopped-up by the windows
Of merchants;   the mirroring store-fronts let us, this one day,
Wear on our heads feet and backs
What we would wish.   This day I have taken in my stride
Swank jogging-suits rayed with bright emblems
Too good for me: have worn in blood-sweating weather
Blizzard-blind parkas and mukluks, a lightning-struck
hairpiece
Or two, and the plumes of displayed Zulu chieftains.

Through the colors of day I move as one must move
        His shadow somewhere on
Farther into the dark.   Any hour now   any minute
        Attend the last rites
     Of pure plod-balance!   Smoke of the sacrificial
Olympic lamb in the Deli!   O swooping and hairline-hanging
   Civic-minded placement of bridges!   Hallelujas of bars!
        Teach those who have trained in the sunrise
        On junk-food and pop, how to rest   how to rise
From the timed city's never-die dead.   Through the
   spattering echo
Of Vulcanized hundreds, being given the finish-line
   hot-foot,
        I am lolloping through to the end,
By man-dressing mannequins clad   by flashes of sun on
   squared rivers

As we breast our own breathless arrival: as we home in,
        Ahead of me   me   and behind me
Winning over the squirrel-wheel's outlasted stillness, on the
   unearthly pull and fall
        Of our half-baked soles, all agony-
        smiles and all winning—

        All winning, one after one.

🌿

ALAN DUGAN

Dedication for a Building

The excavation for the new
clinic of Bellevue Hospital
was littered with knocked bricks,
corrupt plaster, and old ward-

flowers thrown to the blasting-dust.
A cat grinned with the effort
as it chewed a piece of meat
fastened to a Kraft-paper bag
while some man slept off something.
Hell, may the clinic rise to cure
all ills its site is host to,
and not mis-treat the desperate.

ALAN DUGAN

From Rome. For More Public Fountains in New York City

Oh effervescent palisades of ferns in drippage,
the air sounds green by civic watered bronze
fountains in New York City. Hierarchs of spray
go up and down in office: they scour the noons
when hot air stinks to itself from Jersey's smoke
and the city makes itself a desert of cement.
Moses! Command the sun to august temperance!
When water rises freely over force and poises,
cleaning itself in the dirty air, it falls back
on the dolphins, Poseidon, and moss-headed nymphs,
clean with the dirt of air left cleansed by its
clear falling, and runs down coolly with the heat
to its commune, pooling. What public utility!
The city that has working fountains, that lights
them up at night electrically, that does not say
to thirsters at its fountains: DO NOT DRINK!—
that city is well ordered in its waters and drains
and dresses its corruption up in rainbows, false
to the eye but how expressive of a cool truth being.

The unitary water separates, novel on its heights,
and falls back to its unity, discoursing. So let
New York City fountains be the archives of ascent
that teach the low high styles in the open air
and frondage of event! Then all our subway selves
could learn to fall with grace, after sparkling,
and the city's life acknowledge the water of life.

ALAN DUGAN

On Visiting Central Park Zoo

The animals, hanging around in forms,
are each resigned to be what each one is,
imprisoned twice, in flesh first, then in irons.
The Bactrian camel is adjusted or is not
as, with his humps collapsed for lack of need
for water and with useless tufts of hair
like hummocks on the great plains of his flanks,
he stands around in shape and chews
a curd of solace, whether bitter, bland, or sweet,
who knows? Such is his formal pride,
his gargoyle's face remains a stone
assertion as he pisses in between his splayed,
seemingly rachitic legs and stays
that way, in place, for want of something else
to do, caught in his double prison all the time.
Whatever he is, he goes on being what he is,
although ridiculous in forced review,
perseverant in not doing what he need not do.

RICHARD EBERHART

The Tobacconist of Eighth Street

I saw a querulous old man, the tobacconist of Eighth Street.
Scales he had, and he would mix tobacco with his hands
And pour the fragrance in a paper bag.
You walked out selfishly upon the city.

Some ten years I watched him. Fields of Eire
Or of Arabia were in his voice. He strove to please.
The weights of age, of fear were in his eyes,
And on his neck time's cutting edge.

One year I crossed his door. Time had crossed before.
Collapse had come upon him, the collapse of affairs.
He was sick with revolution,
Crepitant with revelation.

And I went howling into the crooked streets,
Smashed with recognition: for him I flayed the air,
For him cried out, and sent a useless prayer
To the disjointed stones that were his only name:

Such insight is one's own death rattling past.

RICHARD EBERHART

Reading Room,
The New York Public Library

In the reading room in the New York Public Library
All sorts of souls were bent over silence reading the past,
Or the present, or maybe it was the future, persons
Devoted to silence and the flowering of the imagination,
When all of a sudden I saw my love,
She was a faun with light steps and brilliant eye
And she came walking among the tables and rows of persons,

Straight from the forest to the center of New York,
And nobody noticed, or raised an eyelash.
These were fixed on imaginary splendours of the past,
Or of the present, or maybe of the future, maybe
Something as seductive as the aquiline nose
Of Eleanor of Aquitaine, or Cleopatra's wrist-locket in Egypt,
Or maybe they were thinking of Juliana of Norwich.

The people of this world pay no attention to the fauns
Whether of this world or of another, but there she was,
All gaudy pelt, and sleek, gracefully moving,
Her amber eye was bright among the porticoes,
Her delicate ears were raised to hear of love,
Her lips had the appearance of green grass
About to be trodden, and her shanks were smooth and sleek.

Everybody was in the splendor of his imagination,
Nobody paid any attention to this splendour
Appearing in the New York Public Library,
Their eyes were on China, India, Arabia, or the Balearics,
While my faun was walking among the tables and eyes
Inventing their world of life, invisible and light,
In silence and sweet temper, loving the world.

FREDERICK FEIRSTEIN

The Boarder

Stubborn Spring pushed through the cold twigs
In the small park across the street
From where Yud Schwartz, the poet, lived
With a deaf butcher and the butcher's wife
In one room cluttered as his grief:
Pictures of his dead wife on his desk
And of Schwartz, Sholem Aleichem and Sholem Asch—
Three cypresses on a Bronx street,
Two of them dead, Yud Schwartz
Cut down as well. His bookcase was
A crypt; his Yiddish tongue was dust;
And she dead a week—
Ruts for the skidding wheels of a Ford.

"How do I feel? I woke at dawn
In a yellow sweat, my sheets wet,
My guts wood, my head stuffed with grass,
With bluebird bones, fragments of poems.
I dressed. Buttoning my shirt was hard,
Believe me. 'There's one choice,' I said.
'Make up your mind!' and I half-walked
Down to the park. Forty-six steps—
I counted every one of them.
The clouds were rinsed of simile,
The sky bluer than Galilee.
The buds were out. I touched them: frail
As a wren's tongue, pale. The earth felt
Like bear's fur. Good, damn it, it's good.

"How do I feel?" He read a poem:
About wind, papers wrapped tight on his calves —
As he walked Sholem Aleichem's streets, the old shops
Gone, slush soaking his shoes—gone poor.
Spanish in the tenement rooms
Where he spent the Sabbath afternoons
With his young wife, his poet-friends,
Peeled yellow apples and munched nuts,
Munched figs, and vowed to eat the world.

In Fall I telephoned. "Who?" said the butcher's wife.
"The poet." "Who?" "The boarder!" "Dead.
Last Spring. He left no money and no clothes."

🌿

FREDERICK FEIRSTEIN

"Grandfather" In Winter

The overcoats are gone from Central Park
—In the sudden Spring.
A clump of leaves, that lay in a white crypt
Of roots for months, loosens, looking for life.
Bare feet of hippies on the sunny walks,
Rock-heaps of pigeons bursting like corn, food
From brown bags, from white hands, from black hands,
Black and white kids kissing in the high rocks,
In the Rodin laps, in the hands of God
Above. Below, an old man, in a rough coat,
Wearing my grandfather's frown, lifts his face
Up to the sun and smiles smacking his lips.
His sky-blue Buchenwald tattoo has healed.
Below him, in the skating-rink, a small

Girl, Jewish, repeats the rings of the park:
The ring of her father skating around her,
The guard around him, the border of the rink
Around him, the rings of the pigeon-walks,
The rings of clouds, of jets, of the young
Sun around it. Me on the parapet,
The blood of the false Spring ringing my heart.
My wife beside me aims her camera at
The girl. The girl falls. The rope jerks. Nine
Iraqi Jews are falling through the air,
The Arab horde around them cheers. *Shema.*
The feet clump like leaves. The eyes turn up: white
Rocks. Israel in winter prepares again
For war. Around the gas-house are the guards,
Around the guards, pogroms: Deserts of dead,
Miles wide and miles thick. The rings around
Her border are of time. Grandfather knows.
His dead eyes scrutinize my eyes. He knows
Tomorrow snow will fall like lead, the news
Will be obituaries, Kaddish will
Be sung. It is the eve of war again:
Shema.

🌱

IRVING FELDMAN

The Handball Players at Brighton Beach

TO DAVID RITZ

And then the blue world daring onward
discovers them, the indigenes, aging,
oiled, and bronzing sons of immigrants,
the handball players of the new world

on Brooklyn's bright eroding shore
who yawp, who quarrel, who shove,
who shout themselves hoarse, don't
get out of the way, grab for odds,
hustle a handicap, all crust,
all bluster, all con and gusto all
on show, tumultuous, blaring,
grunting as they lunge. True,
their manners lack grandeur, and
yes, elsewhere under the sun legs
are less bowed, bellies are less
potted, pates less bald or blanched,
backs less burned, less hairy.
                                    So?
So what! the sun does not snub,
does not overlook them, shines,
and the fair day flares,
the blue universe booms and blooms,
the sea-space, the summer high, focuses
its great unclouded scope in ecstatic
perspection—and you see it too
at the edge of the crowd, edge of the sea,
between multitudes and immensity:
from gray cement ballcourts under
the borough's sycamores' golden boughs,
against the odds in pure speculation
Brighton's handball heroes leap up half
a step toward heaven in burgundy, blue,
or buttercup bathing trunks, in black
sneakers still stylish after forty years,
in pigskin gloves buckled at the wrist
to keep the ball alive, the sun up,
the eye open, the air ardent,
festive, clear, crowded with delight.

EDWARD FIELD

New York

I live in a beautiful place, a city
people claim to be astonished
when you say you live there.
They talk of junkies, muggings, dirt, and noise,
missing the point completely.

I tell them where they live it is hell,
a land of frozen people.
They never think of people.

Home, I am astonished by this environment
that is also a form of nature
like those paradises of trees and grass

but this is a people paradise
where we are the creatures mostly
though thank God for dogs, cats, sparrows, and roaches.

This vertical place is no more an accident
than the Himalayas are.
The city needs all those tall buildings
to contain the tremendous energy here.
The landscape is in a state of balance.
We do God's will whether we know it or not:
Where I live the streets end in a river of sunlight.

Nowhere else in the country do people
show just what they feel—
we don't put on any act.
Look at the way New Yorkers
walk down the street. It says,
I don't care. What nerve,
to dare to live their dreams, or nightmares,
and no one bothers to look.

True, you have to be an expert to live here.
Part of the trick is not to go anywhere, lounge about,
go slowly in the midst of the rush for novelty.
Anyway, beside the eats the big event here
is the streets which are full of love—
we hug and kiss a lot. You can't say that
for anywhere else around. For some
it is the sex part they care about and get—
there's all the opportunity in the world if you want it.
For me it is different:
Out walking, my soul seeks its food.
It knows what it wants.
Instantly it recognizes its mate, our eyes meet,
and our beings exchange a vital energy,
the universe goes on Charge
and we pass by without holding.

EDWARD FIELD

Roaches

An old decrepit city like London
doesn't have any.
They ought to love it there
in those smelly, elegant buildings.
Surely I myself have smuggled some in my luggage
but they obviously don't like the English—
for that alone I should love them.

They are among the brightest
and most attractive of small creatures
though you have to be prepared
for the look of horror
on the faces of out-of-town guests
when a large roach walks across the floor
as you are sipping drinks.
You reach out and swat,
and keeping the conversation going
pick up the corpse and drop it into an ashtray
feeling very New Yorky doing it.
After all, you've got to be tough to live here—
the visitor didn't make it.

Roaches also thrive on it here:
They set up lively communes
in open boxes of rice, spaghetti, and matzohs.
You come in to make coffee in the morning
and find a dead one floating in the kettle
and dots of roach shit on the dishes,
hinting at roachy revels the night before.

If you let them alone
they stop running at the sight of you
and whisker about
taking a certain interest in whatever you are doing,
and the little ones, expecting like all babies to be adored,
frolic innocently in the sink,
even in daytime when grownup roaches rest
after a night of swarming around the garbage bag.
The trouble with this approach is
they outbreed you and take over,
even moving sociably right into your bed.

Which brings up the question, Do they bite?
Some say yes, and if yes,
do they carry oriental diseases?
Even though you have tried to accept them
there comes a point when you find your eyes
studying labels of roach killers on supermarket shelves,
decide to try a minimal approach, buy one,
but when you attack with spray can aimed
they quickly learn to flee.
The fastest of course live to multiply
so they get cleverer all the time
with kamikaze leaping into space,
or zigzagging away,
race into far corners of the apartment
where they drop egg-sacks in their last throes
and start ineradicable new colonies.

When you light the oven
they come out and dance on the hot stove top
clinging with the tips of their toes,
surviving by quick footwork until you swat them.
Or if you spray it first
you have the smell of roaches roasting slowly.

And when you wash them down the drain
without their being certifiably dead
do they crawl up when the coast is clear?
Some even survive the deadliest poisons devised by man
and you have weird, white mutations running about.
Dying, they climb the walls, or up your legs, in agony,
making you feel like a dirty rat,
until they fall upside down with frail legs
waving in the air.

No more half-measures—
it's them or us you finally realize
and decide on nothing less than total fumigation:
The man comes while you are out
and you return to a silent apartment, blissfully roach-free.
You vacuum up the scattered bodies of the unlucky,
pushing down guilty feelings, lonely feelings,
and congratulate yourself.

                                                          You booby,
they have only moved over to the neighbor's
and she too is forced to fumigate,
and just when you are on the princess phone crowing to your
        friends,
back they come, the whole tribe of them,
many gone now
due to their trivial life-span and chemical adversaries
but more numerous than ever with the new born
and all the relatives from next door and the neighborhood with
        them,
you standing there outraged, but secretly relieved
as they swarm into the kitchen from every crevice,
glad to be home, the eternal innocents,
greeting you joyfully.

ROBERT FITZGERALD

Park Avenue

BETWEEN dinner and death the crowds shadow the loom of steel.
Engines dwell among the races; the tragic phrase
Falls silent in the tune and tremble of them.
Spun beyond the sign of the Virgin and bloomed with light
The globe leans into spring;
The daughter from the dead land returns.
Between the edges of her thighs desire and cruelty
Make their twin temples, whereof the columns sunder
In the reverberations of time past and to come.
A pestilence among us gives us life.
Sparks shot to the cylinders explode softly
Sheathing speed in sleep.

JEAN GARRIGUE

Bleecker Street

Two infants vis-à-vis
Laughing, striking softly out
At one another in their carriage,
The American flag set out in bulbs—
The crookt stars and tawdry stripes,
Aren't they bizarre
To advertise a church bazaar
By backs of Spanish melons?
That child in the butcher shop
With lids so fine-cut over such a blue—

Inviolate—
Out of where?
O pure and neat, severe
Sentinel angel!
Life! Sister! A kitten sleeping
Ready to paw out if I scratch behind his ear!
I'm laden with your bread, your milk,
I'm thinking of you just the way
I'd think of lips, hair . . .
I'd sense like a kiss upon the cheek
The way you seem to be upon the air
Like one come from far
To favor us with careless smiles and blinks
Inscrutable!
But where the lamb hangs in his wool
I meet the waiter taking dinner
To my blind old neighbor,
Sick, blind, alone.
Yes, but we're disabled
To meet the many that you are,
You'd stifle us in backrooms of the soul!
There's no strutting we can do
Like my neighbor's pigeons who've brought down
Some straw of snatched-up sunlight in their beaks.
Nothing that you do not contradict,
Our gentle, murderous Enigma!
And night comes round the corner after you . . .

CYNTHIA KRAMAN GENSER

Club 82: Lisa

They're dancing. two step. They let go grab on snap apart
like magnets. And the queens are getting it on all over
New York.

A little dance step there
a little Fred Astaire,

       LISA QUEEN OF QUEENS
       LISA QUEEN SUPREME
       LISA THE NEW MAHOGANY

He spins. catches himself in the mirror figures to win.
hands down. her hips. Brushes her lip with a blue lip.
Her muscles ripple under her black skirt. hip slit.
She works this place with a big blonde in a black kimono.
The blonde leans over the bar two butch old women making
drinks Lisa kisses their hands. The blonde wants to dance.
takes Lisa's man and tells him

      THIS TIME FOR LISA
      O DARLING IT'S YOUR LOVE I NEED
      O GIMME SOME
      GIMME GIMME GIMME SOME

the blonde flashes her gold tooth. tells him the truth but
he's past truth. looped. He's alone on the dance floor.
Gone on splendor her long legs the dead have such long
spanish legs.

At another table sits Frank the Snake. Been sneaking
around before he was born. been snaking till he got
so forlorn and Jimmy, nineteen. Father sells clothes
$180 a week. I live. I live I ain't a freak. Jimmy D.
got the initials to move with. And Lisa well Lisa's
moving on nothing and high heels. fake tits and she
squeals o honey not not yet let's save it for later.

His hands slide off her hips like wind off a tar road
up around Fairbanks. Everyone a 49er everyone a oneliner
who's got a joke? c'mon whose got a joke well I do lisps
Lisa pure Castilian back arching teeth white the line down
a tar road the car stops. Dead. The dead have such long
spanish cars. And her heels leave a mark in the tar six
inches deep while six feet under a ghost wonders who will
take him in her arms, hold him through the long night.

Lisa's boy's a Bronx wop like the rest. First he was
awed by the women now he's charmed by the man. Doesn't
matter what sex he sees the scar on her forehead her arms
flex she's good. Moves. She really moves. To the streets.
Six AM she wants a cab. They stand on the Bowery pale
grey cars pass. Horses of the night. Joey pulls up pulls
it out "got something nice" he says. Flashing. A smile.
Lisa and he talk clothes. "Terry-cloth skirts gonna be
big." Then he sees Jimmy coming up the street the clothier
becomes a father pulling it in his zipper up "What you doin
here? It's fuckin 6 o'clock you and that slut daughter of
mine drinkin your fuckin heads off get in." Motions
to the car hits the daughter Jimmy pulls a knife. Joey
grabs it kicks his gut they drive away minutes later Lisa
laughing like a hawk on fire "Get a cab" she says laughing
"I gotta fix I'm feeling it." The smile goes but the
laughter rolls on down the Bowery expires around Wall Street
where the Neutrals are just beginning a new day.

When he wakes up he feels bad. feels like crying. he
sick/ drunk/ he's paralyzed. hands don't work. When he
reaches for his shirt it feels heavy, stinks, moves like
a shroud over his pale wet head. Grabs his pants, his
shoes, Lisa's spread on the sheets. The light falls on
her dick her long legs head flamed in black the hands of
a workman hips of a dancer the blue-veined neck of a dreamer
lost in dreams and it seems he loves her he loves her he
pulls the covers over her and catches the double C back
home. Sleeps through the white afternoon falling till
he's back on his feet in Málaga the Neutrals holding him
to the wall he closes his eyes. sweet smile playing around
his lips Lisa from a crowd coming to him with deliverance
in her hands his head on a plate the smell of burning in
the leveche blowing out from the hills.

Takes two pills and it goes away a headache he has his
whole life. Says to the wife "I remember something but
I don't know what it is" reaching for a limb of the
imagination, there's nothing there. And he moves over the
land a marked man crying "O my friends have pity on me.
Have pity on me. For I am one touched by the hand of God."

☙

ALLEN GINSBERG

I Am a Victim of Telephone

When I lay down to sleep dream the Wishing Well it rings
"Have you a new play for the brokendown theater?"
When I write in my notebook poem it rings
"Buster Keaton is under the brooklyn bridge on Frankfurt and
    Pearl . . ."
When I unsheath my skin extend my cock toward someone's
    thighs fat or thin, boy or girl
Tingaling—"Please get him out of jail . . . the police are crashing
    down"
When I lift the soupspoon to my lips, the phone on the floor
    begins purring
"Hello it's me—I'm in the park two broads from Iowa . . .
    nowhere to sleep last night . . . hit 'em in the mouth"
When I muse at smoke crawling over the roof outside my street
    window
purifying Eternity with my eye observation of grey vaporous
    columns in the sky
ring ring "Hello this is Esquire be a dear and finish your political
    commitment manifesto"

When I listen to radio presidents roaring on the convention floor
the phone also chimes in "Rush up to Harlem with us and see the
  riots"
Always the telephone linked to all the hearts of the world beating
  at once
crying my husband's gone my boyfriend's busted forever my
  poetry was rejected
won't you come over for money and please won't you write me a
  piece of bullshit
How are you dear can you come to Easthampton we're all here
  bathing in the ocean we're all so lonely
and I lay back on my pallet contemplating $50 phone bill, broke,
  drowsy, anxious, my heart fearful of the fingers dialing, the
  deaths, the singing of telephone bells
ringing at dawn ringing all afternoon ringing up midnight ringing
  now forever.

🌿

ALLEN GINSBERG

Waking in New York

PART II

On the roof cloudy sky fading sun rays
          electric torches atop —
        auto horns — The towers
    with time-hands giant pointing
        late Dusk hour over
          clanky roofs

Tenement streets' brick sagging cornices
        baby white kite fluttering against giant
        insect face-gill Electric Mill
                smokestacked blue & fumes drift up
Red messages, shining high floors,
        Empire State dotted with tiny windows
        lit, across the blocks
of spire, steeple, golden topped utility
        building roofs — far like
        pyramids lit in jagged
                desert rocks —

The giant the giant city awake
        in the first warm breath of springtime
Waking voices, babble of Spanish
        street families, radio music
        floating under roofs, longhaired
                announcer sincerity squawking
                        cigar voice
        Light zips up phallos stories
        beneath red antennae needling
                thru rooftop chimnies' smog
                        black drift thru the blue air —
Bridges curtained by uplit apartment walls,
        one small tower with a light
        on its shoulder below the "moody,water-loving
                                giants"
The giant stacks burn thick grey
        smoke, Chrysler is lit with green,
down Wall street islands of skyscraper
        black jagged in Sabbath quietness —
Oh fathers, how I am alone in this
        vast human wilderness
Houses uplifted like hives off
        the stone floor of the world —
the city too vast to know, too
        myriad windowed to govern
                from ancient halls —

"O edifice of gas!" — Sun shafts
    descend on the highest building's
      striped blocktop a red light
        winks buses hiss & rush
        grinding, green lights
        of north bridges,
            hum roar & Tarzan
            squeal, whistle
            swoops, hurrahs!

Is someone dying in all this stone building?
Child poking its black head out of the womb
    like the pupil of an eye?
Am I not breathing here frightened
          and amazed — ?
Where is my comfort, where's heart-ease,
    Where are tears of joy?
Where are the companions? in
      deep homes in Stuyvesant Town.
      behind the yellow-window wall?
I fail, book fails, — a lassitude,
      a fear — tho I'm alive
and gaze over the descending — No!
peek in the inky beauty of the roofs.

NIKKI GIOVANNI

Nikki Rosa

childhood remembrances are always a drag
if you're Black
you always remember things like living in Woodlawn
with no inside toilet
and if you become famous or something
they never talk about how happy you were to have your mother
all to yourself and
how good the water felt when you got your bath from one of those
big tubs that folk in chicago barbecue in
and somehow when you talk about home
it never gets across how much you
understood their feelings
as the whole family attended meetings about Hollydale
and even though you remember
your biographers never understand
your father's pain as he sells his stock
and another dream goes
and though you're poor it isn't poverty that
concerns you
and though they fought a lot
it isn't your father's drinking that makes any difference
but only that everybody is together and you
and your sister have happy birthdays and very good christ-
masses and I really hope no white person ever has cause to
write about me because they never understand Black love
is Black wealth and they'll probably talk about my hard
childhood and never understand that all the while I was
quite happy

ANDREW GLAZE

Fantasy Street

Feeling all at once imprisoned, I stalk for the door,
as I go closing my coat up. Three gin-and-tonics—
no, I never should have allowed myself to have them.
But the hell with it.
Go!—get out!—get through the blunt glass
and off into the incalculable darkness.
Sure enough: as I burst out, there it is—
freedom! freedom! freedom!

It seems I am going to explode out of my skin,
to shout! By some miracle, I keep my silence.
The lights are amazing and flashing—Fifth Avenue!
The cold is like being struck by a soprano bell:
clear, fine, trembling, penetrating.
An Irish policeman outside Canada House supports the dusk
like a dark column or pedestal.
Shuffling his slow black feet he looks at me warily.
Am I too happy, too feverish? Might I be the camouflage
for our next I.R.A. bomber? Shaking with careless excess,
I push my bike across the south corner
toward 53rd Street, pass St. Thomas Church.
This morning three young French artists
had drawn in chalk near the staircase Delacroix's
portrait of a peasant girl. It is almost half walked-off now,.
ragged in the sodium-vapor light mixed with late sun,
but somehow still thumping with life, like an angry heart.
Suddenly I look up and have
stepped into a furious cockpit of battling cacophonous music.
A bagpiper on the church steps is squawling "Scotland the
    Brave."
The clanless Highland vestment is Macspinningmill tartan.

"Help me get hame" says his sign. A boon he's been asking six
   months.
There's talk he lives on East 76th Street with a Neapolitan
   mother.
Tonight he will not have the street to himself.
Six yellow trucks across the way—
pasted prow to taffrail with signs—squall, screech,
swarmed about by crowds of little men in beards,
tieless shirts, black coats. The speakers jitter and skid,
throwing away horas between the Chassidic hymns.
It is the Lubavitcher bringing us messages from the Rebbe.
They inquire of every soul who passes,
"Are you Jewish?" They shout after us, "Wear phylacteries!
Observe dietary laws!" Shy little men with burning eyes,
they pop like skyrockets showering down on us with
flashing religious courage.
And straight ahead on the corner by the Tishman Building
the steel band won't give up: it hammers wildly, dexterously,
mellifluously, pouring out, over the already earthquake-torn ears
of our intersection, "Yellow Bird."
It is battered to fragments by horas,
diced in the knives of the pipe chanters,
shot down over the crossway by up-to-date piety.
Enough! I run to the corner, almost throw the bike
ahead of me into the street,
fling myself on it like a demon.
A taxi klaxons by, coughing in my ear. Get out!
Fly! from the hell of this music! fly! fly!
At the end of such a day, give me a wonderful gift!
It is given. It's as though a door closes—
silence—all the madness trapped in the intersection
turns in upon itself. Only a hundred feet away
a single violinist scratches at Bach arpeggios
under the beggar's arcade at the back of the church,
uninterrupted, watched over by one serious girl.
And the Museum of Modern Art on the right gleams and billows

like a wave of quiet illumination. Through the ground-floor
    window
Marilyn Monroe's enormous lips poise to eat
a nameless art student looking somewhere else in a timid beret.
And now up the left of the street advances that old beggar
who looks like Khrushchev. He bangs his vicious
steel cane upon the sidewalk like a shoe.
He pierces you with malevolent eyes, snarls.
"Hee!" he whines. "Hee!," jabbing his hand like a threat.
Now I'm gathering speed; everything begins to hurry into a blur,
the people in red, purple, yellow-green, violet
sew themselves along the quilt-strip of the sidewalk like checks.
My time of day! Excitement and events
bob in and out of windows like winking eyes!

Ahead, Sixth Avenue, and the hour
and the kind of weather that makes me take a fierce breath.
The sky is full of clouds weighing hundreds of millions of tons,
overwhelming us like a wonderful painting.
Down southwest, vast new buildings glow with strange colors
like ice-colored blocks of honeycomb candy riddled with yellow
    bees.
Now they fall over toward me under the weight
of enormous lilac and puce cotton cumuli streaked with smoke,
and salmon edges sliding along between upper surfaces of hazy
    blue.
I put my hands up to protect my head.
I look out and nothing has moved—
and yet—don't I know absolutely everything has moved?

So it's all right. On! On! Across the street
fresh kitchen odors from the Hilton:
shrimp and cinnamon from this imitation New Orleans,
bay and thyme, garlic and parsley from that pretension of Paris,
and a smoky broiled steak from a mock Kansas City.
The kitchen ducts snuffle over the marquees like wet commercial
    noses.

I glare at the animal doctor's office across the way.
My wife stood there the other day shouting at the nurse,
who would not ask her boss to look at Peter's gerbil.
Poor thing, with a paw swollen the size of a raisin,
all the local blood stopped by a tangled thread.
What kind of vicious snobbery chooses pet cats over pet mice?
On the second floor above is a sign,
"Stairway to the Stars Bellydance Studio."
I imagine them practicing their Phrygian birth dances,
palpitating from shaking diaphragm to the splay of the groin,
bent over backwards like some antique climax,
an ancient Busby Berkeley musical improvidence
with thousands of finger gongs tingle-ringing,
thousands of stars in galaxies ascending
out of silver quiverings up into the black empyrean.
Where are they now?
I am buffeted by the wind past the Americana Hotel.
I wave to the doorman of the old CBS building.
Proving his manhood, he sneers back.
Why is it I am slowly encroached upon by I don't know what?
The immense trenches of something going to happen
are about to swallow me.
It's after six, I go home like this every day, but still
my heart pounds like a riot policeman's feet, rapidly, gloomily.
By the side of Roseland stands the old black man
I see here often slapping his tennis ball
off the back of the Dance Palace,
catching it again on his worn racquet through the weft of traffic.
His T-shirt says "Old Men Need Love Too."
He holds back his arm till I've passed by.
Thank you! I shake my head to drive away the fear
that relentlessly extends its wires.
Eighth Avenue at 6:15, and traffic like Ney's final
cavalry charge at Waterloo. Stupid, enormous, brutal,
meaningless—you can almost see the empty-headed marshal
whacking the brass guns with the furious butt of his sword.

And now I know something *is* happening. From across the
     boulevard
it catches my ear and eye.
Underneath bilious street lights some vast mob
is pouring out of the church in the center of the block,
each carrying a vespers candle.
And over them the sky has poured closer
as the buildings droop, against a half-darkness
of invisible sunset in front of which the clouds
dip and rise, stately, like great black-and-orange whales
spuming with anger.
Beyond the choir and the escort of police cars
I hear a flapping torn screaming,
a red banner of fire sirens and police cars
pasting together toward me across the extremities of sound.
What's happening? Is the Last Judgment arriving?
On a ragged spring evening when we know it's impossible
to put up with one more day of the old winter's ugliness?
No! No!—I get down, I hurry my bicycle
along past the army of illuminated penitents.
I drift beside them watching, presided over
by a sky full of brooding, distant, frightened wails.
Their soft faces over the candles are peaceful,
even earnestly fatuous, overborne with importance and duty.
"What we are doing"—they shine—"is so
very urgently necessary for this city—for us!"

But now I hurry past them
to the place where there are sounds of everything burning up
and thieves coming through all the windows.
Vast rivers of candles are turning north.
I wait, biting my lip as they pass by to the last baby.
I catapult my imagination
to the front of the Bodega Garcia,
where twenty-five of my neighbors wait quietly
standing on the sidewalk with beer cans.
It's cocktail hour.

Frantically I urge them, Look up at the windows of my house!
Find out what's happening!
Is everyone there broken on the floor?
Is my kitchen crammed with policemen
looking at cut throats? Or are they—Is everyone gone?
Snatched away to Little Neck or Patchogue?
"Wait! Wait! Christ, don't go, even if you are dying,
wait for me! I'm coming, I want to go, too!"
My heart crowded with catastrophes, I vault across,
half running, half riding,
thick with foreboding and excitement,
pick up my bicycle and stumble up the stairs,
face full of tears.

PAUL GOODMAN

The Lordly Hudson

"Driver, what stream is it?" I asked, well knowing
it was our lordly Hudson hardly flowing,
"It is our lordly Hudson hardly flowing,"
he said, "under the green-grown cliffs."

Be still, man! no one needs your passionate
suffrage to select this glory,
this is our lordly Hudson hardly flowing
under the green-grown cliffs.

"Driver! has this a peer in Europe or the East?"
"No no!" he said. Home! home!
be quiet, heart! this is our lordly Hudson
and has no peer in Europe or the East,

this is our lordly Hudson hardly flowing
under the green-grown cliffs
and has no peer in Europe or the East.
Be patient, Paul! home! home!

HORACE GREGORY

The Lunchroom Bus Boy Who Looked Like Orson Welles

FROM *THE PASSION OF M'PHAIL*

The lunchroom bus boy who looked like Orson Welles,
Romeo, Brutus, and a man from Mars in his two eyes,
the bellhop who was Joe Louis to the life,
the Greek fruit peddler who in church on Sundays
was a lightning-struck dead image of J. P. Morgan,
the Italian barber who in a mirror was more like
John Barrymore than Barrymore himself,
the Woolworth demonstration cold-cream girl
who was Garbo at a glance, only more real,
the shoe clerk who in midnight rain outside of Lindy's
should have been Clark Gable,
the Second Avenue ex-Baptist minister
who was born to have a face like Cordell Hull's—
why do they look at me like that,
why do they stare, sleepwalking through my dreams?
What was the big mistake?

They looked like power and fame,
like love, like everything you need;
and you would think their looks would put them where
they could dictate a letter or run a bank
or kiss a microphone or float a yacht or sleep in
a genuine imitation Marie Antoinette bed
or get somewhere before they die
instead of dropping into dreams too deep
to tell themselves who, what, or where they are
until a fire turns them out into the street
or a shot is heard and the police are at the door.

BARBARA GUEST

The Location of Things

Why from this window am I watching leaves?
Why do halls and steps seem narrower?
Why at this desk am I listening for the sound of the fall
of color, the pitch of the wooden floor
and feet going faster?
Am I to understand change, whether remarkable
or hidden, am I to find a lake under the table
or a mountain beside my chair,
and will I know the minute water produces lilies
or a family of mountaineers scales the peak?

Recognitions

On Madison Avenue I am having a drink, someone
with dark hair balances a carton on his shoulders
and a painter enters the bar. It reminds me
of pictures in restaurants, the exchange of hunger
for thirst, art for decoration, and in a hospital
love for pain suffered beside the glistening rhododendron
under the crucifix. The street, the street bears light
and shade on its shoulders, walks without crying,
turns itself into another and continues, even
cantilevers this barroom atmosphere into a forest
and sheds its leaves on my table
carelessly as if it wanted to travel somewhere else
and would like to get rid of its luggage
which has become in this exquisite pointed rain
a bunch of umbrellas. An exchange!

That head against the window
how many times one has seen it. Afternoons
of smoke and wet nostrils,
the perilous make-up on her face and on his,
numerous corteges. The water's lace creates funerals,
it makes us see someone we love in an acre of grass.

The regard of dramatic afternoons

through this floodlit window
or from a pontoon on this theatrical lake,
you demand your old clown's paint and I hand you
from my prompter's arms this shako,
wandering as I am into clouds and air
rushing into darkness as corridors
who do not fear the melancholy of the stair.

JORGE GUILLÉN

Metropolitan Night

Above a surface of stars,
Night and the city, fabulous,
Shine with great heat.

Upon the asphalt, pale
Jewelry shops reveal
Their depths to all.

Letters of light pronounce—
Grammar of vertigo—
Their fretful rigmarole.

The glistening streets
Are acts of masquerade
That want to be part of earth.

Operas, yes, divine indeed;
Opening out through night
Upon the living stars!

Translated, from the Spanish, by Barbara Howes

THOM GUNN

New York

It wasn't ringworm he
explained it was speed
made those blotches all
over his body
            On the catwalk
above the turning wheels, high
on risk
        his luck
and the resources of the body
kept him going we were
balancing
            up there
                    all night
grinning and panting
hands black with machine oil
grease monkeys of risk
and those wheels were turning *fast*

I return to the sixth floor
where I am staying: the sun
ordering the untidy kitchen,
even the terraced black circles
in the worn enamel are bright,
the faucet dripping,
the parakeets chirping quietly
domestic about their cage,
my dear host in the bed and
his Newfoundland on it, together
stretching, half-woken, as
I close the door.
                        I calm down,
undress, and slip
in between them and think
of household gods.

MARILYN HACKER

Elektra on Third Avenue
FOR LINK

At six, when April chills our hands and feet
walking downtown, we stop at Clancy's Bar
or Bickford's, where the part-time hustlers are,
scoffing between the mailroom and the street.
Old pensioners appraise them while they eat,
and so do we, debating half in jest
which piece of hasty pudding we'd like best.

I know you know I think your mouth is sweet
as anything exhibited for sale,
fresh coffee cake or boys fresh out of jail,
which tender hint of incest brings me near
to ordering more coffee or more beer.
The homebound crowd provides more youth to cruise.
We nurse our cups, nudge knees, and pick and choose.

MARILYN HACKER

Living in the Moment

This is a seasick way,
this almost/never touching, this
drawing-off, this to-and-fro.
ADRIENNE RICH

Two blue glasses of neat
whiskey, epoxy-mended Japanese
ashtray accruing Marlboro and Gauloise
butts, umber and Prussian blue ceramic cups
of Zabar's French Roast, cooling. You acquired
a paunch; I am almost skinny
as I'd like to be. You are probably
right, leaving. We've been here
thousands of miles away, hundreds of times before.

I try to be a woman I could love.
I am probably wrong, asking
you to stay. Blue cotton jersey
turtleneck, navy corduroy Levis,
nylon briefs, boy's undershirt, socks, hiking shoes:
inside (bagged opals, red silk swaddles a
Swiss Army knife) a body nobody sees.
Outside, cars and men screech on Amsterdam Avenue
hundreds of times, before, thousands of miles away,

hidden in cropped hair like a lampshade,
I try to hear what I think I mean.
My thirty-five-year-old white skin wants you
to stroke back twenty-seven-year-old certainty
I'd better doubt. The time-stopped
light hours ago on the smelly East River
glazes my eyes with numbers, years. We both
wear glasses. We both have children
thousands of miles away. Hundreds of times before,

we agree, the nerves' text tricked us
to bad translation. My wrapped sex cups
strong drink. A woman honed words
for this at an oak desk above the Hudson
River in November; cross-legged on woven straw
in a white room in a stucco house; locked
in the bathroom away from the babies, notebook
on her knees. I repeat what we were asking
hundreds of times before. Thousands of miles away

I am leaving you at Heathrow. Revolution
of a dozen engines drowns parting
words, ways: "I should be asking you to stay."
I shouldn't be asking you to stay. We finish
our courage. Tumblers click on the table.
Tumblers click in the lock. I unwrap
cotton and corduroy, nylon and cotton,
wrap up in flannel for the night that started
thousands of miles before, hundreds of times away.

MARILYN HACKER

September

The umber dowagers of Henry Street
gossip from windows while they rest their feet.
The Jew on East Broadway sells rotten fruit.
Last night the cops busted a prostitute;
broke up the crap game in the hall next door—
woke the kids up at almost half past four.
As taken with the ripened fall of words
against the yard as what they saw or heard,
their voices scoop the sun like beautiful
harsh birds, until the cindered yard is dull
with evening, and the regularities
of grubby men and children home to eat.
Two laminated toucans pepper meat
as sunlight sheaths behind the sumac trees.

DANIEL HALPERN

Street Fire

It is past midnight in a thick fog when sirens
call us to the terrace.
We look down onto blossoms of bright fire
opening from manholes on Fifth Avenue.
There are men standing and smoking in rubber jackets
outside a garment-district café,

the lights fluttering, the fire
offering us its electric smoke.
In bare feet and robes—the cat
and dog at our feet—we hear
the heat pound tubes stuffed with wire.
And somewhere down there, under the softening blacktop,
the gas mains wait to take in the whole block.
We bring the two or three small relics of our lives,
the dog and cat, and the elevator to the street.
There is a cold wind and ice in the gutters.
There is the street's midnight population
leaning against the wall of Reverend Peale's Sunday Church.
We note the taxis that deliver strangers
to watch with us as the street shrivels and begins
to flow around the manhole covers.
They are all there: men of the brigade, the police,
women from nearby hotels, their furred men,
the strangers from the city
What we see is the tip of the iceberg,
they tell us—and underneath
the tubes alive with flames.
For an hour we watch from the corner—
in this weather tragedies are distant.
The elevator back up contains the momentary explosion
in the eye where disasters flare—
our section of New York, between the flowers and furs,
is full of bright red petals.
We reach the ninth floor and step into air
powdered with radiator heat.
The tiny, muffled beats of fire below the street
pant through the window an even pulse.
The dog moves into the living room where the fire is dying
on bricks. The cat takes the warm tiles
of the bathroom. We stand silently, listen
a few minutes, then move to each other.

Our own fire is watered by the conviction
that things are right. Later, we listen to the small puffs
of heat spit from the manholes outside, smell
the smoke from live wires
bound with rubber that smolders into morning.

ANTHONY HECHT

Fifth Avenue Parade

Vitrines of pearly gowns, bright porcelains,
Gilded dalmatics, the stone balconies
Of eminence, past all of these and past
The ghostly conquerors in swirls of bronze,
The children's pond, the Rospigliosi Cup,
Prinked with the glitter of day, the chrome batons
Of six high-stepping, slick drum-majorettes,
A local high school band in Robin's Egg Blue,
Envied by doormen, strippers, pianists,
Frogged with emblazonments, all smiles, advance
With victorious booms and fifings through a crowd
Flecked with balloons and flags and popsicles
Toward some weak, outnumbered, cowering North
That will lay down its arms at Eighty-sixth.

ANTHONY HECHT

Third Avenue in Sunlight

Third Avenue in sunlight. Nature's error.
Already the bars are filled and John is there.
Beneath a plentiful lady over the mirror
He tilts his glass in the mild mahogany air.

I think of him when he first got out of college,
Serious, thin, unlikely to succeed;
For several months he hung around the Village,
Boldly T-shirted, unfettered but unfreed.

Now he confides to a stranger, "I was first scout,
And kept my glimmers peeled till after dark.
Our outfit had as its sign a bloody knout,
We met behind the museum in Central Park.

Of course, we were kids." But still those savages,
War-painted, a flap of leather at the loins,
File silently against him. Hostages
Are never taken. One summer, in Des Moines,

They entered his hotel room, tomahawks
Flashing like barracuda. He tried to pray.
Three years of treatment. Occasionally he talks
About how he almost didn't get away.

Daily the prowling sunlight whets its knife
Along the sidewalk. We almost never meet.
In the Rembrandt dark he lifts his amber life.
My bar is somewhat further down the street.

JOHN HOLLANDER

Movie-Going

Drive-ins are out, to start with. One must always be
Able to see the over-painted Moorish ceiling
Whose pinchbeck jazz gleams even in the darkness, calling
The straying eye to feast on it, and glut, then fall
Back to the sterling screen again. One needs to feel
That the two empty, huddled, dark stage-boxes keep
Empty for kings. And having frequently to cope
With the abominable goodies, overflow
Bulk and (finally) exploring hands of flushed
Close neighbors gazing beadily out across glum
Distances is, after all, to keep the gleam
Alive of something rather serious, to keep
Faith, perhaps, with the City. When as children our cup
Of joys ran over the special section, and we clutched
Our ticket stubs and followed the bouncing ball, no clash
Of cymbals at the start of the stage-show could abash
Our third untiring time around. When we came back,
Older, to cop an endless series of feels, we sat
Unashamed beneath the bare art-nouveau bodies, set
High on the golden, after-glowing proscenium when
The break had come. And still, now as always, once
The show is over and we creep into the dull
Blaze of mid-afternoon sunshine, the hollow dole
Of the real descends on everything and we can know
That we have been in some place wholly elsewhere, a night
At noonday, not without dreams, whose portals shine
(Not ivory, not horn in ever-changing shapes)
But made of some weird, clear substance not often used for gates.
Stay for the second feature on a double bill
Always: it will teach you how to love, how not to live,
And how to leave the theater for that unlit, aloof

And empty world again. "B"-pictures showed us: shooting
More real than singing or making love; the shifting
Ashtray upon the mantel, moved by some idiot
Between takes, helping us learn beyond a trace of doubt
How fragile are imagined scenes; the dimming-out
Of all the brightness of the clear and highly lit
Interior of the hero's cockpit, when the stock shot
Of ancient dive-bombers peeling off cuts in, reshapes
Our sense of what is, finally, plausible; the grays
Of living rooms, the blacks of cars whose window glass
At night allows the strips of fake Times Square to pass
Jerkily by on the last ride; even the patch
Of sudden white, and inverted letters dashing
Up during the projectionist's daydream, dying
Quickly—these are the colors of our inner life.

Never ignore the stars, of course. But above all,
Follow the asteroids as well: though dark, they're more
Intense for never glittering; anyone can admire
Sparklings against a night sky, but against a bright
Background of prominence, to feel the Presences burnt
Into no fiery fame should be a more common virtue.
For, just as Vesta has no atmosphere, no verdure
Burgeons on barren Ceres, bit-players never surge
Into the rhythms of expansion and collapse, such
As all the flaming bodies live and move among.
But there, more steadfast than stars are, loved for their being,
Not for their burning, move the great Characters: see
Thin Donald Meek, that shuffling essence ever so
Affronting to Eros and to Pride; the pair of bloated
Capitalists, Walter Connolly and Eugene Pallette, seated
High in their offices above New York; the evil,
Blackening eyes of Sheldon Leonard, and the awful
Stare of Eduardo Cianelli. Remember those who have gone—
(Where's bat-squeaking Butterfly McQueen? Will we see again
That ever-anonymous drunk, waxed-moustached, rubber-legged

Caught in revolving doors?) and think of the light-years logged
Up in those humbly noble orbits, where no hot
Spotlight of solar grace consumes some blazing hearts,
Bestowing the flimsy immortality of stars
For some great distant instant. Out of the darkness stares
Venus, who seems to be what once we were, the fair
Form of emerging love, her nitrous atmosphere
Hiding her prizes. Into the black expanse peers
Mars, whom we in time will come to resemble: parched,
Xanthine desolations, dead Cimmerian seas, the far
Distant past preserved in the blood-colored crusts; fire
And water both remembered only. Having shined
Means having died. But having been real only, and shunned
Stardom, the planetoids are what we now are, humming
With us, above us, ever into the future, seeming
Ever to take the shapes of the world we wake to from dreams.

Always go in the morning if you can; it will
Be something more than habit if you do. Keep well
Away from most French farces. Try to see a set
Of old blue movies every so often, that the sight
Of animal doings out of the clothes of 'thirty-five
May remind you that even the natural act is phrased
In the terms and shapes of particular times and places.
Finally, remember always to honor the martyred dead.
The forces of darkness spread everywhere now, and the best
And brightest screens fade out, while many-antennaed beasts
Perch on the housetops, and along the grandest streets
Palaces crumble, one by one. The dimming starts
Slowly at first; the signs are few, as "Movies are
Better than Ever," "Get More out of Life. See a Movie" Or
Else there's no warning at all and, Whoosh! the theater falls,
Alas, transmogrified: no double-feature fills
A gleaming marquee with promises, now only lit
With "Pike and Whitefish Fresh Today" "Drano" and "Light
Or Dark Brown Sugar, Special." Try never to patronize
Such places (or pass them by one day a year). The noise

Of movie mansions changing form, caught in the toils
Of our lives' withering, rumbles, resounds and tolls
The knell of neighborhoods. Do not forget the old
Places, for everyone's home has been a battlefield.

I remember: the RKO COLONIAL; the cheap
ARDEN and ALDEN both; LOEW'S LINCOLN SQUARE'S bright
    shape;
The NEWSREEL; the mandarin BEACON, resplendently arrayed;
The tiny SEVENTY-SEVENTH STREET, whose demise I rued
So long ago; the eighty-first street, sunrise-hued,
RKO; and then LOEW'S at eighty-third, which had
The colder pinks of sunset on it; and then, back
Across Broadway again, and up, you disembarked
At the YORKTOWN and then the STODDARD, with their dark
Marquees; the SYMPHONY had a decorative disk
With elongated 'twenties nudes whirling in it;
(Around the corner the THALIA, daughter of memory! owed
Her life to Foreign Hits, in days when you piled your coat
High on your lap and sat, sweating and cramped, to catch
"La Kermesse Heroique" every third week, and watched
Fritz Lang from among an audience of refugees, bewitched
By the sense of Crisis on and off that tiny bit
Of screen) Then north again: the RIVERSIDE, the bright
RIVIERA rubbing elbows with it; and right
Smack on a hundredth street, the MIDTOWN; and the rest
Of them: the CARLTON, EDISON, LOEW'S OLYMPIA, and best
Because, of course, the last of all, its final burst
Anonymous, the NEMO! These were once the pearls
Of two-and-a-half miles of Broadway! How many have paled
Into a supermarket's failure of the imagination?

Honor them all. Remember how once their splendor blazed
In sparkling necklaces across America's blasted
Distances and deserts: think how, at night, the fastest
Train might stop for water somewhere, waiting, faced
Westward, in deepening dusk, till ruby illuminations

Of something different from Everything Here, Now, shine
Out from the local Bijou, truest gem, the most bright
Because the most believed in, staving off the night
Perhaps, for a while longer with its flickering light.

These fade. All fade, Let us honor them with our own fading
    sight.

𝒴

JOHN HOLLANDER

Sunday Evenings

All this indigo, nonviolent light will triumph.

Uneven shadows have fallen out of the darkness' that waits,
Continuously created there, as in the whiteness
Of the kitchen two rooms away, icecubes are being made
With a humming of generation. Whether, earlier, it had been
Fine, with sunlight infusing the hints of ice incipient
In the blue air, with promises of gleaming winters
Already trumpeting through the blood and singing *"l'Avenir!"*
Unheard, but pounding somewhere within the inner ear,
Or whether the delaying rains and the two-day-old
Grayness of sky, grayness of generality, had
Spoiled the earlier day for being outside an apartment,
Outside a self—no matter. With night unfolding now
In every corner wherever walls meet or dust collects,
What has just been is obscured. The trickle of time and loss
Condenses along the outside of things: this icy glass
Sweats drops of terror not its own; this room diffuses
Tiny patches of light through its half-shaded windows
Into the winking, myriad galaxies of all

New York on clear October nights—bits of a brightness
It has not, let alone can give; this world inside
These walls, condensing on the outside of my mind,
Has corners and darkenings quite unimaginable,
But visible as Presences in gray and purple light
At this time of day, of week, of year, of life, of time.
Even the usual consolations of Sunday become
A part of all its general threat: symphonic music
On heavy afternoons; the steam-heat, blanketing
A brown couch and a bridge-lamp and dark bookshelves;
No need for a meal, and too much newspaper to be read;
Rooms around this one, full of what is still undone
And what may never be; the glimpses out at tiny,
Unwise revelations of light, from rooms as high up as this,
Several blocks away. And to put an end to the near-
Darkness would hurt too much—a senseless, widening light
From an unfrosted lamp would do it.
                                        But then what?
Why, blinking. Then numbing to the icy fire of incandescence,
Lidded blinds lowering over the windows that overlook
Darknesses of the Park, this room being all the light
In the world now. And then, perhaps, Sunday will have been
        over.

But then what? Oh yes, once, perhaps, in a month of Sundays,
The exciting stars against a clear, cold, black sky
Shone down like promising, wise and truthful splinters of mirror.
We saw that the light was good, and meteored across
The starlight of high Manhattan to ordered arrangements of taxis
And blocks of apartments, and parties of frosty eyes like wide,
Entire mirrors, reflecting in joy the twinkling, burning
High overhead at the end of some windy afternoon.

But then what? The next week was full of itself, and ended,
Inevitable, in the darkening late afternoon, indoors,
On Sunday. Ended? Or was it merely the new week's beginning
Come to a bad end? No matter. Whatever ends up like this—

The day, week, year; the life; the time—can't be worth much.
On Sunday afternoons, one can have followed the blackening
Water of the river from eyes along the Drive
And then climbed up a concrete hill to one's own walls
And quietly opened a vein. *"It would be no crime in me*
To divert the Nile or Danube from its course, were I able
To effect such purposes. Where then is the crime
Of turning a few ounces of blood from their natural channel?"
Or the crime of emptying this late-afternoon room
Of all its indigo, not by the light of common
Illumination, but by a long pouring of darkness?
Yes, if it is permitted, everything is. So let it
Be. And let it be night now, at very long last,
A night outside the cycle of light and dark and Sunday,
A night in despite of fiery life, or icy time
That starts its chilling-out of the heart each week at five
Or five-thirty or so on Sunday, when the big, enlightening myths
Have sunk beyond the river and we are alone in the dark.

JOHN HOLLANDER

West End Blues

The neon glow escapes from
Inside; on a cracked red leather
Booth poets are bursting
Into laugher, half in
Death with easeful love. They
Feign mournful ballads
Made to their mistresses' highbrows

"Lalage, I have lain with thee these many nights"
For example (but I hadn't,
Really, only once, and
When we got to the room
I'd borrowed from a logician
We left all the lights off,
And so in the cloudy morning
She gasped at the sudden, grey sight
Of the newspaper picture of Henry
Wallace tacked up on the wall)

You bastards, my girl's in there,
Queening it up in the half-light

O salacious tavern!
Festus taught me the chords of "Milenberg Joys" there
Far from mid-western places where red sunsets fall
Across railroad tracks, beyond the abandoning
Whistles of trains.   .

They've taken out the bar that lay along the wall
And put one in the middle
Like a bar in Indiana
(Not the old Regulator where there were hardboiled eggs)

"Approchez-vous, Néron, et prenez votre place"
Said Gellius, and there I was, skulking like Barrault
After his big dance in *Les Enfants du Paradis*
When Lemaître takes him out for coffee: "Yes, Ma," I said
While the frightfully rare breed of terrier waddled
From lap to lap, ignoring his dish of sorrowful beer.
And later on in the evening, swimming through the smoke,
Visions of others came upon us as we sat there,
Wondering who we were: Drusus, who followed a dark
Form down along the steps to the water of the river,
Always seemed to have just left for his terrible moment;
Gaius in Galveston, setting out for Dakar,

Was never away. As a bouncy avatar
Of "Bye, Bye Blackbird" flew out of its flaming cage
Of juke-box colored lights yet once more, finally
I would arise in my black raincoat and lurch my way
Out to the street with a shudder. The cold and steamy air
Carrying protein smells from somewhere across the river
Hovered about me, bearing me out of Tonight into
A late hour like any other: as when at five in the morning,
Clatter of milk cans below his window on the street
Measured with hushed, unstressed sounds of her long hair,
Her pillowslip, beside his window on the bed,
Suddenly the exhausted undergraduate sees his prize
Poem taking its shape in a horribly classical meter
—So would the dark of common night well up around me
As the revolving door emptied me onto the street.

Salax taberna! And all you, in there, past the third
Corner away from Athena's corny little owl
Hiding for shame in the academic skirt-folds of Columbia,
Alma Mater, who gazes longingly downtown—
All you, all you in there, lined up along the bar
Or queening it up in the half-light,
Listen to me! No, don't!

Across Broadway and down a bit, the painfully bright
Fluorescence and fierce tile of Bickford's always shone
Omnisciently, and someone sad and crazy said
"God lives in Bickford's"

But that was after we had all become spectres, too,
And eyes, younger eyes, would glisten all unrecognizing
As heads turned,
Interrupting the stories innocently and inaccurately
Being told about us, to watch the revolving door make a tired,
Complete turn, as the shape huddled inside it hardly
Bothered to decide not to go in at all,
Having been steered there only by the heart's mistakes
In the treasonable night; by a kind of broken habit.

RICHARD HOWARD

209 Canal

Not hell but a street, not
Death but a fruit-stand, not
Devils just hungry devils
Simply standing around the stoops, the stoops.

We find our way, wind up
The night, wound uppermost,
In four suits, a funny pack
From which to pick ourselves a card, any card:

Clubs for beating up, spades
For hard labor, diamonds
For buying up rough diamonds,
And hearts, face-up, face-down, for facing hearts.

Dummies in a rum game
We count the tricks that count
Waiting hours for the dim bar
Like a mouth to open wider After Hours.

BARBARA HOWES

At 79th and Park

A cry!—someone is knocked
Down on the avenue;
People don't know what to do
When a walker lies, not breathing.

I watch, 10 storeys high,
Through the acetylene air:
He has been backed up over;
Still the accident

Is hard to credit. A group
Of 14 gathers; the Fire
Department rains like bees,
Visored, black-striped on yellow

Batting, *buzz*—they clamber
Around that globule; somebody
Brings out a comforter
For shroud; a woman's puce

Scarf bobs, from my 10th-floor view,
Desperately; by the backed truck
An arm explains, hacks air
In desperation, though no

One takes much notice. As through
A pail of glass, I see —
Far down—an ambulance,
A doctor come; they slide

Away the stretcher . . . In minutes
The piston-arm, the truck,
Puce, police, bees, group
All have been vacuumed up.

LANGSTON HUGHES

Dive

Lenox Avenue
by daylight
runs to dive in the Park
but faster . . .
faster . . .
after dark.

RICHARD HUGO

Graves in Queens

How long will these graves go on?
How long will my head ache from
that who's-for-loving booze?
Things went well until—but then
time's a damn sad thing—
time and the time it brings—
selection of a casket
in the mid-price range.

God knows I've curbed responses
in response to current trends
and practiced automatic ones.
Secretaries think I'm nice
except that one, but she—
This.curve shows the cost of love
went up in late November
and where it intersects this line
representing the rate of pain
we call point kiss. A damn sad thing.
The stones go on and on.
Caskets must be touching underground.

Now we're welcome at the homes
of those who never spoke before.
Whee. Success. Money coming in.
Welcome at the homes of grovelers
I'm sure. Pigeons I have fed
found better pickings at the dump.
Molding apricots. The faded sign.
Big Lil. Dancer. On at nine.
Eleven. One. Last show. Last gala
strip-down strip-off strip-skin
show with count 'em twenty
gorgeous straight from Vegas and
above all clean cats on at three.
        A damn sad thing.

The morning after a reading
at the YMHA Poetry Center

From my room, a splendid view
of a statue of a stuffy man
who founded Uruguay, a land
I don't believe in although maps
still show it red below Brazil.
Should I say with noble waving
of my arms I'm free? Ah, liberty.
A gasper goo among nonentities.
A bone the dogs are tossing
to the dogs. Big Lil was a cat.
I believe in Paraguay, Peru.
It's the P that makes them real.
The U that starts out Uruguay
is not a P. UP. United Press.
           A damn sad thing.

I never told you. Greenland floats.
Is often Africa when no one looks.
Has been Russia in its time and France.
Is never Italy because of snobbery.
I believe in Greenland. It's the G.
Gee. I'd give the world to see
that old gang of mine. A damn
sad bunch of damn sad things.
Lynn is less one eye in Singapore.
Winslow waits behind the door
that opens only at his feeding time,
a time time's sure to bring.

Last night what poem was it where
Joe Langland brought so many birds
down stone dead through the air?
And where did Claire McAllister
get such blond hair? And still
the graves go on. In Mukilteo,
Washington, the graveyard holds
twenty, maybe, all who died
as I recall by 1910.

I'll not die of course. My health
is perfect. I'll admit the jet
we're on our way to get
might crash in Iowa,
I smoke too much, and once
when thirteen at a seance
a spirit scared me half-to-death
forecasting I'd be killed
by rain. Such a damn sad thing.
And I'll select my casket
in the mid-price range.

The bus and graves go on. Millions—
and the lines of stone all point our way.
A damn sad thing. Let's go home to bed.
You didn't mean a thing when you were living
and you don't mean nothing now you're dead.

DAVID IGNATOW

How Come?

I'm in New York covered by a layer of soap foam.
The air is dense from the top of skyscrapers
to the sidewalk in every street, avenue
and alley, as far as Babylon on the East,
Dobbs Ferry on the North, Coney Island
on the South and stretching far over
the Atlantic Ocean. I wade
through, breathing by pushing
foam aside. The going is slow,
with just a clearing ahead
by swinging my arms. Others are groping

from all sides, too. We keep moving.
Everything else has happened here
and we've survived: snow storms,
traffic tieups, train breakdowns, bursting
water mains; and now I am writing
with a lump of charcoal stuck between my toes,
switching it from one foot to the other—
this monkey trick learned visiting
with my children at the zoo of a Sunday.
But soap foam filling the air,
the bitter, fatty smell of it . . . How come?
My portable says it extends to San Francisco!
Listen to this, and down to the Mexican border
and as far north as Canada. All the prairies,
the Rocky Mountains, the Great Lakes, Chicago,
the Pacific Coast. No advertising stunt
could do this. The soap has welled out of the ground
says the portable suddenly. The scientists report
the soil saturated. And now what?
We'll have to start climbing for air,
a crowd forming around the Empire State Building
says the portable. God help the many
who will die of soap foam.

JOSEPHINE JACOBSEN

49th & 5th, December 13

I passed between the bell and the glass
window. Santa rang his bell. The wax girl leaned
forward: she was naked and had red nails.
Santa wore spectacles and rang his bell.
The second-floor trees raised rainbows in the dusk.

The snow fell lightly. I did not stop to ask
the scarlet man a favor; the girl leaned as if to give
from her wax body blood or heat or love.
But she was wax. Her belly and breasts were shaped;
she wore black pumps and leaned, above the pavement.

The unique snowflake died on the cement.
I passed between her wax eyes and his clapper.
The steelrimmed eyes watched me, the wax eyes watched the
    watcher.

He rang, she leaned, to give me my message: that I must breed
alive unique love from her wax and his steel.

RANDALL JARRELL

The Subway from New Britain to the Bronx

Under the orchid, blooming as it bloomed
In the first black air: in the incessant
Lightning of the trains, tiled swarming tubes
Under the stone and Reason of the states;

Under the orchid flowering from the hot
Dreams of the car-cards, from the black desires
Coiled like converters in the bowels of trade
To break to sunlight in one blinding flame
Of Reason, under the shaking creepers of the isles;

Under the orchid, rank memorial,
From the armature about which crystallized
A life—its tanks, its customers, its Christ—
The rain-forest's tepid siftings leach
Its one solution: of lust, torment, punishment—
Of a man, a man.

Here under the orchid
Of florists, Geography, and flesh,
A little water and a little dirt
Are forever urban, temperate: a West
Dead in the staring Orient of earth.

The air-fed orchid, the unquestioning
Trades of the leaf, of longing, of the isles
Sigh for you, sparrow, the same yearning sigh
Their beasts gave once, in summer, to the bars
And peoples of the Bronx, their conquerors.

🌿

JUAN RAMÓN JIMÉNEZ

Deep Night
NEW YORK, APRIL 27TH

New York deserted—without a person! I walk down Fifth
Avenue, with lots of time, singing aloud. From time to time, I
stop to look at the gigantic and complicated locks in the banks,
the department store windows being changed, the flags flapping
in the night . . . And this sound which my ears, as if inside some
enormous cistern, have taken in unconsciously, coming from I
don't know which street, gets nearer, harder, louder. The sounds
are footsteps, shuffling and limping, they seem to be coming from
above, they constantly approach and never manage to get here. I
stop again and look up the avenue and down. Nothing. The moist
spring moon, with circles under its eyes, the sounds, and I.

Suddenly, I can't tell if far off or near, like the solitary soldier
I saw on the sands of Castille, that evening when the sea wind
was strong, a point or a child, or an animal, or a dwarf—What?
And slowly it comes closer. About to pass. I turn my face and
meet his gaze, the eyes bright, black, red and yellow, larger than

his face, all he is is his gaze. An old Negro, crippled, with a shrunken overcoat and a hat with a faded top, greets me ceremoniously, and then, smiling, goes on up Fifth Avenue . . . A brief shudder goes through me, and with my hands in my pockets I go on, the yellow moon in my face, half singing to myself.

The echo of the crippled Negro, king of the city, makes a turn around the night in the sky, now toward the west.

Translated, from the Spanish, by Robert Bly

JUAN RAMÓN JIMÉNEZ

"In the Subway"
NEW YORK, APRIL 2ND

In the subway. The suffragette, with an ugliness that is positively exhibitionistic, and some stale pastry for a hat, rises toward a red-faced old man who comes in and, with a domineering dignity, offers him her seat. He resists, looking with divine humility at the snow between two Negro women's hats. She takes him by the arm. He becomes indignant and looks as though he might hit someone. She sits him down, once and for all, without speaking. He goes on talking soundlessly, moving his raised hands furiously, a final spark of blood in his clear eyes that are weak and blue.

Translated, from the Spanish, by Robert Bly

PATRICIA JONES

14th St/new york
[EXCERPTS]

I

on the corner where s. klein's used to be
this old woman sits in the summertime/sells
dirty pretzels and antique shopping bags
her wares go untouched
she mumbles to the wind
there should be a sign:

HERE IS A HAVEN FOR FLIES

II

the procession for San Martin de Porres the only
Black Saint I know of was not accompanied by police
escort   it moved through the street oblivious to
the Saturday afternoon traffic the priests wore black
the acolytes wore white over black   the parishioners
wore cloth coats and sensible shoes   the garb of the
religious poor   the statue of San Martin de Porres
bobbed over the heads of the marchers   the cabbies
cursed and swerved   the truckers honked horns the marchers
moved slowly singing a dirge like hymn   two pretty
black girls wore purest white flowers carried flowers   often
smiled *el procesion* de San Martin de Porres shifted
the traffic gently till the cars and trucks till the
curses and sighs joined the slow music   the sad funereal
song for San Martin de Porres the only Black Saint I
know of

IV

on second avenue even in november the corner stays hot
some sister always be signifying between sips of straw-
berry hill or wild irish rose wine
blonde or near blonde women fight with their black pimps
it's a game of defeat plus defeat equals terror—SHUT
UP BITCH/DONCHA KNOW WHO'S TALKING TO
    YOU—slap—
police
shiver on the corner   young latinos chant loose joints
loose joints
once at 3 a.m. or was it four there was a Latin brother
hugging the lamppost on the corner screaming METHADONE
METHADONE   he had on a light cotton shirt colorful snow
was on the ground nobody else on the street 'cept lovers
quarreling or kissing

VI

on the bus the medical personnel: two women and a man
discuss the deterioration of the neighborhood   my black
face before them   they do not mention race there is no
telling   i could be one of them militants or worse just
plain angry   they hint over and around this sorrow but
who can be blamed? why me   why they/the spanish speaking
men at the back of the bus   why us huh   no one says what
they are truly thinking   everyone avoids an incident it's
winter and no one wants an incident on the
crosstown bus

VII

off First Avenue the filipinos sell freshly cut pineapple
there is this fishy sweet scent from the fish and fruit stands
the bank on the corner guards the smells
the clock on the bank's facade almost always is correct
the crosstown bus is almost always slow
a furniture store greets the ascending passengers from the bmt
the wind shifts repeatedly
someone is singing   even late at night
it's lovely here
really
                like a medieval bazaar

ERICA JONG

Walking through the Upper East Side

All over the district, on leather couches
& brocade couches, on daybeds
& "professional divans," they are confessing.
The air is thick with it,
the ears of the analysts must be sticky.

Words fill the air above couches & hover there
hanging like smog. I imagine
impossible Steinberg scrolls,
unutterable sounds suspended in inked curlicues
while the Braque print & the innocuous Utrillo
look on look on look on.

My six analysts, for example—

the sly Czech who tucked his shoelaces
under the tongues of his shoes,
the mistress of social work with orange hair,
the famous old German who said:
"You sink, zerefore you are,"
the bouncy American who loved to talk dirty,
the bitchy widow of a famous theoretician,
& another—or was it two?—I have forgotten—
they rise like a Greek chorus in my dreams.
They reproach me for my messy life.
They do not offer to refund my money.

& the others—siblings for an hour or so—
ghosts whom I brushed in & out of the door.
Sometimes the couch was warm from their bodies.
Only our coats knew each other,
rubbing shoulders in the dark closet.

JUNE JORDAN

Towards a City That Sings

Into the topaz the crystalline signals
of Manhattan
the nightplane lowers my body
scintillate with longing to lie positive
beside
the electric waters of your flesh
and
I will never tell you the meaning of this poem:
Just say, "She wrote it and I recognize
the reference." Please
let it go at that. Although

it is all the willingness you lend
the world
as when you picked it up
the garbage scattering the cool
formalities of Madison Avenue
after midnight (where we walked
for miles as though we knew the woods
well enough to ignore the darkness)
although it is all the willingness you lend
the world
that makes me want
to clean up everything
in sight
(myself included)

for your possible
discovery

VICKIE KARP

The Last Farmer in Queens

Forty years ago a saloon stood where the church is.
Now when he really needs a drink
He walks around to the greenhouse.

He hears, in the glass cold, a trickling hose
Near the pail with the gin bottle in it.
Then, by a tangle of tools, the thick step of a possum
As it backs behind some stacks of shelving.

No distaste more plain than that of the intruder
Intruded upon. Bedded down on the dirt mattress
Of its own shadow, the possum bats its eyes
And lounges on the belief that it can wait forever
To get free.

When he leaves, the empty bottle rattling around
Like an alarm in the tipped pail, the possum
Lumbers out behind: old man and odd sidekick
Avoiding the neighbors
In morning's first blush.

WELDON KEES

Aspects of Robinson

Robinson at cards at the Algonquin; a thin
Blue light comes down once more outside the blinds.
Gray men in overcoats are ghosts blown past the door.
The taxis streak the avenues with yellow, orange, and red.
This is Grand Central, Mr. Robinson.

Robinson on a roof above the Heights; the boats
Mourn like the lost. Water is slate, far down.
Through sounds of ice cubes dropped in glass, an osteopath,
Dressed for the links, recounts an old Intourist tour.
—Here's where old Gibbons jumped from, Robinson.

Robinson walking in the Park, admiring the elephant.
Robinson buying the *Tribune*, Robinson buying the *Times*.
    Robinson
Saying, "Hello. Yes, this is Robinson. Sunday
At five? I'd love to. Pretty well. And you?"
Robinson alone at Longchamps, staring at the wall.

Robinson afraid, drunk, sobbing. Robinson
In bed with a Mrs. Morse. Robinson at home;
Decisions: Toynbee or luminal? Where the sun
Shines, Robinson in flowered trunks, eyes toward
The breakers. Where the night ends, Robinson in East Side bars.

Robinson in Glen-plaid jacket, Scotch-grain shoes,
Black four-in-hand, and oxford button-down,
The jewelled and silent watch that winds itself, the brief-
Case, covert topcoat, clothes for spring, all covering
His sad and usual heart, dry as a winter leaf.

WELDON KEES

from The Hourglass

V

The crew is changed, the stone's face notched in darkness.

Held in the rouged and marketable glow
Beyond Third Avenue, the city hums
Like muffled bees. Sheeted, we lie
Above the streets, where headlights
Search the mirrors through the heat
And move on, reverential over the cement.
—Sleep. But there is no sleep. Far down on Lexington,
A siren moans and dies. A drunk is sobbing
In the hall. Upstairs, an organ record
Of a Baptist hymn comes on. Past one o'clock.
It is the time of seconal, of loss, of
Heartbeats of a clock, enormous, by your bed,
Of noises in the walls,
Of one more drink.—A shadow slides.

Drawn toward the window, I look down like one
Who sees his life spread out upon the pavements
And finds a death renewed. Here, for a time,
I lived, to circumscribe and praise
Such residue of splendor as remained
In the soft mornings and the glow of rooms
At nightfall, ardent with music and the speech of friends,
Knowing, through all that harbored time, the light was lessening.

Now from a corner of the street there comes
A sound like old seeds shaken in a gourd,
Where ghosts take up their wanderings
On routes the owls improvised. A shadow
Slides. And the past instant, charged with loss,
A speck in time, secured, sustained
Between the future and the past
By space—by headlights and the haunted streets—
Endures and is not lost. In Prague,
Above the City Hall, Death's figure stands
Against the dial of a calendar, and sounds a bell
Before the hour strikes. The scythe-man cuts
The old in two, a woodcut on a yellowed page,
Preparing for the young, who will arrive
To find the city marbled with desire. Time
Mows the brittle stalks of autumn as
It stirs the fresh grass, heals all things
And shapes the blood of new wounds. Shadows slide.
The squirrel turns in his cage, shale
Tumbles from a mountain to a road,
A planet surges, plunging, and goes out.

WELDON KEES

Problems of a Journalist

"I want to get away somewhere and re-read Proust,"
Said an editor of *Fortune* to a man on *Time*.
But the fire roared and died, the phoenix quacked like a goose,
And all roads to the country fray like shawls
Outside the dusk of suburbs. Pacing the halls
Where mile-high windows frame a dream with witnesses,
You taste, fantast and epicure, the names of towns along the
     coast,
Black roadsters throbbing on the highways blue with rain
Toward one lamp, burning on those sentences.

"I want to get away somewhere and re-read Proust,"
Said an editor of *Newsweek* to a man on *Look*.
Dachas with telephones, Siberias with bonuses.
One reads, as winter settles on the town,
The evening paper, in an Irving Place café.

WELDON KEES

Relating to Robinson

Somewhere in Chelsea, early summer;
And, walking in the twilight toward the docks,
I thought I made out Robinson ahead of me.

From an uncurtained second-story room, a radio
Was playing *There's A Small Hotel*; a kite
Twisted above dark rooftops and slow drifting birds.
We were alone there, he and I,
Inhabiting the empty street.

Under a sign for Natural Bloom Cigars,
While lights clicked softly in the dusk from red to green,
He stopped and gazed into a window
Where a plaster Venus, modeling a truss,
Looked out at Eastbound traffic. (But Robinson,
I knew, was out of town: he summers at a place in Maine,
Sometimes on Fire Island, sometimes the Cape,
Leaves town in June and comes back after Labor Day.)
And yet, I almost called out, "Robinson!"

There was no chance. Just as I passed,
Turning my head to search his face,
His own head turned with mine
And fixed me with dilated, terrifying eyes
That stopped my blood. His voice
Came at me like an echo in the dark.

"I thought I saw the whirlpool opening.
Kicked all night at a bolted door.
You must have followed me from Astor Place.
An empty paper floats down at the last.
And then a day as huge as yesterday in pairs
Unrolled its horror on my face
Until it blocked—" Running in sweat
To reach the docks, I turned back,
For a second glance. I had no certainty,
There in the dark, that it was Robinson
Or someone else.

The block was bare. The Venus,
Bathed in blue fluorescent light,
Stared toward the river. As I hurried West,
The lights across the bay were coming on.
The boats moved silently and the low whistles blew.

WELDON KEES

Testimonies

"Others at their porches . . ."

I

"I baited bears and prayed. The Queen
Grew inky on Boethius. Between
The angels and the animals we lived and died.
The sun, the King, and my own being blazed as one.
I spoke occasionally to God."

II

"I circumcise my son and laud
The covenant. The massacres go on.
And now, plunder, expulsion. Poisoned fountains drown
The Synagogue. Blood stains the font;
The staff breaks toward the desert in my hands."

III

"I did not see the Grail. Sir John
Lay dying at the bridge. When barbers cut away
Those spongy growths from the poor soldiers' gums,
The whole camp echoed with our cries.
I place the cauldron of God's wrath upon the coals."

IV

"I watch the world contract to this
Gray winter Grub Street where the scavengers
Drop in the cold. The famine spreads more every day.
God save the King, the Army, and the House of Lords!
The rags fall from my arms outside the coffee-house.

V

"I live. The Elevated shudders to a stop
At Twenty-Eighth and Third. Among
The nuns and crippled Negroes, we descend
The stairway to the street, to red-cheeked chromo Christ,
Hung with the bloody calves' heads in the butcher shop."

GALWAY KINNELL

The River That Is East

1

Buoys begin clanging like churches
And peter out. Sunk to the gunwhales
In their shapes tugs push upstream.
A carfloat booms down, sweeping past
Illusory suns that blaze in puddles
On the shores where it rained, past the Navy Yard,
Under the Williamsburg Bridge
That hangs facedown from its strings
Over which the Jamaica Local crawls,
Through white-winged gulls which shriek
And flap from the water and sideslip in
Over the chaos of illusions, dangling
Limp red hands, and screaming as they touch.

2

A boy swings his legs from the pier,
His days go by, tugs and carfloats go by,
Each prow pushing a whitecap. On his deathbed
Kane remembered the abrupt, missed Grail
Called Rosebud, Gatsby must have thought back
On his days digging clams in Little Girl Bay
In Minnesota, Nick fished in dreamy Michigan,
Gant had his memories, Griffeths, those
Who went baying after the immaterial
And whiffed its strange dazzle in a blonde
In a canary convertible, who died
Thinking of the Huck Finns of themselves
On the old afternoons, themselves like this boy
Swinging his legs, who sees the *Ile de France*
Come in, and wonders if in some stateroom
There is not a sick-hearted heiress sitting
Drink in hand, saying to herself his name.

3

A man stands on the pier.
He has long since stopped wishing his heart was full
Or his life dear to him.
He watches the snowfall hitting the dirty water.
He thinks: Beautiful. Beautiful.
If I were a gull I would be one with white wings,
I would fly out over the water, explode, and
Be beautiful snow hitting the dirty water.

4

And thou, River of Tomorrow, flowing . . .
We stand on the shore, which is mist beneath us,
And regard the onflowing river. Sometimes
It seems the river stops and the shore
Flows into the past. Nevertheless, its leaked promises
Hopping in the bloodstream, we strain for the future,
Sometimes even glimpse it, a vague, scummed thing
We dare not recognize, and peer again
At the cabled shroud out of which it came,
We who have no roots but the shifts of our pain,
No flowering but our own strange lives.

What is this river but the one
Which drags the things we love,
Processions of debris like floating lamps,
Towards the radiance in which they go out?
No, it is the River that is East, known once
From a high window in Brooklyn, in agony—river
On which a door locked to the water floats,
A window sash paned with brown water, a whisky crate,
Barrel staves, sun spokes, feathers of the birds,
A breadcrust, a rat, spittle, butts, and peels,
The immaculate stream, heavy, and swinging home again.

GALWAY KINNELL

Room of Return

Room over the Hudson
Where a naked light bulb
Lights coat hangers, whisky bottles,
Umbrellas, anti-war tracts, poems,
A potted plant trimmed to a crucifixion,

From which, out the front window,
You sometimes see
The *Vulcania* or the *France*
Or a fat *Queen*
Steaming through the buildings across the street,

To which every night
The alleycat sneaks up
To slop his saucer
Of fresh milk on the fire escape,
Washing down his rat,

Room crossed by winds from
Air conditioners' back ends,
By the clicking at all hours of invisible looms,
By cries of the night-market, hoofbeats, horns,
By bleats of boats lost on the Hudson,

Room, anyway,
Where I switch the light on
After an absence of years
Tiny glimmer again in this city
Pricking the sky, shelled by the dirty sea.

GALWAY KINNELL

Under the Williamsburg Bridge

1

I broke bread
At the riverbank,
I saw the black gull
Fly back black and crossed
By the decaying Paragon sign in Queens,
Over ripped water, it screamed
Killing the ceremony of the dove,
I cried those wing muscles
Tearing for life at my bones.

2

Tomorrow,
There on the Bridge,
Up in some riveted cranny in the sky,
It is true, the great and wondrous sun will be shining
On an old spider wrapping a fly in spittle-strings.

STANLEY KUNITZ

The Hemorrhage

The people made a ring
Around the man in the park.
He was our banished king
Of blames and staunchless flows,
Exhibitor of the dark
Abominable rose,

Our chief, returned at last
From exile, with the grim
Stamina of the lost,
To show his sovereign hurt.
Wildly we dreaded him
And the strong god of his heart

Escaping, crawling down
Ditches where papers blow,
Smearing the sills of the town,
Strangling the hydra-drains
Coiled under. Stop! We know
How much a man contains.

We picnicked all that day,
Dishonored signs that nayed us,
Pulled marigolds, were gay
Before the apes, smashed glass.
Rifles could not have made us
Keep off the bloody grass;

For we were sick of crimes
Against us, and the head
Pitched on the absorbing Times,
And no one to accuse,
And nothing paid for, and we read,
We read that day what blotted out the news.

SYDNEY LEA

Accident

Never to remember
New York City
Mingus's splendid tirades
Chico   Max
The MJQ   or early Gerry
He rides
His bike shooting out of woods like a switchblade
Onto the lane
In our meadow   where night air
Leaves a slick on the gravel.   This dawn
Has no steam breathing through pavement cobbles
But a purple moth struggles
With the wet burden like Elvin
Jones in a gin-soaked club
And with his half-shucked shell
Into such brief improvisation
Of beauty that if the boy were nearer
Or it were an hour later
(Daytime frogs on the beat
Like morning cops—Ninth at Broadway, dawn,
Twenty years gone—
Or our daughter doing her scat
Voices drowning
The riff of wings like tiny high-hat cymbals)
I would never have noticed

The muted sun like Miles cuts through
The mistflumes' chorus
On the river where mayflies
Loose their shifting hold on pebbles
At the bottom and make their way up
And trout at their stations hover like trebles
In the haysweet hills
The I I think I am
Beats against the snare of the past
And sleep and dream
Hard case
My son repeats
The terrible solo again
And again in his seventh summer
That decrescendo
Dreaming his bike a flyer
Set for the moon like Diz
Last night our baby daughter
Poked a thumb at the ofay moon
And sang, "I want it." She thinks
It's Big Rock Candy. Meatfat and drink
Clash in my sour intestines
Like Monk's odd clusters in the old Half Note
The moth flies up
And clings in splendor to a screen

Hanging in country air
There's the boy's high wail
As his fender shivers like a tambourine

AL LEE

In the Yellow Light of Brooklyn,

When October gets too chilly
At lunch hour,

He is not hungry.
He sleeps more than he wants to,

More than you or I do,
But he thinks of sleep now

Lingering on Court Street.
The rhythm of his job

Is the short breath
He will hear

When he tells her
What he has thought through.

She will choke too.
He will have to tell her

Soon. "Love is not you
And I on a dreamy bed.

Life is not. I love
The girl you dreamed in girlhood

You would become, and the girl
You are at night near a bed lamp

And when we turn it out,
But not when you have things to do.

You are what getting by
Has made of you; I

Am Canarsie. We have come
To ourselves in window envelopes.

The first star of twilight
Cannot be touched. Its twinkling

Blinds me and I fall alone
To my knees on Kings Highway.

I love you. Goodbye. Goodbye."

🖋

AL LEE

Maiden Lane

FOR HILDA, JENNIFER, AND CHRISTINE

Caged back of iron grilles
And ninety-ton doors,
The golden American canary sings
In Lorenzo's limestone palace.

* * *

Children, one boy or girl in twenty
Is American. The gray sky
Is a cloud, it is bathwater—
Above it another sky is blue
Like a summer dress.
Jets whoosh by in polish up there
Bigger than the Santa Maria.

Speak low,
For this is Saturday Downtown,
Where kids had better not holler
At the heroic ambiance of finance.
Deep inside their air-conditioned walls,
The grand dreamers never roll up their sleeves
As they labor on paper with the world's work.

Of the whole world's pretty
And helpful things, half-plus are ours.
They are lumped unevenly on the avenues.
If there were periscopes on the IRT,
We could eye ridges of riches,
We could snort at the arroyos
Of uncollected garbage. Girls,
Worry that the train roars deeper,
The wheels squealing like the hull
Of a submarine about to burst.

RIKA LESSER

527 Cathedral Parkway

Squatting under the weight
of the balcony they support,
four gargoyles in need of cleaning:

The first, hunched over a bowl,
raises a spoon to his gaping mouth—
the Black Hole of Cathedral Parkway.
His right foot has four toes
with lots of dirt between them.
His nose is long, blunt at the tip.
He must be very hungry—lids
lowered, eyes only for his food.

The second is bald, bends
over a book, his filthy beard
caught among the pages. One
eyebrow raised, both eyes dart
to the left; they have a knowing look.
In his right hand a heavy plume.
If he's an artist, the arts are black.

The third, alchemist or cook,
clutches a cauldron. Flames lick
its bottom. He looks younger
than the others, lacks a tooth,
sticks out his tongue, touches
it with a finger.

The fourth, greedy, *very* greedy,
has a whole roast chicken on a platter.
He is not intent on eating, only
on keeping it for himself. His legs
bend in the lotus position; in every
other way he's a dog.

Eastward, their four twin brothers hold up
another balcony, but in a different order:
The Cook, Jack Sprat, Rover, The Leery Sage.
Higher up, over us all,
ten heads as well as two gryphons
drop their blessings on all who pass.

DENISE LEVERTOV

The Cabdriver's Smile

Tough guy. Star of David
and something in Hebrew—a motto—
hang where Catholics used to dangle
St. Christopher (now discredited).
No smile. White hair. American-born,
I'd say, maybe the Bronx.
When another cab pulls alongside
at a light near the Midtown Tunnel, and its driver
rolls down his window and greets this guy
with a big happy face and a first-name greeting,
he bows like a king, a formal acknowledgement,
and to me remarks,
                        deadpan,
            'Seems to think he knows me.'

'You mean you don't know him?'—I lean forward laughing,
close to the money-window.
                        'Never seen him before in my life.'
Something like spun steel floats invisible, until
                                questions strike it,
all round him, the way light gleams webs among
                                grass in fall.

And on we skim
in silence past the cemeteries, into
the airport, ahead of time. He's beat
the afternoon traffic. I tip him well.
A cool acceptance. Cool? It's
cold as ice.

Yet I've seen,
squinting to read his license,
how he smiled—timidly?—anyway,
smiled, as if hoping to please,
at the camera. My heart
stabs me. Somewhere this elderly
close-mouthed skeptic hides
longing and hope. Wanted
—immortalized for the cops, for his fares, for the world—
to be looking his best.

$\mathcal{V}$

PHILIP LEVINE

Get Up

Morning wakens on time
in sub-freezing New York City.
I don't want to get out,
thinks the nested sparrow,
I don't want to get out
of my bed, says my son,
but out in Hudson Street
the trucks are grinding and honking
at United Parcel, and the voices
of loud speakers command us all.
The woman downstairs turns
on the TV and the smoke
of her first sweet joint rises
toward the infinite stopping
for the duration in my nostrils.
The taxpayers of hell are voting
today on the value of garbage,

the rivers are unfreezing
so that pure white swans may ride
upstream toward the secret source
of sweet waters, all the trains
are on time for the fun of it.
It is February of the year 1979
and my 52nd winter is turning
toward spring, toward cold rain
which gives way to warm rain
and beaten down grass. If I
were serious I would say I
take my stand on the edge
of the future tense and offer
my life, but in fact I stand
before a smudged bathroom mirror,
toothbrush in hand, and smile
at the puffed face smiling
back out of habit. Get up,
honey, I say, it could be a lot worse,
it could be a lot worse,
it could be happening to you.

PHILIP LEVINE

My Son and I

In a coffee house at 3 am
and he believes
I'm dying. Outside the wind
moves along the streets
of New York City picking up
abandoned scraps of newspapers

and tiny messages of hope
no one hears. He's dressed
in worn corduroy pants
and shirts over shirts,
and his hands are stained
as mine once were
with glue, ink, paint.
A brown stocking cap
hides the thick blond hair
so unlike mine. For forty
minutes he's tried not
to cry. How are his brothers?
I tell him I don't know,
they have grown away
from me. We are Americans
and never touch on this
stunned earth where a boy
sees his life fly past
through a car window. His mother?
She is deaf and works
in the earth for days, hearing
the dirt pray and guiding
the worm to its feasts. Why
do I have to die? Why
do I have to sit before him
no longer his father, only
a man? Because the given
must be taken, because
we hunger before we eat,
because each small spark
must turn to darkness.
As we said when we were kids
and knew the names of everything
. . . just because. I reach
across the table and take
his left hand in mine.
I have no blessing. I can

tell him how I found
the plum blossom before
I was thirty, how once
in a rooming house in Alicante
a man younger than I,
an Argentine I barely understood,
sat by me through the night
while my boy Teddy cried out
for help, and how when he slept
at last, my friend wept
with thanks in the cold light.
I can tell him that his hand
sweating in mine can raise
the Lord God of Stones,
bring down the Republic of Lies,
and hold a spoon. Instead
I say it's late, and he pays
and leads me back
through the empty streets
to the Earle Hotel, where
the room sours with the mould
of old Bibles dumped down
the air-shaft. In my coat
I stand alone in the dark
waiting for something,
a flash of light, a song,
a remembered sweetness
from all the lives I've lost.
Next door the TV babbles
on and on, and I give up
and sway toward the bed
in a last chant before dawn.

FEDERICO GARCÍA LORCA

Blind Panorama of New York

If not birds,
covered with ashes,
if not cries beating the bridegroom's windows,
they are delicate creatures of air
oozing fresh blood in unquenchable darkness.
But these are no birds,
for almost the bird metamorphosed, is ox;
white boulders, perhaps, with the help of a moon—
but always the stabbed adolescent
awaiting the judges' approach and the lifting of cloth.

The kinships of woe and mortality, we know,
but grief absolute is not given to spirit.
Not air, nor our lifetime's duration,
nor the smoke-laden terrace retains it.
Grief absolute, grief of the wakened awareness of things,
is a part of eternity's burning,
in the eyes of the guilelessly onlooking systems.

So heavy the weight of the castaway cloth on our shoulders
that sometimes the firmament packs them in hard constellations.
Those dead in their birth-pangs understand, in the last hour of
    all,
that all utterance is stone and each footfall, convulsion.
Ours never to know meditation's frontiers
where larvae and mandarin devour the philosopher.
And idiot children discover in kitchens
little swallows on crutches
adept in the single word: love.

These are no birds.
Bird cannot encompass the fever and murk of lagoons
nor the murderous dread that oppresses us, moment by moment,
nor metallic reports of self-slaughter that quicken us, morning by
    morning.
What stays, is a capsule of air where we groan on the rack of the
    world,
an interval warm to the lunatic fusion of light,
an equivocal scale where the clouds and the roses forget
Chinese pandemonium that boils through an outlet of blood.
Oftentimes I have lost myself wholly
in the track of the burning that wakens awareness of things,
and found only the sailor, tossed on the taffrail,
and the skies' little creatures lying buried in snow.
But woe absolute was always a village square distant,
where crystallized fish perished under the tree trunk;
courtyards of sky unknown to the statue's unblemished antiquity,
and the tender advance of volcanoes.

No woe in our voices. Only the teeth, set,
teeth to be stilled in a fold of black satin.
No woe in our voices. Here only our planet persists.
Our earth, with its gates of forever,
that give on the flush of its fruits.

Translated, from the Spanish, by Ben Belitt

FEDERICO GARCÍA LORCA

The King of Harlem

With a spoon
he gouged out the crocodile's eyes
and thumped on the monkey-rumps,
with a spoon.

Eternity's spark still slept in the flint
and the scarabs that tippled on anise
had forgotten the moss of the parish.

And that patriarch, covered with mushrooms,
went on to the place where the black men were weeping
while the king's ladle crackled
and the tanks of the pestilent water arrived.

Roses fled on the blades
of the last loops of air
and on hummocks of saffron
the little boys smashed little squirrels
in the flush of a soiled exaltation.

Yes: the bridge must be crossed
and the florid black found
if the perfume we bear in our lungs
is to strike, in its guises of peppery pine,
on our temples.

We must murder the yellow-haired hawkers of brandy
and the comrades of apple and sand;
we must batter with fistblows
the gone little jewesses, in a lather of bubbles:
for the king and his hosts must come singing from Harlem,
the crocodiles sleep in the great enfilades,
in a moon of asbestos,
so that none may discredit the infinite beauty
of the dusters, the graters, the kitchenware coppers and
        casseroles.

You Harlem! You Harlem! You Harlem!
No anguish to equal your thwarted vermilions,
your blood-shaken, darkened eclipses,
your garnet ferocity, deaf and dumb in the shadows,
your hobbled, great king in the janitor's suit.

        *   *   *   *   *   *   *   *   *   *

Night opened a fissure; ivory salamanders were mute.
The American girls
carried children and coins in their bellies
and the boys lay inert on the cross of a yawn and stretched
        muscle.

Take note of them:
They drink silver whiskey within sight of volcanoes
and devour little slivers of heart on the frozen ascents of the bear.

King Harlem that night, with the hardest of spoons,
gouged out the crocodile's eyes
and thumped on the monkey-rumps.
With a spoon.
The black men, befuddled, went wailing,
between gold sun and umbrellas,
the mulattoes pulled rubber, impatient to gain a white torso,
and wind blurred the mirrors
and ruptured the veins of the dancers.

    Negroes, Negroes, Negroes, Negroes.

Blood has no doors in your night, lying face to the sky.
Nowhere a blush. But under the skins, blood is raging,
alive in the spine of a dagger and the breast of a landscape,
under the pincers and brackens of Cancer's heavenly moon.

Blood on its thousand pathways, seeking powder-meal deaths,
        ashes of spikenard,
skies fixed in a slant, where the planets' assemblages
toss on the beach with the castaway things.

Blood that looks long, through a corner of eye,
blood pressed out of matweed, subterranean nectars.
Blood rusting the tracks of the negligent trade wind
and melting the moth on the panes.

Blood flows; and will flow
on the rooftops and sheds everywhere;
to burn off the chlorophyl blondes,
to sob at the foot of the bed by insomniac washbowls
and explode in a low-yellow dawn of tobacco.

Escape, since you must:
escape in the corners, hole up in the uppermost stories,
for a marrow of forests will enter the crevices
and leave in your flesh a tentative trail of eclipse,
mock mourning: the discoloring glove and the chemical rose.

     *   *   *   *   *   *   *   *   *   *

In the shrewdest of silences
go the cooks and the valets, and those who would cleanse with
    their tongues
the millionaire's wounds,
seeking a king in the streets, or on crossways of nitre.

A wooden south wind, atilt on black slime
spits upon boatwrecks and tacks down its shoulders;
a southerly wind bearing
alphabets, sunflowers, incisors,
a storage-cell powered with a smother of wasps.

Oblivion spoke in three ink-droppings spotting a monocle,
and love, in the lonely, invisible face, on the rind of a rock.
Medullas, corollas, contrived on the cloud
a rose-barren desert of stubble.

     *   *   *   *   *   *   *   *   *   *

To left and to right, southward, northward,
looms up the impassable wall
for the mole and the water-jet.
Black man, never search in its cleft
the immemorial mask.
Seek out the great sun of the center,
be the hum in the cluster.
Sun gliding through groves
with no expectation of dryads,
sun that undoes all the numbers, yet never crossed over a dream,
sun dropping tattooed on the river,
hallooing, with crocodiles after.

Negroes, Negroes, Negroes, Negroes.

Never serpent or zebra or mule
That paled at death's imminence.
Not even the woodcutter knows
when the death of the thunderous tree he brings down is
        accomplished.
Abide in the vegetal shade of your king
till the hemlock and thistle and thorn rock the furthermost roofs.

Black man: only then, only then, only then
can you kiss out your frenzy on bicycle-wheels
or pair off the microscopes in the caves of the squirrels,
and assuredly dance out the dance while the flower-stems stiffen
and murder our Moses—almost into bulrushes' heaven.

You Harlem in masquerade!
You Harlem, whom torsos of street-clothing menace!
Your murmur has come to me,
your murmur has come over tree trunks and dumb-waiters,
over grey metal-plate
where float all your tooth-covered speed-cars,
across the dead horses and the petty offenses,
past your noble and desperate king
whose beard-lengths go down to the sea.

Translated, from the Spanish, by Ben Belitt

FEDERICO GARCÍA LORCA

Landscape of the Vomiting Multitudes
CONEY ISLAND DUSK

The fat lady came on,
pulling up roots and wetting the drum-skins;
the fat lady
who turns up the cuttlefish and leaves them to die, wrong side
    out.
The fat lady, hostile to moons,
raced through the streets and the tenantless levels,
leaving pigeon-skull trails in the corners,
kindling the furies of obsolete feasts,
calling the demon of bread from the slopes of swept sky
and sifting light's ardor into underground transits.
They are graveyards. I know it. They are graveyards,
a sadness of kitchens sunk deep under silt;
another time's pheasants and apples; those who tighten our
    throats are the dead.

A muttering came from the forest of vomit:
woman's sterility, molten-wax children,
fermentation of trees, and unwearying waiters
serving platters of salt under harps of saliva.
No help for it! Vomit it up, boy! No other way.
Not the vomit of hussars on the breasts of their harlots,
or the vomit of cats unmindfully gulping down frogs.
Those who scratch with the clay of their hands
on the doorways of flint and the rotting confections and clouds,
    are the dead.

The fat lady came on
with the crowds from the boats and the bars and the gardens.
The fanfare was light on the drumheads of vomit
by the daughters of blood
who seek the protection of moons.
Welladay! Welladay! Welladay!
My gaze, that was one time my own, is no longer my own,
a gaze trembling naked in alcohol,
launching incredible navies
on quays of anemone.
The gaze that preserves me
must issue on waves where dawn never ventures:
I, poet and armless, adrift
in the vomiting multitudes,
lacking even the spirit of horses to crop
the rank moss of my temples.

But the fat lady came on, as before,
and the crowds called for druggists
where the tropical bitters were waiting.
And not till the first curs arrived, and they broke out the flags,
did the city swarm out to the rails of the jetty, as one.

New York, December 29, 1929
Translated, from the Spanish, by Ben Belitt

FEDERICO GARCÍA LORCA

New York

Office and Attack

TO FERNANDO VELA

Beneath all the statistics
there is a drop of duck's blood.
Beneath all the columns
there is a drop of a sailor's blood.
Beneath all the totals, a river of warm blood;
a river that goes singing
past the bedrooms of the suburbs,
and the river is silver, cement, or wind
in the lying daybreak of New York.
The mountains exist, I know that.
And the lenses ground for wisdom,
I know that. But I have not come to see the sky.
I have come to see the stormy blood,
the blood that sweeps the machines to the waterfalls,
and the spirit on to the cobra's tongue.
Every day they kill in New York
ducks, four million,
pigs, five million,
pigeons, two thousand, for the enjoyment of dying men,
cows, one million,
lambs, one million,
roosters, two million
who turn the sky to small splinters.
You may as well sob filing a razor blade
or assassinate dogs in the hallucinated foxhunts,
as try to stop in the dawnlight
the endless trains carrying milk,
the endless trains carrying blood,
and the trains carrying roses in chains

for those in the field of perfume.
The ducks and the pigeons
and the hogs and the lambs
lay their drops of blood down
underneath all the statistics;
and the terrible bawling of the packed-in cattle
fills the valley with suffering
where the Hudson is getting drunk on its oil.
I attack all those persons
who know nothing of the other half,
the half who cannot be saved,
who raise their cement mountains
in which the hearts of the small
animals no one thinks of are beating,
and from which we will all fall
during the final holiday of the drills.
I spit in your face.
The other half hears me,
as they go on eating, urinating, flying in their purity
like the children of the janitors
who carry delicate sticks
to the holes where the antennas
of the insects are rusting.
This is not hell, it is a street.
This is not death, it is a fruit-stand.
There is a whole world of crushed rivers and unachievable
    distances
In the paw of a cat crushed by a car,
and I hear the song of the worm
in the heart of so many girls.
Rust, rotting, trembling earth.
And you are earth, swimming through the figures of the office.
What shall I do, set my landscapes in order?
Set in place the lovers who will afterwards be photographs,
who will be bits of wood and mouthfuls of blood?
No, I won't; I attack,

I attack the conspiring
of these empty offices
that will not broadcast the sufferings,
that rub out the plans of the forest,
and I offer myself to be eaten by the packed-up cattle
when their mooing fills the valley
where the Hudson is getting drunk on its oil.

Translated, from the Spanish, by Robert Bly

FEDERICO GARCÍA LORCA

Unsleeping City

BROOKLYN BRIDGE NOCTURNE

No sleep in the sky; nobody, nobody.
No one lies sleeping.
The spawn of the moon sniff the cabins, and circle.
The living iguanas arrive and set tooth on the sleepless.
The heartstricken one who takes flight will meet on the corners
the incredible mute crocodile under the timid reproach of the
    stars.

No sleep upon earth; nobody, nobody.
No one lies sleeping.
The corpse in the furthermost graveyard
that was three years berating
the landscape of drought that he held on his knees,
and the boy that they buried this morning—he whimpered so
    much
they called out the mastiffs to quiet him.

Life is no dream! Beware and beware and beware!
We tumble downstairs to eat of the damp of the earth
or we climb to the snowy divide with the choir of dead dahlias.
But neither dream nor forgetfulness, is:
brute flesh is. Kisses that tether our mouths
in a mesh of raw veins.
Whomsoever his woe brings to grief, it will grieve without
    quarter.
Whom death brings to dread will carry that death on his
    shoulders.

On a day,
the horses will thrive in the taverns,
the ravening ant
will assail yellow heavens withheld in the eyes of a cow.

On a time
we shall see, rearisen, the anatomized butterflies,
and walking the ways of gray sponge and a stillness of boats,
behold our rings glisten and the roses gush forth from our
    tongues.

Beware and beware and beware!
Those still keeping watch on the print of the paw and the
    cloudburst,
the boy in his tears, who cannot interpret the bridge's invention,
the dead with no more than a head and a shoe now—
drive them all to the wall where snake and iguana are waiting,
where the bear's fang lies ready
and the mummified hand of the child
and the pelt of the camel in a raging blue ague, stands on end.

No sleep under heaven; nobody, nobody.
No one lies sleeping.
And should one shut an eye,
lay on the whip, my boys, lay on the whip!
Let eye's panorama be open, I say,
let the bitter sores rankle!
No sleep upon earth; nobody, nobody,
no one, I tell you.
No one lies sleeping.
But if any should find in the night the mosses' excess on his
    temples—
down with the trapdoors and let there be seen in the moon
the perfidious goblets, the theater's skull, and the bane.

Translated, from the Spanish, by Ben Belitt

AUDRE LORD

When the Saints Come Marching In

Plentiful sacrifice and believers in redemption
are all that is needed
so any day now
I expect some new religion
to rise up like tear gas
from the streets of New York
erupting like the rank pavement smell
released by the garbage-trucks'
baptismal drizzle.

The high priests have been ready and waiting
with their incense pans full of fire.
I do not know the rituals
the exhaltations
nor what name of the god
the survivors will worship
I only know she will be terrible
and very busy
and very old.

𝒴

ROBERT LOWELL

Central Park

Scaling small rocks, exhaling smog,
gasping at game-scents like a dog,
now light as pollen, now as white
and winded as a grounded kite—
I watched the lovers occupy
every inch of earth and sky:
one figure of geometry,
multiplied to infinity,
straps down, and sunning openly . . .
each precious, public, pubic tangle
an equilateral triangle,
lost in the park, half covered by
the shade of some low stone or tree.
The stain of fear and poverty
spread through each trapped anatomy,
and darkened every mote of dust.
All wished to leave this drying crust,
borne on the delicate wings of lust
like bees, and cast their fertile drop
into the overwhelming cup.

Drugged and humbled by the smell
of zoo-straw mixed with animal,
the lion prowled his slummy cell,
serving his life-term in jail—
glaring, grinding, on his heel,
with tingling step and testicle . . .

ℒ

ROBERT LOWELL

The Mouth of the Hudson
FOR ESTHER BROOKS

A single man stands like a bird-watcher,
and scuffles the pepper and salt snow
from a discarded, gray
Westinghouse Electric cable drum.
He cannot discover America by counting
the chains of condemned freight-trains
from thirty states. They jolt and jar
and junk in the siding below him.
He has trouble with his balance.
His eyes drop,
and he drifts with the wild ice
ticking seaward down the Hudson,
like the blank-sides of a jig-saw puzzle.

The ice ticks seaward like a clock.
A Negro toasts
wheat-seeds over the coke-fumes
in a punctured barrel.
Chemical air
sweeps in from New Jersey,
and smells of coffee.

Across the river,
ledges of suburban factories tan
in the sulphur-yellow sun
of the unforgivable landscape.

✤

ROBERT LOWELL

New York 1962: Fragment
FOR E.H.L.

This might be nature—twenty stories high,
two water tanks, tanned shingle, corseted
by stapled pasture wire, while bed to bed,
we two, one cell here, lie
gazing into the ether's crystal ball,
sky and a sky, and sky, and sky, till death—
my heart stops . . .
This might be heaven. Years ago,
we aimed for less and settled for
a picture, out of style then and now in,
of seven daffodils. We watched them blow:
buttercup yellow were the flowers, and green
the stems as fresh paint, over them the wind,
the blousy wooden branches of the elms,
high summer in the breath that overwhelms
the termites digging in the underpinning . . .
Still over us, still in parenthesis,
this sack of hornets sopping up the flame,
still over us our breath,
sawing and pumping to the terminal,
and down below, we two, two in one waterdrop

vitalized by a needle drop of blood,
up, up, up, up and up,
soon shot, soon slugged into the overflow
that sets the wooden workhorse working here below.

ROBERT LOWELL

The Opposite House

All day the opposite house,
an abandoned police stable,
just an opposite house,
is square enough—six floors,
six windows to a floor,
pigeons ganging through
broken windows and cooing
like gangs of children tooting
empty bottles.

Tonight, though, I see it shine
in the Azores of my open window.
Its manly, old-fashioned lines
are gorgeously rectilinear.
It's like some firework to be fired
at the end of the garden party,
some Spanish *casa*, luminous
with heraldry and murder,
marooned in New York.

A stringy policeman is crooked
in the doorway, one hand on his revolver.
He counts his bullets like beads.
Two on horseback sidle
the crowd to the curb. A red light
whirls on the roof of an armed car,
plodding slower than a turtle.
Deterrent terror!
Viva la muerte!

🌿

CYNTHIA MACDONALD

Apartments on First Avenue

"Cemeteries are becoming so crowded in the New York area that
    a conglomerate has filed plans to construct a block-square
    above-ground facility."
                                    —WYNC News broadcast

Underground space, like water, is running out
So they are building apartment houses for the dead.
That ad: "Keep your loved ones safe from seepage," is
Obsolete; these marble skyscrapers have
No cracks and point in the right direction.
Here, where the municipal station tolls the hour with
"This is New York where more than eight million people
Live and work and enjoy the fruits of democracy,"
The question now becomes where can you afford
To live and where to live and die?

Persephone, her lips stained with pomegranate juice,
Runs in her shift (it is 8—4) through the hall.
The seeds from that seedy red globe litter;
They cannot root in marble fields. She plays
Her lyre and the single strand of plaint
Turns polyphonous, echo's counterpoint off
Blue-veined cleavage. Here in the clouds, strains
Of the lyre suffuse the thin air, using it up.
But Zeus, her father, angry at the music of women,
Tells her to go to Hades again even though
The bright stamens of her hair make him want to
Stroke it. She resists his direction. Lightning bolts.
O Lord, the hardness of this place.
She takes the elevator down, abasing herself.

O Lord, the hardness of this place.
Galleries fitted to entomb feeling and bodies,
Sky catacombs where love's declensions stiffen into
Fixity. But I play my lyre and it tells the truth.
Gluck's single strand of happiness resounds.
If you, walking ahead, searching for a bridge to
That most circular of Museums, turn and
Look at me too long, we may both become marble—
Statues for our funerary niche—but we must risk it.
Pluto, Zeus, our parents, the archangel Michael,
Mayor Koch: to Hell with them. Or not.
You reach out your hand and turn. Pulses deny marble.
The ignited fires have no lick of burning.
Defying the Storm King Power Co., we walk out into
The light fantastic, trip the sidewalks. Within our
Bodies' compass there is no need to fight gravity.

VLADIMIR VLADIMIROVICH MAYAKOVSKY

Brooklyn Bridge

Hey, Coolidge boy,
make a shout of joy!
When a thing is good
                then it's good.
Blush from compliments
                   like our flag's calico,
even though you're
                the most super-united states
                         of
America.
Like the crazy nut
          who goes
               to his church
or retreats
       to a monastery
              simple and rigid—
so I
   in the gray haze
            of evening
humbly
     approach
          the Brooklyn Bridge.
Like a conqueror
         on cannons with muzzles
                  as high as a giraffe
jabbing into a broken
          city beseiged,
so, drunk with glory,
          alive to the hilt,

I clamber
        proudly
                upon Brooklyn Bridge.
Like a stupid painter
                  whose enamored eyes pierce
a museum Madonna
            like a wedge.
So from this sky,
            sowed into the stars,
I look at New York
             through Brooklyn Bridge.
New York,
       heavy and stifling
              till night,
has forgotten
         what makes it dizzy
               and a hindrance,
and only
       the souls of houses
rise in the transparent
             sheen of windows.
Here the itching hum
         of the 'el'
             is hardly heard,
and only by this
        hum,
          soft but stubborn,
can you feel the trains
         crawl
           with a rattle
as when dishes
        are jammed into a cupboard.
And when from
        below the started river

a merchant
         transports sugar
                   from the factory bins—
then
     the masts passing under the bridge
are no bigger
              in size
                      than pins.
I'm proud
         of this
               mile of steel.
In it my visions
                are alive and real—
a fight
       for structure
                     instead of arty 'style',
the harsh calculation
                     of bolts
                             and steel.
If the end
          of the world
                      comes—
and chaos
         wipes out
                  this earth
and if only this
                bridge
                      remains
rearing over the dust of death,
then
    as little bones,
                    thinner than needles,
clad with flesh,
                standing in museums,
                           are dinosaurs,—

so from this
                    bridge
                              future geologists
will be able
                    to reconstruct
                                   our present course.
They will say:
                         —this
                              paw of steel
joined seas,
                    prairies and deserts,
from here,
                    Europe
                              rushed to the West,
scattering
               to the wind
                              Indian feathers.
This rib here
                    reminds us
                              of a machine—
imagine,
               enough hands, enough grip
while standing,
                    with one steel leg
                              in Manhattan
to drag
          toward yourself
                              Brooklyn by the lip!
By the wires
               of electric yarn
I know this
               is
                    the Post-Steam Era.

Here people
            already
                        yelled on the radio,
here people
            already
                        flew by air.
For some
            here was life
                        carefree,
                                    unalloyed.
For others
            a prolonged
                        howl of hunger.
From here
            the unemployed
jumped headfirst
                        into
                                    the Hudson.
And finally
            with clinging stars
                        along the strings of cables
my dream comes back
                        without any trouble
and I see—
            here
                        stood Mayakovsky,
here he stood
            putting
                        syllable to syllable.

I look,
      as an eskimo looks at a train.
I dig into you,
            like a tick into an ear.
Brooklyn Bridge.
Yes,
      you've got something here.

Translated, from the Russian, by
Vladimir Markov and Merrill Sparks

❦

JANE MAYHALL

Surfaces

At four o'clock in the afternoon
the night came early with clouds
like flaming tarlatons, heavy skirts
of Spanish color, in the slow whirl
of New York's West Side winter sky.
Low little shops glowed in festival
and the traffic stood at a standstill,
car occupants with visages like angels
fiercely golden, and watching nothing.
We could bet our lives on this illusion,
raise families, make love in dances

of meaning, the surfaces of mauve
and tinsel splashing, and out to
the torn, magnificent Hudson. These
were only surfaces, the mind's aberra-
tion as the slow custom of sunset departed.
But we bet our lives on it and glowed
for an instant, heard voices like a religion,
an apocalypse renewal, or like choirs
of people straight out of Walt Whitman—
this was at about Columbus Ave. & 92nd:
Japanese, Greek, Hindustani, Puerto Rican.
It was the red sky light that had made
the connection; until darkness quenched
the vision, the traffic wild and stilled.

HERMAN MELVILLE

The House-Top: A Night Piece
JULY, 1863 —THE DRAFT RIOTS

No sleep. The sultriness pervades the air
And binds the brain—a dense oppression, such
As tawny tigers feel in matted shades,
Vexing their blood and making apt for ravage.
Beneath the stars the roofy desert spreads
Vacant as Libya. All is hushed near by.
Yet fitfully from far breaks a mixed surf
Of muffled sound, the Atheist roar of riot.
Yonder, where parching Sirius set in drought,
Balefully glares red Arson—there—and there.
The Town is taken by its rats—ship-rats
And rats of the wharves. All Civil charms

And priestly spells which late held hearts in awe—
Fear-bound, subjected to a better sway
Than sway of self; these like a dream dissolve,
And man rebounds whole aeons back in nature.
Hail to the low dull rumble, dull and dead,
And ponderous drag that shakes the wall.
Wise Draco comes, deep in the midnight roll
Of black artillery; he comes, though late;
In code corroborating Calvin's creed
And cynic tyrannies of honest kings;
He comes, nor parleys; and the Town, redeemed,
Gives thanks devout; nor, being thankful, heeds
The grimy slur on the Republic's faith implied,
Which holds that Man is naturally good,
And—more—is Nature's Roman, never to be scourged.

WILLIAM MEREDITH

At the Natural History Museum

Past a swim-by of deep-sea fish,
cold rockets in a tank of air, tamed
by their right names and their Latin underneath,
he walks toward the cafeteria. It grows dark.
October clouds shadow the frosted-glass roof,
the dinosaurs appear, mahogany bones.
The family died out.

On the far wall, a fierce one rears erect,
his shoulders thrown back like a man's
when he is loved or seeks high office.
His jaws are strong pliers. Dawn men watch in awe
from the bushes this blood cousin
in a world of crusty things.

But the family dies out before his eyes,
grass-eaters first, then taloned meat-eaters.
Some of the bones have been fleshed out with plaster
but Hazard and the guard are the oldest living things
here. Even the author of the comic verse
about extinction, copied at the monster's feet,
has gone his bony way.

We descend by chosen cells that are not lost,
though they wander off in streams and rivulets.
Not everyone has issue in this creation.
Cousins-german are everywhere in the shale
and marshes under this dry house. In slime, in sperm,
our living cousins flow.

And grazers or killers, each time we must stoop low
and enter by some thigh-lintel, gentle as rills.
Who consents to his own return, Nietzsche says,
participates in the divinity of the world.
Perhaps I have already eddied on, out of this backwater,
man, on my way to the cafeteria, Hazard thinks.
Perhaps nothing dies but husks.

WILLIAM MEREDITH

Effort at Speech

Climbing the stairway gray with urban midnight,
Cheerful, venial, ruminating pleasure,
Darkness takes me, an arm around my throat and
       Give me your wallet.

Fearing cowardice more than other terrors,
Angry, I wrestle with my unseen partner,
Caught in a ritual not of our own making,
       panting like spaniels.

Bold with adrenaline, mindless, shaking,
God damn it, no! I rasp at him behind me,
Wrenching the leather wallet from his grasp. It
       breaks like a wishbone

So that, departing (routed by my shouting,
Not by my strength or inadvertent courage),
Half of the papers lending me a name are
       gone with him nameless.

Only now turning, I see a tall boy running,
Fifteen, sixteen, dressed thinly for the weather.
Reaching the street light, he turns a brown face briefly
       phrased like a question.

I, like a questioner, watch him turn the corner
Taking the answer with him, or his half of it.
Loneliness, not a sensible emotion,
       breathes hard on the stairway.

Walking homeward, I fraternize with shadows,
Zigzagging with them where they flee the street lights,
Asking for trouble, asking for the message
       trouble had sent me.

All *fall down* has been scribbled on the street in
Garbage and excrement—so much for the vision
Others taunt me with, my untimely humor,
           so much for cheerfulness.

Next time don't wrangle, give the boy the money,
Call across chasms what the world you know is.
Luckless and lied to, how can a child master
           human decorum?

Next time a switch-blade, somewhere he is thinking,
I should have killed him and took the lousy wallet.
Reading my cards, he feels a surge of anger
           blind as my shame.

Error like Babel mutters in the places,
Cities apart, where now we word our failures.
Hatred and guilt have left us without language
           who might have held discourse.

JAMES MERRILL

An Urban Convalescence

Out for a walk, after a week in bed,
I find them tearing up part of my block
And, chilled through, dazed and lonely, join the dozen
In meek attitudes, watching a huge crane
Fumble luxuriously in the filth of years.
Her jaws dribble rubble. An old man
Laughs and curses in her brain,
Bringing to mind the close of *The White Goddess*.

As usual in New York, everything is torn down
Before you have had time to care for it.
Head bowed, at the shrine of noise, let me try to recall
What building stood here. Was there a building at all?
I have lived on this same street for a decade.

Wait. Yes. Vaguely a presence rises
Some five floors high, of shabby stone
—Or am I confusing it with another one
In another part of town, or of the world?—
And over its lintel into focus vaguely
Misted with blood (my eyes are shut)
A single garland sways, stone fruit, stone leaves,
Which years of grit had etched until it thrust
Roots down, even into the poor soil of my seeing.
When did the garland become part of me?
I ask myself, amused almost,
Then shiver once from head to toe,

Transfixed by a particular cheap engraving of garlands
Bought for a few francs long ago,
All calligraphic tendril and cross-hatched rondure,
Ten years ago, and crumpled up to stanch
Boughs dripping, whose white gestures filled a cab,
And thought of neither then nor since.
Also, to clasp them, the small, red-nailed hand
Of no one I can place. Wait. No. Her name, her features
Lie toppled underneath that year's fashions.
The words she must have spoken, setting her face
To fluttering like a veil, I cannot hear now,
Let alone understand.

So that I am already on the stair,
As it were, of where I lived,
When the whole structure shudders at my tread
And soundlessly collapses, filling
The air with motes of stone.
Onto the still erect building next door
Are pressed levels and hues—
Pocked rose, streaked greens, brown whites.
Who drained the pousse-café?
Wires and pipes, snapped off at the roots, quiver.

Well, that is what life does. I stare
A moment longer, so. And presently
The massive volume of the world
Closes again.

Upon that book I swear
To abide by what it teaches:
Gospels of ugliness and waste,
Of towering voids, of soiled gusts,
Of a shrieking to be faced
Full into, eyes astream with cold—

With cold?
All right then. With self-knowledge.

Indoors at last, the pages of *Time* are apt
To open, and the illustrated mayor of New York,
Given a glimpse of how and where I work,
To note yet one more house that can be scrapped.

Unwillingly I picture
My walls weathering in the general view.
It is not even as though the new
Buildings did very much for architecture.

Suppose they did. The sickness of our time requires
That these as well be blasted in their prime.
You would think the simple fact of having lasted
Threatened our cities like mysterious fires.

There are certain phrases which to use in a poem
Is like rubbing silver with quicksilver. Bright
But facile, the glamour deadens overnight.
For instance, how 'the sickness of our time'

Enhances, then debases, what I feel.
At my desk I swallow in a glass of water
No longer cordial, scarcely wet, a pill
They had told me not to take until much later.

With the result that back into my imagination
The city glides, like cities seen from the air,
Mere smoke and sparkle to the passenger
Having in mind another destination

Which now is not that honey-slow descent
Of the Champs-Elysées, her hand in his,
But the dull need to make some kind of house
Out of the life lived, out of the love spent.

JAMES MERRILL

18 West 11th Street

In what at least
Seemed anger the Aquarians in the basement
Had been perfecting a device

For making sense to us
If only briefly and on pain
Of incommunication ever after.

Now look who's here. Our prodigal
Sunset. Just passing through from Isfahan.
Filled by him the glass

Disorients. The swallow-flights
Go word by numbskull word
—Rebellion . . . Pentagon . . . Black Studies—

Crashing into irreality,
Plumage and parasites
Plus who knows what of the reptilian,

Till wit turns on the artificial lights
Or heaven changes. The maid,
Silent, pale as any victim,

Comes in, identifies;
Yet brings new silver, gives rise to the joint,
The presidency's ritual eclipse.

Take. Eat. His body to our lips. The point
Was anger, brother? Love? Dear premises
Vainly exploded, vainly dwelt upon.

Item: the carpet.
Identical bouquets on black, rose-dusted
Face in fifty funeral parlors,

Scentless and shaven, wall-to-wall
Extravagance without variety . . .
That morning's buzzing vacuum be fed

By ash of metropolitan evening's
Smoker inveterate between hot bouts
Of gloating over scrollwork,

The piano (three-legged by then like a thing in a riddle)
Fingered itself provocatively. Tones
Jangling whose tuner slept, moon's camphor mist

On the parterre compounding
Chromatic muddles which the limpid trot
Flew to construe. Up from camellias

Sent them by your great-great-grandfather,
Ghosts in dwarf sateen and miniver
Flitted once more askew

Through *Les Sylphides*. The fire was dead. Each summer,
While onto white keys miles from here
Warm salt chords kept breaking, snapping the strings,

The carpet—its days numbered—
Hatched another generation
Of strong-jawed, light-besotted saboteurs.

A mastermind
Kept track above the mantel. The cold caught,
One birthday in its shallows, racked

The weak frame, glazed with sleet
Overstuffed aunt and walnut uncle. Book
You could not read. Some utterly

Longed-for present meeting other eyes'
Blue arsenal of homemade elegies,
Duds every one. The deed

Diffused. Your breakfast *Mirror* put
Late to bed, a fever
Flashing through the veins of linotype:

NIX ON PEACE BID PROPHET STONED
FIVE FEARED DEAD IN BOMBED DWELLING
—Bulletin-pocked columns, molten font

Features would rise from, nose for news
Atwitch, atchoo, God bless you!
Brought to your senses (five feared? not one bit)

Who walking home took in
The ruin. The young linden opposite
Shocked leafless. Item: the March dawn.

Shards of a blackened witness still in place.
The charred ice-sculpture garden
Beams fell upon. The cold blue searching beams.

Then all you sought
No longer, B came bearing. An arrangement
In time known simply as That June—

Fat snifter filled with morbidest
Possibly meat-eating flowers,
So hairy-stemmed, red-muscled, not to be pressed.

Pinhead notions underwater, yours,
Quicksilvered them afresh.
You let pass certain telltale prints

Left upon her in the interim
By that winter's person, where he touched her.
Still in her life now, was he, feeling the dim

Projection of your movie on his sheet?
Feeling how you reached past B towards him,
Brothers in grievance? But who grieves!

The night she left ("One day you'll understand")
You stood under the fruitless tree. The streetlight
Cast false green fires about, a tragic

Carpet of shadows of blosssoms, shadows of leaves.
You understood. You would not seek rebirth
As a Dalmation stud or Tiny Tim.

Discolorations from within, dry film
Run backwards, parching, scorching, to consume
Whatever filled you to the brim,

Fierce tongue, black
Fumes massing forth once more on
Waterstilts that fail them. The

Commissioner unswears his oath. Sea serpent
Hoses recoil, the siren drowns in choking
Wind. The crowd has thinned to a

Coven rigorously chosen from so many
Called. Our instant trance. The girl's
Appearance now among us, as foreseen

Naked, frail but fox-eyed, head to toe
(Having passed through the mirror)
Adorned with heavy shreds of ribbon

Sluggish to bleed. She stirs, she moans the name
Adam. And is *gone*. By her own
Broom swept clean, god, stop, behind this

Drunken backdrop of debris, airquake,
Flame in bloom—a pigeon's throat
Lifting, the puddle

Healed. To let:
Cream paint, brown ivy, brickflush. Eye
Of the old journalist unwavering

Through gauze. Forty-odd years gone by.
Toy blocks. Church bells. Original vacancy.
O deepening spring.

W. S. MERWIN

The Rock

Saxophone and subway
under waking and sleeping
then few hundred feet down nobody

sound of inner stone
with heart on fire

on top of it where it would dream
in the light on its head
and in its shadow
we know one another
riding deaf together
flying up in boxes
through gray gasses
and here pause
to breathe

all
our walls shake if we
listen
if we stop even
to rest a hand on them

when we can love it happens here too
where we tremble
who also are running like white grass
where sirens bleed through us
wires reach to us
we are bottles smashing in paper bags
and at the same time live standing in many windows
hearing under the breath the stone
that is ours alone

W. S. MERWIN

St. Vincent's

Thinking of rain clouds that rose over the city
on the first of the year

in the same month
I consider that I have lived daily and with
eyes open and ears to hear
these years across from St. Vincent's Hospital
above whose roof those clouds rose

its bricks by day a French red under
cross facing south
blown-up neoclassic facades the tall
dark openings between columns at
the dawn of history
exploded into many windows
in a mortised face

inside it the ambulances have unloaded
after sirens' howling nearer through traffic on
Seventh Avenue long
ago I learned not to hear them
even when the sirens stop

they turn to back in
few passersby stay to look
and neither do I

at night two long blue
windows and one short one on the top floor
burn all night
many nights when most of the others are out
on what floor do they have
anything

I have seen the building drift moonlit through geraniums
late at night when trucks were few
moon just past the full
upper windows parts of the sky
as long as I looked
I watched it at Christmas and New Year
early in the morning I have seen the nurses ray out through
arterial streets
in the evening have noticed internes blocks away
on doorsteps one foot in the door

I have come upon the men in gloves taking out
the garbage at all hours
piling up mountains of
plastic bags white strata with green intermingled and
black
I have seen the pile
catch fire and studied the cloud
at the ends of the jets of the hoses
the fire engines as near as that
red beacons and
machine-throb heard by the whole body

I have noticed molded containers stacked outside
a delivery entrance on Twelfth Street
whether meals from a meal factory made up with those
mummified for long journeys by plane
or specimens for laboratory
examination sealed at the prescribed temperatures
either way closed delivery

and approached faces staring from above
crutches or tubular clamps
out for tentative walks
have paused for turtling wheelchairs
heard visitors talking in wind on each corner
while the lights changed and
hot dogs were handed over at the curb
in the middle of afternoon
mustard ketchup onions and relish
and police smelling of ether and laundry
were going back

and I have known them all less than the papers of our days
smoke rises from the chimneys do they have an incinerator
what for
how warm do they believe they have to maintain the air
in there
several of the windows appear
to be made of tin
but it may be the light reflected
I have imagined bees coming and going
on those sills though I have never seen them

who was St. Vincent

SARA MILES

Portrait in Available light

Frame it. Everyone lies, you say. The light's bad.
Behind us the Hudson's cool spring roll, at our feet
artifacts, rubble, oil spill. There are shadows
on my face; sun beats on the face of a brick tenement

where someone else mounts snapshots at her oilcloth kitchen
    table.
This is a portrait, you say. Nobody smiles in my pictures.
We're walking by the rotting waterfront, a man
behind a machine, a woman with bad light in her eyes,
trying not to lie. Your negative burns
with what's left out: dust from the traffic, the urgent shine
of bodies at work, the rattle of our own bad nerves
that swerve out and fade focus. This is a portrait of what we want,
what we can't see, made in available light with tools
of the trade, instruments of illusion between us. Between us
no smiles. Behind us history of the marketplace, memories of
    travel,
the grief and conversation of eight million people
getting through another day. Across the river,
to the north, parallel worlds loom, you say: hold it.
Fine hair across my face I'm looking through
as clearly as I can at what is available,
at what is left to use; this is a portrait
of a woman who is trying to tell the truth.

MARIANNE MOORE

Carnegie Hall: Rescued

"It spreads," the campaign—carried on
by long-distance telephone,
        with "Saint Diogenes
        supreme commander."
    At the fifty-ninth minute
        of the eleventh hour, a rescuer

makes room for Mr. Carnegie's
music hall, which by degrees
 became (becomes)
  our music stronghold
 (accented on the "né," as
  perhaps you don't have to be told).

Paderewski's "palladian
majesty" made it a fane;
 Tschaikovsky, of course,
  on the opening
 night, 1891;
  and Gilels, a master, playing.

With Andrew C. and Mr. R.,
"our spearhead, Mr. Star"—
 in music, Stern—
  has grown forensic,
 and by civic piety
  has saved our city panic;

rescuer of a music hall
menaced by the "cannibal
 of real estate"—bulldozing potentate,
  land-grabber, the human crab
 left cowering like a neonate.

As Venice "in defense of children"
has forbidden for the citizen,
 by "a tradition of
  noble behavior,
 dress too strangely shaped or scant,"
  posterity may impute error

to our demolishers of glory. Jean Cocteau's "Preface
to the Past" contains the phrase
    "When very young my dream
        was of pure glory."
    Must he say "was" of his "light
        dream," which confirms our glittering story?

They need their old brown home. Cellist,
violinist, pianist—
    used to unmusical
        impenetralia's
    massive masonry—have found
        reasons to return. Fantasias

of praise and rushings to the front
dog the performer. We hunt
    you down, Saint Diogenes—
        are thanking you for glittering,
    for rushing to the rescue
        as if you'd heard yourself performing.

MARIANNE MOORE

New York

the savage's romance,
accreted where we need the space for commerce—
the centre of the wholesale fur trade,
starred with tepees of ermine and peopled with foxes,
the long guard-hairs waving two inches beyond the body of the
    pelt;
the ground dotted with deer-skins—white with white spots,

                        NEW YORK:

'as satin needlework in a single colour may carry a varied
    pattern',
and wilting eagle's-down compacted by the wind;
and picardels of beaver-skin; white ones alert with snow.
It is a far cry from the 'queen full of jewels'
and the beau with the muff,
from the gilt coach shaped like a perfume-bottle,
to the conjunction of the Monongahela and the Allegheny,
and the scholastic philosophy of the wilderness
to combat which one must stand outside and laugh
since to go in is to be lost.
It is not the dime-novel exterior,
Niagara Falls, the calico horses and the war-canoe;
it is not that 'if the fur is not finer than such as one sees others
    wear,
one would rather be without it'—
that estimated in raw meat and berries, we could feed the
    universe;
it is not the atmosphere of ingenuity,
the otter, the beaver, the puma skins
without shooting-irons or dogs;
it is not the plunder,
but 'accessibility to experience.'

FREDERICK MORGAN

From a Diary

North of 96th where the tracks come out from under
the sun brightens on morning pavements,
the tired air begins to stir.

Puerto Rican streets in Sunday stillness.
An old fat sofa, guts spilling out,
suns itself on the soiled sidewalk.

From a low doorway deep in soot
a child peers, agate-eyed—
a stray dog lopes along, waving his frazzled tail.

The breeze blows grit into my eyes
as I pass a vacant lot girt with rotting fence-boards.
Stevenson's face looks out from tattered posters
alert and fatigued, somehow beyond it all.
"We must look forward to great tomorrows."

Over on Lexington the bars are closed,
the pawnshops gated tight—but the corner luncheonette,
where you can get the greasiest fried eggs in town,
is doing good business with its counters jammed.

A skinny girl passing by gives me the eye,
I smile and look down. A newspaper blows past.

Down the street a nun—thin, white-faced—
gathers her children about her: but now they're on top of me
in a scraggly column, running and shoving their way
toward the parish school of St. Francis de Sales.
The nun's face is lined, mouth down-drawn, but from the eyes
Something fragile glints that may be happiness.

Or so I propose—as I wonder why it all
happens the way it happens, and what will befall
myself and the world, as time runs out—

and tell myself at last to be still and not mind.
Today, held firm, is my tomorrow.

JOHN MORRIS

In The Hamptons

Much here is historical
And dull, but not therefore.
What has occurred since
Is the rich.
Here, fully clothed,
They summered relentlessly
Miles from the nearest
Jew or serious painter.
All day their trim,
Pictorial waves
Relaxed ashore
In weather clear as gin.

But the last man in America
To play tennis in flannels
Is dead. Beyond Queens,
Borough of cemeteries,
Dressed in an idea
About taste as money,
A future approaches
The invented lanes;
To these few beautiful,
Talkative miles
Of bad behavior
The repressed returns.

Although all night
At Montauk
An end of America,
Washington's light
Still solves again
The pointless, eastward water,
Out of drama of the dark
The snazzy summer theatre takes us in.

JOHN MORRIS

One Snowy Night in December

Penn Station at three in the morning
is empty as Heaven. The clerks
whisper in their cages.
They are waiting for money.
The urinals stand in stiff rows
like men who will win.

I walk out into the stone
talk of the city. Up
Fifth Avenue I am my own band.
The municipal lions listen
to the snow, that white answer.

HOWARD MOSS

A Dead Leaf

Today, the first dead leaf in the hall
Is surprised, taking on its second nature,
To find that trees are forms of furniture;
The earliest message to arrive from winter,
It's too far gone, indoors or out,
To eat the sun or drink the water,
And I, I am more desperate than ever,
Reading the memoirs that Madame Blank
Keeps sending on in thick installments.
Twelve publishers have firmly declined . . .

(Thank God! For I am thinly disguised
As yet another form of furniture:
My name is Harrod—a character
Who at one point rather stupidly remarks,
"Only a Fool could love King Lear.")
Madame would hate these opening lines;
She is against both cadence and meter.

Armories, windows,
Days and weeks
Of peering out, then drawing back—
Is there enough artillery
To blast the gossips of this block?
Paranoia is a borderline
Without a country on either side.
That fortress of brownstones across the way
Is money talking
With nothing to say.

Rectitude and impropriety!
I have given them both up,
And settled for a sleazy mysticism,
Befuddled rain and poisoned mist;
Sometimes I'm so depressed I think
It's *life* that's the anesthetist.
But then I wake quite sane, as if
A bicycle race were about to start:
I'm in the park, the sun is bright,
Water ravishes the eye, and soon
I've won the race, I've made my mark!
Then, once again, the telephone
Is my one lifeline out of the dark.

I'm sick of being obsessed by B.
Whose muffled cryptograms grow hoarse
Explaining themselves, outwitting me.
Does that mean this? Does this mean that?
Temperamental unclarity!

This week, drinks and dinner with M.
Lunch with L. Dinner with P.
A party for C.'s new Argentine.
Handel on Thursday. A *vernissage*.
Next week, drinks and dinner with M.
Tuesday I think I'll watch TV.

To retire from it all! To sit and sit
In a wheelchair, old, in Central Park,
Only a lens that drinks the sun,
Or on a bench in southern France,
The first cassis at four o'clock. . . .

August was green, November brown.
Someday soon I'll awake to see
The world go white from head to toe,
A tablecloth at first, and then
A slab of pockmarked travertine—

The first snow.

HOWARD MOSS

The Roof Garden

A nervous hose is dribbling on the tar
This morning on this rooftop where I'm watching you
Move among your sparse, pinchpenny flowers,
Poor metronomes of color one month long
That pull the sun's rays in as best they can
And suck life up from one mere inch of dirt.
There's water in the sky but it won't come down.

Once we counted the skyline's water towers,
Barrels made of shingle, fat and high,
An African village suspended above
The needle hardness of New York that needs
More light than God provides to make it soft,
That needs the water in the water towers
To snake through pipe past all the elevators
To open up in bowls and baths and showers.

Soon our silence will dissolve in talk,
In talk that needs some water and some sun,
Or it will go the same way as before:
Dry repetitions of the ill we bear
Each other, the baited poles of light
Angling through the way the sun today
Fishes among the clouds.

                              Now you are through
Watering geraniums, and now you go
To the roof edge to survey the real estate
Of architectured air—tense forms wrought up,
Torn down, replaced, to be torn down again . . .
So much like us. Your head against the sky
Is topped by a tower clock, blocks away,
Whose two black hands are closing on the hour,
And I look down into the street below,
Rinsed fresh this morning by a water truck,
Down which a girl, perky in high heels,
Clops by, serenely unaware of us,
Of the cables, gas lines, telephone wires,
And water mains, writhing underfoot.

☙

STANLEY MOSS

SM

With spray can paint,
I illuminate my name
on the subway cars and handball courts,
in the public schoolyards of New York,
S M
written in sky-above-the-ocean blue,
surrounded by a valentine splash
of red and white, not for Spiritus Mundi,
but for a life and death, part al fresco,
part catacomb,
against the city fathers
who have made a crime of signaling
with paint to passengers and pedestrians.
From the ghetto population of my city
I spray my name
with those who stand for a public art
that doesn't disillusion our sacred lives.
In secret if I must,
and wearing sneakers, I sign with those
who have signed for me.

HOWARD NEMEROV

Central Park

The broad field darkens, but, still moving round
So that they seem to hover off the ground,
Children are following a shadowy ball;
Shrill, as of birds, their high voices sound.

The pale December sky at darkfall seems
A lake of ice, and frozen there the gleams
Of the gaunt street-lamps and the young cold cries,
The ball falling in the slow distance of dreams.

Football, long falling in the winter sky,
The cold climate of a child's eye
Had kept you at the height so long a time;
His ear had kept the waiting player's cry,

That after years, coming that way then,
He might be pity's witness among men
Who hear those cries across the darkening field,
And see the shadow children home again.

FRANK O'HARA

A Step Away from Them

It's my lunch hour, so I go
for a walk among the hum-colored
cabs. First, down the sidewalk
where laborers feed their dirty
glistening torsos sandwiches

and Coca-Cola, with yellow helmets
on. They protect them from falling
bricks, I guess. Then onto the
avenue where skirts are flipping
above heels and blow up over
grates. The sun is hot, but the
cabs stir up the air. I look
at bargains in wristwatches. There
are cats playing in sawdust.
                        On
to Times Square, where the sign
blows smoke over my head, and higher
the waterfall pours lightly. A
Negro stands in a doorway with a
toothpick, languorously agitating.
A blonde chorus girl clicks: he
smiles and rubs his chin. Everything
suddenly honks: it is 12:40 of
a Thursday.
              Neon in daylight is a
great pleasure, as Edwin Denby would
write, as are light bulbs in daylight.
I stop for a cheeseburger at JULIET'S
CORNER. Giulietta Masina, wife of
Federico Fellini, *è bell' attrice.*
And chocolate malted. A lady in
foxes on such a day puts her poodle
in a cab.

There are several Puerto
Ricans on the avenue today, which
makes it beautiful and warm. First
Bunny died, then John Latouche,
then Jackson Pollock. But is the
earth as full as life was full, of them?
And one has eaten and one walks,
past the magazines with nudes
and the posters for BULLFIGHT and
the Manhattan Storage Warehouse,
which they'll soon tear down. I
used to think they had the Armory
Show there.

      A glass of papaya juice
and back to work. My heart is in my
pocket, it is Poems by Pierre Reverdy.

FRANK O'HARA

The Day Lady Died

It is 12:20 in New York a Friday
three days after Bastille day, yes
it is 1959 and I go get a shoeshine
because I will get off the 4:19 in Easthampton
at 7:15 and then go straight to dinner
and I don't know the people who will feed me

I walk up the muggy street beginning to sun
and have a hamburger and a malted and buy
an ugly NEW WORLD WRITING to see what the poets
in Ghana are doing these days
                                I go on to the bank
and Miss Stillwagon (first name Linda I once heard)
doesn't even look up my balance for once in her life
and in the GOLDEN GRIFFIN I get a little Verlaine
for Patsy with drawings by Bonnard although I do
think of Hesiod, trans. Richmond Lattimore or
Brendan Behan's new play or *Le Balcon* or *Les Nègres*
of Genet, but I don't, I stick with Verlaine
after practically going to sleep with quandariness

and for Mike I just stroll into the PARK LANE
Liquor Store and ask for a bottle of Strega and
then I go back where I came from to 6th Avenue
and the tobacconist in the Ziegfeld Theatre and
casually ask for a carton of Gauloises and a carton
of Picayunes, and a NEW YORK POST with her face on it

and I am sweating a lot by now and thinking of
leaning on the john door in the 5 SPOT
while she whispered a song along the keyboard
to Mal Waldron and everyone and I stopped breathing

FRANK O'HARA

Homosexuality

So we are taking off our masks, are we, and keeping
our mouths shut? as if we'd been pierced by a glance!

The song of an old cow is not more full of judgment
than the vapors which escape one's soul when one is sick;

so I pull the shadows around me like a puff
and crinkle my eyes as if at the most exquisite moment

of a very long opera, and then we are off!
without reproach and without hope that our delicate feet

will touch the earth again, let alone "very soon."
It is the law of my own voice I shall investigate.

I start like ice, my finger to my ear, my ear
to my heart, that proud cur at the garbage can

in the rain. It's wonderful to admire oneself
with complete candor, tallying up the merits of each

of the latrines. 14th Street is drunken and credulous,
53rd tries to tremble but is too at rest. The good

love a park and the inept a railway station,
and there are the divine ones who drag themselves up

and down the lengthening shadow of an Abyssinian head
in the dust, trailing their long elegant heels of hot air

crying to confuse the brave "It's a summer day,
and I want to be wanted more than anything else in the world."

FRANK O'HARA

Music

If I rest for a moment near The Equestrian
pausing for a liver sausage sandwich in the Mayflower Shoppe,
that angel seems to be leading the horse into Bergdorf's
and I am naked as a table cloth, my nerves humming.
Close to the fear of war and the stars which have disappeared.
I have in my hands only 35¢, it's so meaningless to eat!
and gusts of water spray over the basins of leaves
like the hammers of a glass pianoforte. If I seem to you
to have lavender lips under the leaves of the world,
    I must tighten my belt.
It's like a locomotive on the march, the season
    of distress and clarity
and my door is open to the evenings of midwinter's
lightly falling snow over the newspapers.
Clasp me in your handkerchief like a tear, trumpet
of early afternoon! in the foggy autumn.
As they're putting up the Christmas trees on Park Avenue
I shall see my daydreams walking by with dogs in blankets,
put to some use before all those coloured lights come on!
    But no more fountains and no more rain,
    and the stores stay open terribly late.

FRANK O'HARA

Personal Poem

Now when I walk around at lunchtime
I have only two charms in my pocket
an old Roman coin Mike Kanemitsu gave me
and a bolt-head that broke off a packing case
when I was in Madrid the others never
brought me too much luck though they did
help keep me in New York against coercion
but now I'm happy for a time and interested

I walk through the luminous humidity
passing the House of Seagram with its wet
and its loungers and the construction to
the left that closed the sidewalk if
I ever get to be a construction worker
I'd like to have a silver hat please
and get to Moriarty's where I wait for
LeRoi and hear who wants to be a mover and
shaker the last five years my batting average
is .016 that's that, and LeRoi comes in
and tells me Miles Davis was clubbed 12
times last night outside BIRDLAND by a cop
a lady asks us for a nickel for a terrible
disease but we don't give her one we
don't like terrible diseases, then

we go eat some fish and some ale it's
cool but crowded we don't like Lionel Trilling
we decide, we like Don Allen we don't like
Henry James so much we like Herman Melville
we don't want to be in the poets' walk in
San Francisco even we just want to be rich
and walk on girders in our silver hats
I wonder if one person out of the 8,000,000 is
thinking of me as I shake hands with Leroi
and buy a strap for my wristwatch and go
back to work happy at the thought possibly so

FRANK O'HARA

Rhapsody

515 Madison Avenue
door to heaven? portal
stopped realities and eternal licentiousness
or at least the jungle of impossible eagerness
your marble is bronze and your lianas elevator cables
swinging from the myth of ascending
I would join
of declining the challenge of racial attractions
they zing on (into the lynch, dear friends)
while everywhere love is breathing draftily
like a doorway linking 53rd with 54th
the east-bound with the west-bound traffic by 8,000,000s
o midtown tunnels and the tunnels, too, of Holland

where is the summit where all aims are clear
the pin-point light upon a fear of lust
as agony's needlework grows up around the unicorn
and fences him for milk- and yoghurt-work
when I see Gianni I know he's thinking of John Ericson
playing the Rachmaninoff 2nd or Elizabeth Taylor
taking sleeping-pills and Jane thinks of Manderley
and Irkutsk while I cough lightly in the smog of desire
and my eyes water achingly imitating the true blue

a sight of Manahatta in the towering needle
multi-faceted insight of the fly in the stringless labyrinth
Canada plans a higher place than the Empire State Building
I am getting into a cab at 9th Street and 1st Avenue
and the Negro driver tells me about a $120 apartment
"where you can't walk across the floor after 10 at night
not even to pee, cause it keeps them awake downstairs"
no, I don't like that "well, I didn't take it"
perfect in the hot humid morning on my way to work
a little supper-club conversation for the mill of the gods

You were there always and you know all about these things
as indifferent as an encyclopedia with your calm brown eyes
it isn't enough to smile when you run the gauntlet
you've got to spit like Niagara Falls on everybody or
Victoria Falls or at least the beautiful urban fountains of Madrid
as the Niger joins the Gulf of Guinea near the Menemsha Bar
that is what you learn in the early morning passing Madison
        Avenue
where you've never spent any time and stores eat up light

I have always wanted to be near it
though the day is long (and I don't mean Madison Avenue)
lying in a hammock on St. Mark's Place sorting my poems
in the rancid nourishment of this mountainous island
they are coming and we holy ones must go
is Tibet historically a part of China? as I historically
belong to the enormous bliss of American death

LINDA PASTAN

The City

My mother calls it
"The City,"
as if there were
no other,
and somewhere beneath
its sidewalks
a single subway car
ferries my father's ghost
across the Hudson.
My dreams remain
storefront dreams:
a bracelet of lights
circling my wrist,
stalagmites rising
1000 feet
in a cave
of streets.

Here in the country
the fanatic blue
of the sky
sends me indoors
where on clear nights
through the static
of insects sacrificed
against screens,
through the honking
of barnfowl,
I pick up the siren call
of WNYC.

❦

ROBERT PHILLIPS

Decks

In the fair fields of suburban
counties there are many decks—
        redwood hacked from hearts
        of California giants, cantilevered
        over rolling waves of green
        land, firm decks which do not
        emulate ships which lean and list,
        those wide indentured boards which
        travel far, visit exotic ports of call.
        No. Modern widow's walks,

these stable decks, stacked with fold-up
chairs, charcoal bags, rotogrills,
        are encumbered as the *Titanic*'s.
        They echo Ahab pacing the *Pequod*,
        the boy who stood on the burning,
        Crane's jump into the heart of ice,
        Noah craning for a sign, a leaf . . .
        These decks are anchored to ports
        and sherries which mortgaged house
        -wives sip, scanning horizons,

ears cocked for that thrilling sound,
the big boats roaring home—
        Riviera, Continental, Thunderbird!
        Oh, one day let these sad ladies
        loose moorings, lift anchor, cast
        away from the cinderblock foundations.
        Let the houses sail down Saw Mill,
        Merritt, Interstate. You will see
        them by the hundreds, flying flags
        with family crests, boats afloat

on hope. Wives tilt forward, figureheads.
Children, motley crew, swab the decks.
> Let the fleet pass down Grand Concourse,
> make waves on Bruckner Boulevard.
> Wives acknowledge crowds, lift pets.
> The armada enters Broadway, continues
> down to Wall. Docked, the pilgrims
> search for their captains of industry. When
> they come, receive them well. They harbor
> no hostilities. Some have great gifts.

❦

PEDRO PIETRI

Underground Poetry

Spitting
on this platform
or other parts
of this station
is unlawful
offenders are
liable to arrest
$500 fine 6 months
in prison or both
by the dept. of health

Notice
all passengers
are forbidden
to enter upon
or cross the tracks

tormenting itch
of hemorrhoidal tissues
promptly relieved
with preparation H

NEW YORK:

If u c rd th msg
u c bkm a sec
& gt a gd jb
learn shorthand
in as little as 6 weeks

refresh your taste
with wrigley spearmint gum
you can help
stamp out hepatitis

this number
can save you
from the tragedy
of an abortion

woolite soaks more
than just sweaters clean
passengers are forbidden
to ride between trains

start fresh
with a bill payers loan
up to 1400 dollars
from household finance

Warning
subway tracks
are dangerous
if the train
stops in between
stations
stay inside
do not get out
follow
instructions
of the train crew
or police

Aviso
la vía del tren
subterraneo
es peligrosa
si el tren
se para
entre estaciones
no salga
a fuera
siga las
instrucciones
de los
operadores
del tren
o la policía

Pride fear
and confusion
are stopping
five million
disabled
from getting
the help
they need
what is
stopping you?

MIGUEL PIÑERO

There is Nothing New in New York

No hay nada nuevo en nueva york
There is nothing new in new york
I tell you in english
I tell you in spanish
the same situation of oppression
it's the only action in all the corners
of this nation
a revolver ghetto shooting
cold bullets against the police
luck is death which comes and has
the same stench of
poverty

There is nothing new in new york
brother don't stick your nose into welfare
believe me because the tar is ugly
and a curse that's a lot of fun
for the investigators

There is nothing new in new york
we solicit and need
a rain of solution
another work of revolution
a second movement.

There is nothing new in new york
bro work without bread
in this poetry factory
to contract and end the station of
this glorious nation is no game
brotherman believe it today and not tomorrow
that
there is nothing new in new york.

KENNETH PITCHFORD

The Queen

Always before, we sped in the same direction,
not even aware we moved until the opposite train
swayed alongside. Then we saw
how full of arcs and spirals the course
webbed out before us: one train dipping
as the other rose out of sight to reappear
on the other side, so that we sat a foot apart,
peering into each other's lives.

Sometimes, when I regained the upper air,
I might look about expecting to see you
ascending the stair a second later,
but we met only underground,
both our trains hissing as though to strike
our illusory, single destination
just ahead in the darkness,
like the intertwining bodies of two snakes.

We met thus often. You never read
a paper or book or even the curved advertisements
of my time's madness above us,
always wearing the same unpleated blue,
wheat-colored hair drawn back by a single comb.
Whenever I saw you, you were already looking
into my gaze as long as the trains allowed.
Perhaps we invented each other. Neither smiled.

Here, this first winter day, I see you motionless
on the other platform, waiting as I,
but now for a train that runs the other way.
Again, you have already seen me when I notice,
but neither goes to the stairway that would lead
to the other's landing. We only stand and cast
a spider web of intersecting gazes,
less beautiful than those our courses wove.

I spin your history, sister, Persephone,
still wearing the color of your fields and skies,
making a stately progress across the river
into the kingdom of sleepless sleep. And yet,
I wonder why you rode so long beside me
and break away forever now, at the season's turning.
I could not be your king, except where dreams erupt
through an uprooted aconite in a field

real trains never reach. As a hiss of brakes
heralds our cars' arrival,
and our brittle net shatters in sympathy,
we wave goodbye, our only recognition,
until our trains curve back upon each other a last time,
you on the way to our impossible meadow
where the springtime's bridegroom waits,
I on my last descent into the dark.

STANLEY PLUMLY

Fifth & 94th

People are standing, as if out of the rain,
holding on. For the last two blocks
the woman across the aisle has wept
quietly into her hands, the whole
of her upper body nodding, keeping time.
The bus is slow enough you can hear,
inside your head, the traffic within
traffic, like another talk.

Someone is leaning down, someone has touched
her shoulder. But by now she has tucked
her legs up under her, grief given over.
She will not lift her face.
Across the park the winter sun is perfect
behind the grill-work of the trees,
as here it is brilliant against buildings.
Above her body the thousand windows blur.

❧

RALPH POMEROY

Corner

The cop slumps alertly on his motorcycle,
Supported by one leg like a leather stork.
His glance accuses me of loitering.
I can see his eyes moving like fish
In the green depths of his green goggles.

His ease is fake. I can tell.
My ease is fake. And he can tell.
The fingers armored by his gloves
Splay and clench, itching to change something.
As if he were my enemy or my death,
I just stand there watching.

I spit out my gum which has gone stale.
I knock out a new cigarette—
Which is my bravery.
It is all imperceptible.
The way I shift my weight,
The way he creaks in his saddle.

The traffic is specific though constant.
The sun surrounds me, divides the street between us.
His crash helmet is whiter in the shade.
It is like a bull ring as they say it is just before the fighting.
I cannot back down I am there.

Everything holds me back.
I am in danger of disappearing into the sunny dust.
My levis bake and my T shirt sweats.

My cigarette makes my eyes burn.
But I don't dare drop it.

Who made him my enemy?
Prince of coolness. King of fear.
Why do I lean here waiting?
Why does he lounge there watching?

I am becoming sunlight.
My hair is on fire. My boots run like tar.
I am hung-up by the bright air.

Something breaks through all of a sudden,
And he blasts off, quick as a craver,
Smug in his power; watching me watch.

EZRA POUND

N.Y.

My City, my beloved, my white! Ah slender,
Listen! Listen to me, and I will breathe into thee a soul.
Delicately upon the reed, attend me!

Now do I know that I am mad,
For here are a million people surly with traffic;
This is no maid.
Neither could I play upon any reed if I had one.

My City, my beloved,
Thou art a maid with no breasts,
Thou art slender as a silver reed.
Listen to me, attend me!
And I will breathe into thee a soul,
And thou shalt live for ever.

ALASTAIR REID

Pigeons

On the crooked arm of Columbus, on his cloak,
they mimic his blind and statuary stare,
and the chipped profiles of his handmaidens
they adorn with droppings. Over the loud square,
from all the arms and ledges of their rest,
only a bread crust or a bell unshelves them.
Adding to Atlas' globe, they dispose themselves
with a portly propriety and pose as garlands
importantly about his burdened shoulders.
Occasionally a lift of wind uncarves them.

Stone becomes them; they, in their turn, become it.
Their opal eyes have a monumental cast,
and, in a maze of noise,
their quiet *croomb croomb* dignifies the spaces,
suggesting the sound of silence. On cobbled islands,
marooned in tantrums of traffic, they know their place—
the faithful anonymity of servants—
and never beg, but properly receive.

Arriving in rainbows of oil-and-water feathers,
they fountain down from buttresses and outcrops,
from Fontainebleau and London,
and, squat on the margin of roofs, with a gargoyle look,
they note from an edge of air, with hooded eyes,
the city slowly lessening the sky.

All praise to them who nightly in the parks
keep peace for us; who, cosmopolitan,
patrol and people all cathedraled places,
and easily, lazily haunt and inhabit
St. Paul's, St. Peter's, or the Madeleine,
the paved courts of the past, pompous as keepers—
a sober race of messengers and preservers,
neat in their international uniforms,
alighting with a word perhaps from Rome.
Permanence is their business, space and time
their special preservations, and wherever
the great stone men we save from death are stationed,
appropriately on the head of each is perched,
as though forever, his appointed pigeon.

JAMES REISS

Approaching Washington Heights

North, near the tip, where the island
raises its head like a factory
worker who has been asleep in a gray cap
and who blinks, his eyes full of sand,
his lips chapped with age,

where the only bridge in America
that can sing Old Man River with the wind
in its cables has an audience of fire
escapes, and the brown ledge
of the land sprouts names
like Chitenden Avenue, Cabrini Boulevard,

I, who have driven three decades of A trains
shotgun to the motorman from midtown
glued to the window
as we highballed sixty blocks without a stop
up the guts of an electric eel

north past stray stations, dimwatted,
mudugly, platforms
that would be the rust-colored scenarios
of nightmares in which I would race
to catch a train but never make it,
my legs churning in the same spot,

I, who am churning now, who have stayed
on, not gotten off pale-faced
in Harlem as if in the middle of a sentence,

I, who will never get off this train
of thought, these silver wheels
                              barreling
north toward the black mammoth elevators
and hammering escalators of 181st Street,

where the man who sells tokens has a life
behind bars that is totally alien
from mine, though his face is also a map
of Israel, his eyes are tiny
dead seas

❧

DONALD REVELL

Central Park South

The way the buildings curve (as if a thought
or big dream you could never really get
your brain to go about fixing for you, had
for once become a grand hotel, an all
forgiving gray exterior like that
which faces north across the park and loves
you) makes you think of any afternoon
at five in late October and of how
the girl you followed used to disappear
into the Plaza. Nothing has changed along
that street. You walk. You watch a limousine
go by and look for actresses. The light
is still what you remember having thought of
when you thought of Venice, Henry James,
or being happy—blue, with a touch of gray
and orange. Only your nerves can rot; the rest
goes on discriminating, particularly

places. There have always been those places,
real corners that can stay there and forgive your
wanting a drink or having once believed
that love should be conducted openly
and in the daytime. If you could wrap your mind
around the park, the way these walls do, you
would rot a little more slowly. Maybe if
you dreamed the way a building dreams you
might even heal. Remembering that girl
was not a bad way to start. Just follow her
along the park side now, but go west, away
from that hotel that always put an end
to everything. At Columbus, turn and head
for the museum where they put the bones
together; you will be glad of bones by then,
or with a bit of luck, be side by side
with the girl, having forgotten. But either way,
romantic Venice is alive in New York
again. The lights are as blue as ever; the park
is colorful at night, in October. What
you came for were the curves. You got them. Look
at how the buildings curve around and close
in lovingly. You had been following love
then. Now it is a street beside the park.

CHARLES REZNIKOFF

Walk about the subway station

Walk about the subway station
in a grove of steel pillars;
how their knobs, the rivet-heads—
unlike those of oaks—
are regularly placed;
how barren the ground is
except here and there on the platform
a flat black fungus
that was chewing-gum.

ADRIENNE RICH

Burning Oneself In

In a bookstore on the East Side
I read a veteran's testimony:

the running down, for no reason
of an old woman in South Vietnam
by a U.S. Army truck

The heat-wave is over
Lifeless, sunny, the East Side
rests under its awnings

Another summer
The flames go on feeding

and a dull heat permeates the ground
of the mind, the burn has settled in
as if it had no more question

of its right to go on devouring
the rest of a lifetime,
the rest of history

Pieces of information, like this one
blow onto the heap

they keep it fed, whether we will it or not,
another summer, and another
of suffering quietly

in bookstores, in the parks
however we may scream we are
suffering quietly

MURIEL RUKEYSER

Trinity Churchyard

FOR MY MOTHER & HER ANCESTOR, AKIBA

Wherever I walked I went green among young growing
Along the same song, Mother, even along this grass
Where, Mother, tombstones stand each in its pail of shade
In Trinity yard where you at lunchtime came
As a young workingwoman, Mother, bunches of your days,
        grapes
Pressing your life into mine, Mother,
And I never cared for these tombs and graves
But they are your book-keeper hours.

You said to me summers later, deep in your shiniest car
As a different woman, Mother, and I your poem-making
     daughter—
"Each evening after I worked all day for the lock-people
"I wished under a green sky on the young evening star—
"What did I wish for?" What did you wish for, Mother?
"I wished for a man, of course, anywhere in my world,
"And there was Trinity graveyard and the tall New York
     steeples."

Wherever I go, Mother, I stay away from graves
But they turn everywhere in the turning world; now,
Mother Rachel's, on the road from Jerusalem.
And mine is somewhere turning unprepared
In the earth or among the whirling air.
My workingwoman mother is saying to me, Girl—
Years before her rich needy unreal years—
Whatever work you do, always make sure
You can go walking, not like me, shut in your hours.

Mother I walk, going even here in green Galilee
Where our ancestor, Akiba, resisted Rome,
Singing forever for the Song of Songs
Even in torture knowing. Mother, I walk, this blue,
The Sea, Mother, this hillside, to his great white stone.
And again here in New York later I come alone
To you, Mother, I walk, making our poems.

CARL SANDBURG

Trinity Place

The grave of Alexander Hamilton is in Trinity yard at the end of
Wall Street.

The grave of Robert Fulton likewise is in Trinity yard where Wall
Street stops.

And in this yard stenogs, bundle boys, scrubwomen, sit on the
tombstones, and walk on the grass of graves, speaking of war
and weather, of babies, wages and love.

An iron picket fence . . . and streaming thousands along Broad-
way sidewalks . . . straw hats, faces, legs . . . a singing,
talking, hustling river . . . down the great street that ends
with a Sea.

. . . easy is the sleep of Alexander Hamilton.
. . . easy is the sleep of Robert Fulton.
. . . easy are the great governments and the great steamboats.

PHILIP SCHULTZ

The Apartment-Hunter

The longing that moves me is a second, heavier body.
In dark rooms I stare at buildings which mirror other buildings.

The single hanger swaying in closets is always the same hanger.
I press my ear to walls & hear my own echo.

Each empty apartment is a legacy of silence.
I meet myself on stairs & pass without nodding.

JAMES SCHUYLER

Dining Out with Doug and Frank

FOR FRANK POLACH

I

Not quite yet. First,
around the corner for a visit
to the Bella Landauer Collection
of printed ephemera
luscious lithos and why did
Fairy Soap vanish and
Crouch and Fitzgerald survive?
Fairy Soap was once a
household word! I've been living
at Broadway and West 74th
for a week and still haven't
ventured on a stroll in
Central Park, two bizarre blocks
away. (Bizarre is for the ex-
town houses, mixing Byzantine
with Gothic and Queen Anne).
My abstention from the Park
is for Billy Nichols who went
bird watching there and, for
his binoculars, got his
head beat in. Streaming blood
he made it to an avenue
where no cab would pick him up
until one did and at
Roosevelt Hospital he waited
several hours before any
doctor took him in hand. A
year later he was dead. But,
I'll make the park: I carry
more cash than I should and

walk the street at night
without feeling scared unless
someone scary passes.

II

Now it's tomorrow,
as usual. Turned out that
Doug (Douglas Crase, the poet)
had to work (he makes his bread
writing speaches): thirty pages
explaining why Eastman Kodak's
semi-slump (?) is just what
the stockholders ordered. He
looked glum, and declined
a drink. By the by did you know
that John Ashbery's grandfather
was offered an investment-in
when George Eastman founded his
great corporation? He turned it
down. Eastman Kodak will survive.
"Yes" and where would our
John be now? I can't imagine him
any different than he is
a problem which does not arise,
so I went with Frank (the poet,
he makes his dough as a librarian,
botanical librarian at Rutgers
and as a worker he's a beaver:
up at 5.30, home after 7, but
over striped bass he said he
had begun to see the unwisdom
of his ways and next week will
revert to the seven hour day
for which he's paid. Good. Time
and energy to write. Poetry
takes it out of you, or you

have to have a surge to bring
to it. Words. So useful and
pleasant) to dine at McFeely's
at West 23rd and 11th Avenue
by the West River, which is
the right name for the Hudson
when it bifurcates from
the East River to create
Manhattan "an isle of joy."
Take my word for it, don't
(shall I tell you about my
friend who effectively threw
himself under a train in
the Times Square station?
No. Too tender to touch. In
fact, at the moment I've blocked
out his name. No I haven't
Peter Kemeny, gifted and tormented
fat man) listen to anyone
else.

III

Oh. At the Battery all
that water becomes the
North River, which seems
to me to make no sense
at all. I always thought
Castle Garden faced Calais.

IV

Peconic Bay scallops, the
tiny, the real ones and cooked
in butter, not breaded and
plunged in deep grease. The food
is good and reasonable (for these

days) but the point is McFeely's
itself—the owner's name or
was it always called that? It's
the bar of the old Terminal Hotel
and someone (McFeely?) has had
the wit to restore it to what
it was: all was there, under
layers of paint and abuse, neglect.
You, perhaps, could put a date
on it: I'll vote for 1881
or 70s. The ceiling is
florid glass, like the cabbage rose
runners in the grand old hotels
at Saratoga: when were they built?
The bar is thick and long and
sinuous, virile. Mirrors: are
the decorations on them cut
or etched? I do remember that
above the men's door the
word Toilet is etched
on a transom. Beautiful lettering
but nothing to what lurks
within: the three most
splendid urinals I've ever
seen. Like Roman steles. I
don't know what I was going
to say. Yes. Does the Terminal Hotel
itself still function? (Did you
know that "they" sold all the
old mirror glass out of Gage
and Tollner's? Donald Droll has
a fit every time he eats there.)
"Terminal," I surmise, because
the hotel faced the terminal
of the 23rd Street ferry, a
perfect sunset sail to Hoboken
and the yummies of the Clam

Broth House, which, thank God,
still survives. Not many do:
Gage and Tollner's, The Clam Broth House,
McSorley's and now McFeely's. Was
that the most beautiful of the
ferry houses or am I thinking
of Christopher Street? And there
was another uptown that crossed
to Jersey and back but docking
further downtown: it sailed
on two diagonals. And wasn't
there one at 42nd? It couldn't
matter less they're gone, all
gone and we are left with just
the Staten Island ferry, all
right in its way but how often
do you want to pass Miss Liberty
and see that awesome spikey postcard
view? The river ferry boats were
squat and low like tugs, old
and wooden and handsome, you
were *in* the water, *in* the shipping:
Millay wrote a lovely poem about
it all. I cannot accept their
death, or any other death. Bill
Aalto, my first lover (five tumultuous
years found Bill chasing me around
the kitchen table—in Wystan Auden's
house in Forio d'Ischia—with
a carving knife. He was serious
and so was I and so I wouldn't go
when he wanted to see me when
he was dying of leukemia. Am I
sorry? Not really. The fear had
gone too deep. The last time I
saw him was in the City Center lobby
and he was jolly—if he just

stared at you and the tears began
it was time to cut and run—
and the cancer had made him lose
a lot of weight and he looked
young and handsome as the night
we picked each other up
in Pop Tunick's long gone gay bar.
Bill never let me forget that
on the jukebox I kept playing
Lena Horne's "Mad About the Boy."
Why the nagging teasing? It's
a great performance but he
thought it was East 50s queen
taste. Funny—or, funnily enough—
in dreams, and I dream about him
a lot, he's always the nice guy
I first knew and loved not
the figure of terror he became.
Oh well. Bill had his hour: he
was a hero, a major in the
Abraham Lincoln Brigade. A dark
Finn who looked not unlike
a butch version of Valentino.
Watch out for Finns. They're
murder when they drink) used
to ride the ferrys all the
time, doing the bars along
the waterfront: did you know
that Hoboken has—or had—
more bars to the square inch
(Death. At least twice when
someone I knew and hated
died I felt the joy of vengeance:
I mean I smiled and laughed out
loud: a hateful feeling.
It passes.) to the square inch
than any other city? "Trivia,

Goddess . . ." Through dinner
I wanted to talk more than we
did about Frank's poems. All it
came down to was "experiment
more" "try collages" and, "write
some skinny poems" but I like
where he's heading now and
Creative Writing has never
been my trip although I understand
the fun of teaching someone
something fun to do although most people
simply have not got the gift
and where's the point? What
puzzles me is what my friends
find to say. Oh forget it. Reading,
writing, knowing other poets
will do it, if there is
anything doing. The reams
of shit I've read. It would
have been so nice after dinner
to take a ferryboat with Frank
across the Hudson (or West River,
if you prefer). To be on
the water in the dark and
the wonder of electricity—
the real beauty of Manhattan.
Oh well. When they tore down
the Singer Building,
and when I saw the Bogardus Building
rusty and coming unstitched in
a battlefield of rubble I deliberately
withdrew my emotional investments
in loving old New York. Except
you can't. I really like
dining out and last night was
especially fine. A full moon
when we parted hung over

Frank and me. Why is this poem
so long? And full of death?
Frank and Doug are young and
beautiful and have nothing
to do with that. Why is this poem
so long? "Enough is as good
as a feast" and I'm a Herrick fan.
I'd like to take that plunge
into Central Park only I'm
waiting for Darragh Park to phone.
Oh. Doug and Frank. One is light,
the other dark.
Doug is the tall one.

JAMES SCHUYLER

Greenwich Avenue

In the evening of a brightly
unsunny day to watch back-lighted
buildings through the slits
between vertical strips of blinds
and how red brick, brick painted
red, a flaky white, gray or
those of no color at all take
the light though it seems only
above and behind them so what
shows below has a slight evening
"the day—sob—dies" sadness and
the sun marches on. It isn't like that
on these buildings, the colors which
seem to melt, to bloom and go and
return do so in all reality. Go

out and on a cross street briefly
a last sidelong shine catches
the faces of brick and enshadows
the grout: which the eye sees only
as a wash of another diluted color
over the color it thinks it knows
is there. Most things, like the sky,
are always changing, always the same.
Clouds rift and a beam falls
into a cell where a future saint
sits scratching. Or a wintry
sun shows as a shallow pan of red
above the Potomac, below Mount Vernon,
and the doctor from Philadelphia
nods and speaks of a further bleeding.

JAMES SCHUYLER

Hudson Ferry

April what an ice-cold promise
I saw a cherry almost in bloom today
one of five magnolias opened all its buds
wide and pointing at the sun
going down in front of City Hall

they cleaned it. It looks new.
Why can't they stop cleaning things
and sweep the streets. Like the April weather
you can't talk about the weather
it's like saying my lady's damask cheek

look at the smoke blazing over Jersey
the flats are on fire it's like a flushed cheek
and nearer a smokestack blows a dense dark blue
smoke is hot it looks cold trailing like hair
the bite-me kind springy or·flung about

you can't get at a sunset naming colors
the depth the change the charge deep out of deep
the flaring upward what it nails on houses
the smoke swiftly pouring at the stack
hangs lazy wide and scarce dispersed

look at Esta, Isador and Alvin bright
rosy-gilded with wind-burnished cheeks
laughing and chatting in the wind
above the slap and river hoots
and there's Miss Strong Arm, toting her torch

it's another city going back
the moon one night past its full
writes signs vanishing hypnotically
downtown the towers block massively
at the rail a man who rests his hands

looks heroic: he works at night: going from or to?
I don't know I hardly know why I'm on the river
late at night. It's a bore, waiting for a train
reading a tabloid. The City Hall all clean
gleams like silver like the magnolias in the moonlight

DELMORE SCHWARTZ

America, America!

I am a poet of the Hudson River and the heights above it,
     the lights, the stars, and the bridges
I am also by self-appointment the laureate of the Atlantic
     —of the peoples' hearts, crossing it
        to new America.

I am burdened with the truck and chimera, hope,
     acquired in the sweating sick-excited passage
       in steerage, strange and estranged
Hence I must descry and describe the kingdom of emotion.

For I am a poet of the kindergarten (in the city)
     and the cemetery (in the city)
And rapture and ragtime and also the secret city in the heart and
    mind.
This is the song of the natural city self in the 20th century.

It is true but only partly true that a city is a "tyranny of numbers"
(This is the chant of the urban metropolitan and metaphysical self
After the first two World Wars of the 20th century)

—This is the city self, looking from window to lighted window
When the squares and checks of faintly yellow light
Shine at night, upon a huge dim board and slab-like tombs,
Hiding many lives. It is the city consciousness
Which sees and says: more: more and more: always more.

JAMES SCULLY

Esperanza

The bony black face
of Esperanza

archaic face
of blood work, chicken
slaughter, pinfeathers, salted carcasses,
of hands condemned to glow
in cold dreamless water,
cold cement
stopping the feet dead,

the look of work
and strike, one more
picket with a slag-foot rhythm
that says, we won't kill ourselves,
we can walk this line forever,
or what amounts to forever. . . .

Esperanza is sick of forever.

On the strict iron
of the fire escape, she bristles
like chilblains in sunlight
resting her bones against the warm brick wall.

Against the world, which is
legal and anglo, she yanks
a lavender vinyl collar across her face.
Not like an ostrich, but an old opera.
They want her soul, her bread,
her food stamps, welfare
check, slave pay,
her 30-dollar-a-week
union dole.
Her man, her coat.

Even at night
she pulls the night over her head.
Even her cunning
gets carried away
on the wings of her innocence.

The cold damp air
is killing her.
She's picking up what she can,
flying back
to Puerto Rico,
wherever it is—

a thin black bird
good morning'd and fed,
have a pleasant trip
as never before, never again,
in the belly lap
of a huge silver bird . . .
coming down into
factory clouds of sunset chemicals,
flecks of ash,
the queasy
blue wrinkled bay water,
skimming and overshooting
rows of stunted
pineapples withering in the field

a few shreds
of fading color,
the same earth
she had come from, gone to, and left.

A swollen superport
rose from the sea, draining the sea.
A third of the women had been sterilized.

Limousines
sped past vacant lots. Gardenias.

A mountain of nickel,

gouged face . . .

Esperanza
shivered to bone
in the throat of restaurants,
in plump *bodega* hearts,
and in the labyrinth of refineries
—high-flying
    torches
        burning off the night—
in the sublime
filaments of computers
that could not swallow her,
and cannot spit her out.

Now all the hand-slapped guitars
put on
smiles of glass.
They have a mouthful
of sharp dark bird, petty
thievery, acrid
envy;
Esperanza
fills their mouths with blood.

. . . Unborn skies
come to stare: at broken
palm fronds, broken words,
at what seem to be
hands
wrung like flags of shame.

To stare and wonder, how so much
wealth made so much poverty
so much alone,
how so much misery
made Esperanza,

who expected
nothing,

scavenge in the cracks
of her own hands.
This
thing that existed only

to bury her face in the dust of Puerto Pobre.

𝒱

LEOPOLD SEDAR SENGHOR

New York
Trumpet Solo For Jazz Orchestra

1

New York! At first I was confounded by your beauty, those tall
                              long-legged golden girls.
Timid at first before your metallic blue eyes, your frosty smile,
So timid, and my anguish at the bottom of your skyscraping
            streets, raising owl-eyes toward the blacked out sun.
Sulfurous your light and the livid shafts whose heads smash up
                              against the sky.
Skyscrapers whose steely muscle and bronzed stony skin chal-
                              lenge cyclones.
Fifteen days on Manhattan's naked sidewalks
—at the third week's end the fever grabs one with a jaguar's leap,
Fifteen days without wellspring or pasture, birds falling suddenly
                              dead from sooty rooftops.
No blossoming child's laughter, his hand in my cool one.
No maternal breast, nyloned legs. Legs and breasts without odor
                              or sweat.
No tender word in the absence of lips, nothing but artificial
                  hearts paid for at high prices.

And no book in which to read wisdom. The painter's palette is
                 bedecked with coral crystals
O insomniac Manhattan nights! So stirred up with lively lights,
                 while auto horns blare forth the empty hours
And murky waters carry past hygienic loves, like flood rivers, the
                 bodies of dead children.

2

Now is the season for rendering and accounts,
New York! Yes, now is the time for manna and hyssop.
Only listen to God's trombones, let your heart beat to the rhythm
                 of blood, your blood.
I have seen in Harlem, humming with sounds, ceremonious col-
                 ors and flamboyant scents
—at teatime in the drugstores.
I have seen the festival of night in preparation at the flight of day.
                 I proclaim the night more truthful than the day.
This is the pure hour when God makes immemorial life spring
                 forth in the streets,
Its amphibious elements radiating like suns.
Harlem! Harlem! This is what I've seen—Harlem, Harlem!
A green breeze of wheat springing from pavements plowed by
        barefoot dancers waving silken rumps and spearhead
        breasts, ballets of waterlilies and fabulous masks.
At the feet of police horses, the mangoes of love rolling from low
                 houses.
And I have seen along the sidewalks rivulets of white rum,
                 rivulets of black milk in the blue fog of cigars.
I have seen snowfalls at night of cotton flowers, seraphic wings
                 and sorcerers' plumes.
Listen, New York! Oh listen to your virile, copper voice, your
                 vibrating
oboe's voice, hear the stopped-up anguish of your tears fall in
                 great clots of blood
Hear the distant beat of your nocturnal heart, rhythm and blood
                 of the tom-tom, tom-tom blood and tom-tom.

New York! I say New York, let black blood flow in your blood,
Let it rub the rust from your steely joints, like a life-giving oil
Till it gives your bridges the curves of buttocks and the supple-
ness of vines.
For then will be refound the unity of ancient times, the reconcili-
ation of Lion, Bull, and Tree,
Idea linked to act, ear to heart, and sign to sense.
There are your rivers rippling with musky crocodiles and
mirage-eyed manatees. And no need to invent any Sirens.
But it is enough to behold an April rainbow
And to hear, especially to hear the Lord, who with a saxophonic
laugh, created heaven and earth in six days.
And on the seventh, slept a great Negro sleep.

Translated, from the French, by Ellen Conroy Kennedy

ANNE SEXTON

Riding the Elevator Into the Sky

As the fireman said:
Don't book a room over the fifth floor
in any hotel in New York.
They have ladders that will reach further
but no one will climb them.
As the New York *Times* said:
The elevator always seeks out
the floor of the fire
and automatically opens
and won't shut.
These are the warnings
that you must forget
if you're climbing out of yourself.
If you're going to smash into the sky.

Many times I've gone past
the fifth floor,
cranking toward,
but only once
have I gone all the way up.
Sixtieth floor:
small plants and swans bending
into their grave.
Floor two hundred:
mountains with the patience of a cat,
silence wearing its sneakers.

Floor five hundred:
messages and letters centuries old,
birds to drink,
a kitchen of clouds.
Floor six thousand:
the stars,
skeletons on fire,
their arms singing.
And a key,
a very large key,
that opens something—
some useful door—
somewhere—
up there.

HARVEY SHAPIRO

National Cold Storage Company

The National Cold Storage Company contains
More things than you can dream of.
Hard by the Brooklyn Bridge it stands
In a litter of freight cars,
Tugs to one side; the other, the traffic
Of the Long Island Expressway.
I myself have dropped into it in seven years
Midnight tossings, plans for escape, the shakes.
Add this to the national total—
Grant's tomb, the Civil War, Arlington,
The young President dead.
Above the warehouse and beneath the stars
The poets creep on the harp of the Bridge.
But see,
They fall into the National Cold Storage Company
One by one. The wind off the river is too cold,
Or the times too rough, or the Bridge
Is not a harp at all. Or maybe
A monstrous birth inside the warehouse
Must be fed by everything—ships, poems,
Stars, all the years of our lives.

HARVEY SHAPIRO

Riding Westward

It's holiday night
And crazy Jews are on the road,
Finished with fasting and high on prayer.
On either side of the Long Island Expressway
The lights go spinning
Like the twin ends of my tallis.
I hope I can make it to Utopia Parkway
Where my father lies at the end of his road.
And then home to Brooklyn.
Jews, departure from the law
Is equivalent to death.
Shades, we greet each other.
Darkly, on the Long Island Expressway,
Where I say my own prayers for the dead,
Crowded in Queens, remembered in Queens,
As far away as Brooklyn. Cemeteries
Break against the City like seas,
A white froth of tombstones
Or like schools of herring, still desperate
To escape the angel of death.
Entering the City, you have to say
Memorial prayers as he slides overhead
Looking something like my father approaching
The ark as the gates close on the Day of Atonement
Here in the car and in Queens and in Brooklyn.

JUDITH JOHNSON SHERWIN

The Fabulous Teamsters

up from West 86 St., banging, against all hope
dark sun, dark sun
                    the buzzing of small rain
nyah nyah, and i outside
not here but fourteen floors down
in the beeping of trucks right onto your windowpane

well, i couldn't go forward, all roads blocked off and worse
midnights of tubes tied
all over this midnight town
so i stripped my gears with a roar into reverse

backed two Allied trailers up your wall / sunshine
if my tailgate falls /
with the shock / off, and this heavy vanload tries
of uninsured housewares to bump clatter up the wall,
what you find that falls

up should be no surprise.
reach, please and now, for the ground, happy love, take hold
of no matter all that flies.

we are too full of eyes
see too much to see each other, we have sold
past taking what's out of the brownout sent to us
truck up the bricks after truck
load not signed for, our lives, too, sent back after a fuss
or just not seen, dark sun.

buoyant, i for you, you for me,
by levity pulled up
in our boisterous negative momentum, honestly,
gently, ridiculously, praise God, let's be

love's teamsters who have found
if you're not sent up you never get off the ground.

CHARLES SIEBERT

City Butterfly

No memory but this new day, dark wings,
a monarch rests here above the window ledge
over tar-roofs, skylights, and railway sledge,
a long sleep away from earthbound things:
the distant flow of cars on a gray swing
of expressway along eaves toward Brooklyn Bridge,
the blurred city, the morning's vague assemblage
of what is lost each day upon waking.
And a man comes to rest after work each night
on his arms in the window across from me.
He looks out on the same street in the same white
shirt, sleeveless, and, from his tired body, leans,
counting again the rows of traffic lights,
dull roofs and condominiums in Queens.

CHARLES SIMIC

Second Avenue Winter

When the horses were no longer found in dreams,
And the country virgins ceased riding them naked.
When their manes ceased to resemble sea-foam,
And the twitching of their ears no longer prophesied great
    battles.

Just then, a horse came pulling a wagon
Piled up high with old mattresses,
Bent under a grey army blanket
On thick sturdy legs the color of winter's twilight,
Partly a ghost, partly a poor man's burial,
Bringing with each step the heaviness
Of a dumb and unknown animal sorrow.

The fresh snow sobbed under the hoofs of the last horse.
The wagon wheels whined their ancient lineage
Of country roads, of drunks left lying in the mud—
A million years of shivering and coughing.

I too went after them
With a slow shuffle
Of sweet sanctified thoughts
Like a bearded pilgrim.

Thinking of the old negro driver,
Of the insanity that makes him keep
A horse in New York city,
Of their night and their supper,
Its ritual and secret life
Where I wish to be anointed.

LOUIS SIMPSON

Stumpfoot on 42nd Street

1

A Negro sprouts from the pavement like an asparagus.
One hand beats a drum and cymbal;
He plays a trumpet with the other.

He flies the American flag;
When he goes walking, from stump to stump,
It twitches, and swoops, and flaps.

Also, he has a tin cup which he rattles;
He shoves it right in your face.
These freaks are alive in earnest.

He is not embarrassed.
It is for you to feel embarrassed,
Or God, or the way things are.

Therefore he plays the trumpet
And therefore he beats the drum.

2

I can see myself in Venezuela,
With flowers, and clouds in the distance.
The mind tends to drift.

But Stumpfoot stands near a window
Advertising cameras, trusses, household utensils.
The billboards twinkle. The time
Is 12:26.

O why don't angels speak in the infinite
To each other? Why this confusion,
These particular bodies—
Eros with clenched fists, sobbing and cursing?

The time is 12:26.
The streets lead on in burning lines
And giants tremble in electric chains.

3

I can see myself in the middle of Venezuela
Stepping in a nest of ants.
I can see myself being eaten by ants.

My ribs are caught in a thorn bush
And thought has no reality.
But he has furnished his room

With a chair and table.
A chair is like a dog, it waits for man.
He unstraps his apparatus,

And now he is taking off his boots.
He is easing his stumps,
And now he is lighting a cigar.

It seems that a man exists
Only to say, Here I am in person.

LOUIS SIMPSON

The Union Barge on Staten Island

The crazy pier, a roof of splinters
Stretched over the sea,
Was a cattle barge. It sailed in the Civil War,
In the time of the Wilderness battles.
The beams are charred, the deck worn soft between the
    knotholes.

When the barge sank offshore
They drove the cattle on land and slaughtered them here.
What tasty titbits that day
For the great squawking seagulls and pipers!
A hooded shuffling over the dark sand . . .

Under your feet, the wood seems deeply alive.
It's the running sea you feel.
Those animals felt the same currents,
And the drifting clouds
Are drifting over the Wilderness, over the still farms.

❦

L. E. SISSMAN

Lüchow's and After

Dinner at Lüchow's. The invisible man—
Replete, clean-shaven, in a quiet tan
Dacron-and-worsted suit—pays up, gets up,
Walks out, dodging a junkie and a drunk
Disintegrating on the sidewalk, and
Heads south to haunt old haunts, a fattening,
Unlikely ghost of his emaciate
Old self. Unriotous Fifth Avenue—
Asleep in almost as profound a sleep
As in its teens, that mammoth cave of mens-
Wear basted in black silk and lined with blue
Star-pattern Bemberg—peels back from my eyes
In skeins of years: Macmillan's, Sixty-Eight,
The church in its iron close, the Grosvenor,
The other church, the old Fifth Avenue,
Apartments unremembered, Number One—
A cut rate *gratte-ciel*—the gash of Eighth

Street bleeding neon, the streetlight-white Arch,
The Square alive with songs and arguing,
The gloomy Reggio, the tough tenderloin
Beyond it: the mean streets of immigrant-
Less tenements now turned to kinky bars,
Tout-fronted supper clubs for out-of-town
Explorers, cafés packed with solid sound
By small groups with big amps, long poster shops,
Wildcat theatres seating sixty-two,
Diggers' free stores, and *boîtes* that promise blue,
Or, rather, experimental, movies by
Great underground directors. Nothing new
About all this, except for the degree
Of license on display; what worries me
Is the parade of faces down these streets:
Young as the morning, white as inky sheets
Of the *East Village Other* smugly fixed
On the next vein of pleasure to be tapped
(Pill, body, bottle, music, pain, or speed)
At unencumbered will, at instant need;
Soft chins and baby cheeks taped tightly up
In a glazed mask of not-quite-cruel, not-
Quite-irresponsible all-knowingness,
Which spits on you and me, or would if it
Troubled to notice us. Not that our aims
Differ so much from theirs, but that our peers—
Doubles and brothers, classmates and colleagues, friends—
Anxious and thoughtless, put into their hands,
Paternally, the lethal weapon of
The gift of things and not the gift of love.

L. E. SISSMAN

Nocturne, Central Park South

Put a rocket up the man in the moon
And send an astronaut to oust all stars.
No trespass! Bolts of night are ours
At an incredible bargain; bales of noon.

It is amazing how the heart locks out
All interference and clear-channels galaxies
Into one-chambered worlds. Doubt
Is the house dick and time whistles taxis.

L. E. SISSMAN

Pepys Bar, West Forty-eighth Street, 8 a.m.

FOR MAEVE BRENNAN

Up and betimes across the asphalt water,
Misted with morning, to where daytime presses
The fortune of these failing buildings harder
Than we would credit, and turns evening dresses
Sodden and draggled on each dancing daughter
Returning to the Bristol with her tresses
Dishevelled, past the grating at whose center
An iron spider waits for his successes.

L. E. SISSMAN

The West Forties: Morning, Noon, and Night

But nothing whatever is by love debarred . . .
PATRICK KAVANAGH.

I. WELCOME TO HOTEL MAJESTY (SINGLES $4 UP)
On this hotel their rumpled royalties
Descend from their cross-country buses, loyalties
Suspended, losses cut, loves left behind,
To strike it lucky in the state of mind
That manufactures marvels out of mud.
Ensanguined by a bar sign selling Bud,
The early-Streamline lobby, in its shell
Of late-Edwardian ornament, with a bell-
Mouthed cupidon extolling every swag
On its tall, fruitful front (a stale sight gag
First uttered by the comic landsmen who
Compounded a Great White Way out of blue
Sky, gneiss, and schist a whole stone age ago,
Before time steeled the arteries we know)—
The lobby washes redly over guests
With rope-bound bags containing their one best
Suit, shirt, tie, Jockey shorts, and pair of socks,
Half-empty pint, electric-razor box,
Ex-wife's still smiling picture, high-school ring,
Harmonica, discharge, and everything.
Amid the alien corn and ruthless tares
I hear a royal cry of horseplayers
Winding their tin horns in a chant of brass,
Their voices claiming in the wilderness.

II. SAL'S ATOMIC SUBMARINES
The Puerto Rican busboy, Jesus, coughs
Above the cutting board where Sal compiles
An outbound order for the Abinger
Associates next door; then, carrying

A pantheon of heroes in a brown
Kraft-paper bag, he sidles by the chrome-
Formica-plastic dinette furniture
And gains the world, where anti-personnel
Gases from crosstown buses, vegetable
Soup simmering at Bickford's, and My Sin
Seeping from Walgreen's silently combine
To addle all outsiders. Only lithe,
Quick indigenes like Jesus (whose tan neck
Is thinner than my wrist) can long survive
And later even prosper in the air
Of these times' squares, these hexahedral hives
Where every worker drudges for his queen.

III. Stage-Door Johnny's

Silvana Casamassima, Vic Blad
(The talent agent), Lance Bartholomey,
Piretta Paul, Max Dove, A. Lincoln Brown,
Samarra Brown, Lil Yeovil, Beryl Cohn
(Theatrical attorney), Johnny Groen
(The owner), Merritt Praed, Morty Monroe,
Dame Phyllis Woolwich, Sir Jack Handel, Bart.,
Del Hector (the producer), Coquetel,
Fab Newcome, Temple Bell, Vanessa Vane,
Burt Wartman, C. R. Freedley, F.R.S.,
Alf Wandsworth (author of "Queer Street"), Mel Hess,
His Honor Judge Perutz, Merced McCall,
Tam Pierce, Jan Stewart, Tom Cobley, and all
The darlings, mirrored in their flourishing
Autographed caricatures on every wall,
Sail on, sealed in, important, bright, serene,
In league in Captain Nemo's submarine.

IV. Penny Arcadia

Live lava, rock erupts to fill the room
From each coäx- coäx- coäxial
Concentric speaker's throat, and rolls like doom
Over the unmoved pinball-playing boys

Whose jaws lightly reciprocate like long-
Stroke pistons coupled to the Tinguely loom
Of augmented electric music, strong
As sexuality and loud as noise,
Which keens across the dingy room at full
Gain and, its coin gone, as abruptly dies.

V. Meyer Wax Loans

Clear and obscure, elbows of saxophones
Shine out like sink traps in an underworld
Of pledges unredeemed—a spectral band
Of brass and nickel marching in the dark
Toward the morning and redemption, where
Known lips will kiss their reeds, familiar hands
Resume their old and loving fingering.
Unlikely. In a hundred rented rooms
From here to Ybor City, pledgers plan
What next to pawn: the Rolleicord, the ring,
The eight-transistor Victor radio,
The travelling alarm. Alarm creeps in-
To all their calculations, now the bloom
Is off their promise, now the honeymoon
Is over with a cry, and time begins
To whittle expectations to a size
Convenient for their carrying to pawn.

VI. Lovemovie

Before the glazed chrome case where Lovelies Swim
Au Natural, and under the sly lights,
Which wink and bump and wink and grind, except
For those that have burned out, the singing strings
Of Madame Violin essay "Caprice,"
Not missing many notes, considering
How cold it is outside the Lovemovie.
Stray pennies in her tin cup punctuate
The music like applause. Play, gypsies! Dance!
The thin strains of a Romany romance
Undaunt the ears of each peajacketed

Seaman on liberty, and of each old
Wanderer slowly losing to the cold,
And of each schoolboy who has come to see
Life in the flesh inside the Lovemovie.
Beneath her stiff green hair, an artist's grin
Knits up the ravelled cheek of Madame Violin.

VII. THE ARGO BUILDING: NEW DELMAN'S GOOD NIGHT
The last bone button in the old tin tea
Box of the Argo Building lastly sees
INVISIBLE REWEAVING peeling off
His street-side window as he locks the door
Of 720 one more night and struts
His septuagenarian stuff down
The corridor, past Aabco Dental Labs,
Worldwide Investigations, Inc., Madame
Lillé, Corsetière, Star School of Tap,
Dr. O'Keefe, Franck Woodwind Institute,
Wink Publications, and Watch Hospital.
Up the wrought shaft, preceded by its wires
Ticking and twittering, the intrepid car
Rises like an old aeronaut to take
Its ballast-passenger aboard beneath
The pointed clear bulbs of its flour flambeaux.
Sweetly attenuated Art Nouveau
Which was *vieux jeu* and is the rage, unknown
To old New Delman, whom it ferries down
In its black cage, funebrially slow,
To Stygian Forty-seventh Street below.

DAVE SMITH

Gramercy Park Hotel

TO MARVIN BELL

*"Offering the only privately owned park
in New York City. Ask at the desk for a key."*

Genteel, elegant once, the place has seen hard times
that leave the walls pocked like an actor
out of make-up. Waiters crawl in uniforms
stained like old fish, their accents
bubbling up countries far distant.
Plumbing knocks, pressure is asleep,
no one answers the phone. Surely
this is home, it has the feel
of arrival, nonchalant
guests whose babble is determined and cool.

One of them, thirteen floors up I arise, shower, shave
to a new man, and feel bravely tall
as the light that filters through
a dirt-spattered window. If they
could see me now, I think—
and see myself as a fist
uncurling after the long night's
flight through dreams
slipped off like loud silks.
But what now? I stand paralyzed,

as if all that I am and have been has burned away to this
curious stranger, this dark stalk in a mirror.
A sound like my teeth on clam-grit comes.
I throw open the window to breathe.
In the dank smell of concrete,
old bricks, raw gas fumes,
it breaks through like a flower,
the upthrusting will to survive,
a park that is all one green
eye, lined with hard silver.

Then there it is, the wink, the ripple over the heart,
a small wind tilting the leaves, perhaps, a gesture
I imagine rising from roots deeply buried,
a light I once saw foam and spread
in sea water where a big thing
waited, sluggish, long, to leap
and convulse the sky. Gone,
was this the same flat green?
The only horizon? As if in answer
comes a swarming cloud of minnows,

joggers, multicolored feeders that surge and flash,
hungrily pouring around the park, sure
there is some death near now. Is this
why I feel my shadow leave my body
to creak down caged
in the gilded elevator,
to burst out luggageless, laughing
among those I will never understand?
What history, what life do we share
that I would want to be running
at Gramercy, who should hail a cab
and do business in the city's dark, gorged heart?

One more look down. The park shrinks again, a sparse
gray-green, more memory of woods than woods,
no bird call or bright flash. What was,
kept below in a locked drawer.
Already the joggers peel off.
I shield my eyes and try to catch
the far, relentless gleam
the Atlantic would be
from here, that promise.
Behind me conversations, doors
slammed, the tick-tick of descent.
I will not be here long, will be
careful, will have no time for the key.

GERALD STERN

At Bickford's

You should understand that I use my body now for everything
whereas formerly I kept it away from higher regions.
My clothes are in a stack over against the orange pine cupboard
and my hair is lying in little piles on the kitchen floor.
I am finally ready for the happiness I spent my youth arguing and
    fighting against.
    Twenty years ago—walking on Broadway—
I crashed into Shaddai and his eagles.
My great specialty was darkness then
and radiant sexual energy.
Now when light drips on me I walk around without tears.
—Before long I am going to live again on four dollars a day
in the little blocks between 96th and 116th.

I am going to follow the thin line of obedience
between George's Restaurant and Salter's Books.
There is just so much feeling left in me for my old ghost
and I will spend it all in one last outburst of charity.
I will give him money; I will listen to his poems;
I will pity his marriage.
—After that I will drift off again to Bickford's
and spend my life in the cracked cups and the corn muffins.
I will lose half my hatred
at the round tables

🌿

GERALD STERN

96 Vandam

I am going to carry my bed into New York City tonight
complete with dangling sheets and ripped blankets;
I am going to push it across three dark highways
or coast along under 600,000 faint stars.
I want to have it with me so I don't have to beg
for too much shelter from my weak exhausted friends.
I want to be as close as possible to my pillow
in case a dream or a fantasy should pass by.
I want to fall asleep on my own fire escape
and wake up dazed and hungry
to the sound of garbage grinding in the street below
and the smell of coffee cooking in the window above.

🌿

GERALD STERN

One Foot in the River

Living on the river I am able to dip my feet in darkness
whenever I want to and touch the bottom with my white hands.

I am able to live for days in a cold state
besides the catfish and the bony shad.

Going to New York I carry the river in my head
and match it with the flow on 72nd Street and the flow on
    Broadway.

I always know where I am when the struggle begins
and a butchered face goes by me in the water.

I walk down as far as I can without sinking
and make my bed in the black sand and the bottles.

I lie there for hours watching the blood come,
one foot on 72nd Street, one foot in the river.

GERALD STERN

Straus Park

If you know about the Babylonian Jews
coming back to their stone houses in Jerusalem,
and if you know how Ben Franklin fretted
after the fire on Arch Street,
and if you yourself go crazy when you walk through the old shell
on Stout's Valley Road,

then you must know how I felt when I saw Stanley's Cafeteria
boarded up and the sale sign out;
and if you yourself mourned when you saw the back wall settling
and the first floor gone and the stairway gutted
then you must know how I felt when I saw the iron fence
and the scaffold and the plastic sheets in the windows
—Don't go to California yet!
Come with me to Stanley's and spend your life
weeping in the small park on 106th Street.
Stay with me all night! I will give you
breast of Lamb with the fat dripping over the edges;
I will give you the prophet of Baal
making the blood come.
Don't go to California with its big rotting sun
and its oleanders;
I will give you Sappho
preparing herself for the wind;
I will give you Mussolini
sleeping in his chair;
I will give you Voltaire
walking in the snow.
—This is the dark green bench
where I read Yeats,
and that is the fountain where the Deuteronomist sat
with his eyes on the nymph's stomach.
I want you to come here one more time
before you go to California;
I want you to see the Hotel Regent again
and the Edison Theater
and the Cleopatra Fruit Market.
Take the iron fence with you
when you go into the desert.
Take Voltaire and the Deuteronomist
and the luscious nymph.
Do not burn again for nothing.
Do not cry out again in clumsiness and shame.

WALLACE STEVENS

Arrival at the Waldorf

Home from Guatemala, back at the Waldorf.
This arrival in the wild country of the soul,
All approaches gone, being completely there,

Where the wild poem is a substitute
For the woman one loves or ought to love,
One wild rhapsody a fake for another.

You touch the hotel the way you touch light
Or sunlight and you hum and the orchestra
Hums and you say "The world in a verse,

A generation sealed, men remoter than mountains,
Women invisible in music and motion and color,"
After that alien, point-blank, green and actual Guatemala.

❧

PAMELA STEWART

Central Park, 1916

Christmas candles confuse the dusk
But the grind of motors softens
As the Avenue
Narrows and fills up with snow.
The parcels in poinsetta paper
Go soggy in my arms as my boots,
Weighted with whiteness, slow
To turn me toward the Park.

There, the darkening branches
Grow thinner and thinner as white treetops
Merge with slopes and hedges. The streetlamps
Pull back, become gaseous
Beyond the brimming light while the snow
Stings itself to death
Along my body. Back on the corner

Two boys are beating a cart-horse—
Their broomsticks fringed with icy straw.

I feel my outline fade, a tree
Embraced by elements, and believe
I've left this world
As the grey metallic pond
Swallows reckless snow: a flurry
Of swans diving under ice.

Behind me, the rhythmic clink of bells
Is gaining. A small sleigh
Hisses from the trees, its bay pony
Lifting high delicate legs. Faint laughter

Drifts from clustered furs and wool.
My footprints
Vanish as if the clouds had simply
Dropped me here. A boy
Cuts from the street dragging
His sled, a delivery piled with meats
And butter in a wooden box.

I stand restful in this vacancy, then
Turn back to the row of lamps
Peering for steps
And a door with light behind it.
My key works easily, four flights up
To a room. Unthinking, I wipe
My boots to strike the match. Two fingers

On protruding brass
Till the flame's blue wedge shakes light
Around me. The unsteady
Circle on the floor quiets
Like the ending of bad weather,
Like that horse

Dying against a brownstone wall, his forelegs
Buckled beneath him as he slides down
Feathered by the falling snow:
A new guardian of the Park's pond, sad

And giant swan!

❦

TERRY STOKES

The Blood Supply in New York City Is Low

There is no surrealist blood
left on this block. Running out
on ourselves was something we never
dreamed. We followed the calves,

the blue tongue disease
across the toothless border. Our
meat sours; our eyes breed
like foreign bodies, & these were

clear canals we once loved. No,
it is, was, nothing like that.
A young woman dressing, in a pink
slip at the moment, making a bed,

her own, perhaps to sleep in.
Perhaps she will rise, & face my window,
my hazel eyes, perhaps she will call
the police, & tell them I have

hazel eyes, or that she, herself,
has hazel eyes. We are in trouble.
Our fingers burn as we turn away
from the rough glass. We don't know why,

how, we have become *we*. Was it something
we ate? Was it a stream of obscenities
we vaguely imagined? A thundering piece
of rust in our hearts? Darting out

into the blue rain we sprain our hips,
we've sprained our lips, & it doesn't end
on such an up-note. No, I was old enough
to pick up the phone, dial the correct

number, make the right connection, &
you said, "The blood supply is low,"
& I said, "The blue tongue disease
is on the rise." Snails are licking

the moon's full body, all the parts
we will never see.

MARK STRAND

Night Piece

(AFTER DICKENS)

A fine bright moon and thousands of stars!
It is a still night, a very still night
and the stillness is everywhere.

Not only is it a still night
on deserted roads and hilltops
where the dim, quilted countryside seems to doze
as it fans out into clumps of trees dark and unbending
against the sky, with the gray dust of moonlight upon them,

not only is it a still night
in backyards overgrown with weeds, and in woods,
and by tracks where the rat sleeps under the garnet-crusted rock,
and in the abandoned railroad station that reeks of mildew and
    urine,
and on the river where the oil slick rides the current
sparkling among islands and scattered weirs,

not only is it a still night
wherever the river winds through marshes and mud flats fouled
by bottles, tires, and rusty cans, and where it narrows
through the sloping acres of higher ground covered with plots
cleared and graded for building,

not only is it a still night
wherever the river flows, where houses cluster in small towns,
but farther down where more and more bridges are reflected in
    it,
where wharves, cranes, warehouses make it black and awful,
where it turns from those creaking shapes and mingles with the
    sea,

and not only is it a still night
at sea and on the pale glass of the beach
where the watcher stands upright in the mystery and motion of
     his life
and sees the silent ships move in from nowhere he has ever been,
crossing the path of light that he believes runs only to him,

but even in this stranger's wilderness of a city
it is a still night. Steeples and skyscrapers grow
more ethereal, rooftops crowded with towers and ducts
lose their ugliness under the shining of the urban moon;
street noises are fewer and are softened, and footsteps
on the sidewalks pass more quickly away.

In this place where the sound of traffic never ceases
and people move like a ghostly traffic from home to work and
     home,
and the poor in their tenements speak to their gods
and the rich do not hear them, every sound is merged,
this moonlight night, into a distant humming, as if
the city, finally, were singing itself to sleep.

JON SWAN

Among Commuters

In the night in the train pulling out of the city,
standing in the swaying club car, drinking with others
whose faces are too familiar, whose names one does not want to
     know,
looking out of the grubby, pocked, three-star window
at the finale of a sunset, the long clouds the color of rust,
at rubble and tenement, at billboards that advertise space,
at space, one feels, or may feel, that at long last
one is escaping what?

Click of wheel assures you that you are leaving, leaving,
that on earth as in heaven flight is still possible,
that the half-seen faces staring from windows into the summer
	night,
enduring the noise of your elevated passing,
will slip from your mind even as they slip out of sight
like a drowning crowd in another forgettable movie,
that you can shed the daily skin of your existence
by being thus transported.

But the sun sinks and around you the faces flare,
ruddy as they celebrate once again the day's end,
the irresponsible interval between office and home,
between the pressure to produce and the pressure to relax,
to be attentive and loving: another man.
Through dark country now we move between our selves, as the
	train moves,
reluctantly, as if it had too often
reached its destination.

ℐ

MAY SWENSON

At the Museum of Modern Art

At the Museum of Modern Art you can sit in the lobby
on the foam-rubber couch; you can rest and smoke,
and view whatever the revolving doors express.
You don't have to go into the galleries at all.

In this arena the exhibits are free and have all
the surprises of art—besides something extra:
sensory restlessness, the play of alternation,
expectation in an incessant spray

thrown from heads, hands, the tendons of ankles.
The shifts and strollings of feet
engender compositions on the shining tiles,
and glide together and pose gambits,

gestures of design, that scatter, rearrange,
trickle into lines, and turn clicking through a wicket
into rooms where caged colors blotch the walls.
You don't have to go to the movie downstairs

to sit on red plush in the snow and fog
of old-fashioned silence. You can see contemporary
Garbos and Chaplins go by right here.
And there's a mesmeric experimental film

constantly reflected on the flat side of the wide
steel-plate pillar opposite the crenellated window.
Non-objective taxis surging west, on Fifty-third,
liquefy in slippery yellows, dusky crimsons,

pearly mauves—an accelerated sunset, a roiled
surf, or cloud-curls undulating—their tubular ribbons
elongations of the coils of light itself
(engine of color) and motion (motor of form).

MAY SWENSON

Fashion in the 70's

Like, everyone wants to look black
in New York these days.
Faces with black lenses, black
frames around the eyes,
faces framed in black

beards. Afros on all the blacks—
beautiful. But like,
everyone looks puff-headed.
Slouching along in black
leather, fake fur, sleazy body-
shirts, floppy pants, wearing black
boots with thick heels. Bootblacks
have disappeared. Good—but like,
everyone wants to look hoody.
Blacks used to want to look
white. And whites used to want
to be pink. That's pig now.
Sharp, neat, crewcut, cleancut,
blonds preferred is out. O.K., but
whites, the women especially,
if they don't want to look black,
want to look dead. Like,
morticians make them up,
in the Ugly Parlors.
Blacks are loose walkers,
relaxed, laughing. For whites
it's hip to look uptight, scowl,
be grimy, wear scary, puffed-out hair.
Crowds of square-toed black
boots, heavy heels crossing the Walk-
Don't-Walk streets. Like, everyone
wants to look ugly in New York
these days. Like, ugly is beautiful.

MAY SWENSON

Snow in New York

It snowed in New York. I walked on Fifth
Avenue and saw the orange snowplow cut the drifts
with rotary sickles, suck up celestial clods into its turning neck,
a big flue that spewed them into a garbage truck.
This gift from the Alps was good for nothing, though scarcely
    gray.
The bright apparatus, with hungry noise,
crumbled and mauled the new hills. Convoys
of dump-cars hauled them away.

I went to Riker's to blow my nose
in a napkin and drink coffee for its steam. Two rows
of belts came and went from the kitchen, modeling scrambled
eggs, corn muffins, bleeding triangles of pie.
Tubs of dirty dishes slid by.
Outside the fogged window black bulking people stumbled
cursing the good-for-nothing whiteness. I thought
of Rilke, having read how he wrote

to Princess Marie von Thurn und Taxis, saying: "The idea haunts
    me—
it keeps on calling—I must make a poem for Nijinski
that could be, so to say, swallowed and then danced." Printed
as on the page, in its
remembered place in the paragraph, that odd name with three
    dots
over the *iji*, appeared—as I squinted
through the moist window past the traveling
dishes—against the snow. There unraveled

from a file in my mind a magic notion
I, too, used to play with: from chosen words a potion
could be wrung; pickings of them, eaten, could make you fly,
    walk

on water, be somebody else, do or undo anything, go back
or forward on belts of time. But then I thought:
Snow in New York is like poetry, or clothes made of roses.
Who needs it, what can you build with snow, who can you feed?
   Hoses
were coming to whip back to water, wash to the sewers the
   nuisance-freight.

🌿

MAY SWENSON

To the Statue

The square-heeled boat sets off for the Statue.
People are stuck up tight as asparagus stalks
inside the red rails (ribbons tying the bunch).

The tips, their rigid heads against the fog,
all yearn toward the Statue; dents of waves
all minimize and multiply to where

she, fifteen minutes afar (a cooky-tin-shaped
mother-doll) stands without a feature
except her little club of flame.

Other boats pass the promenade. It's exciting
to watch the water heave up, clop the pier,
and even off: a large unsteady belly,

oil-scaled, gasping, then breathing normally.
On the curved horizon, faded shapes of ships,
with thready regalia, cobweb a thick sky.

Nearer, a spluttering bubble over the water
(a mosquito's skeletal hindpart, wings detached
and fused to whip on top like a child's whirltoy)

holds two policemen. They're seated in the air,
serge, brass-buttoned paunches behind glass,
serene, on rubber runners, sledding fog.

Coming back, framed by swollen pilings,
the boat is only inches wide, and flat.
Stalk by stalk, they've climbed into her head

(its bronze is green out there, and hugely spiked)
and down her winding spine into their package,
that now bobs forward on the water's mat.

Soon three-dimensional, colored like a drum,
red-staved, flying a dotted flag,
its rusty iron toe divides the harbor;

sparkling shavings curl out from the bow.
Their heads have faces now. They've been to the Statue.
She has no face from here, but just a fist.
(I think of the flame carved like an asparagus tip.)

❧

ALLEN TATE

The Subway

Dark accurate plunger down the successive knell
Of arch on arch, where ogives burst a red
Reverberance of hail upon the dead
Thunder like an exploding crucible!
Harshly articulate, musical steel shell
Of angry worship, hurled religiously
Upon your business of humility
Into the iron forestries of hell:

Till broken in the shift of quieter
Dense altitudes tangential of your steel,
I am become geometries, and glut
Expansions like a blind astronomer
Dazed, while the worldless heavens bulge and reel
In the cold revery of an idiot.

JEAN VALENTINE

Fidelities

1

Up in this quiet room here, reading your letter,
it's as if I'm in your house. I'm reading.
You're working late, downstairs. The children are all asleep.
It's raining. Later we'll have some warm bourbon and water,
and sleep.
            Outside, the streets are white, the rain
shines like glass. Police
cruise by. You hold me in your arms.
Huge planes move off overhead.

It's as if
if I answer your letter I'll have to show them
my passport: New York. October.
Other friends, another life. It's as if I could choose.

2

strange, sad, these letters

not knowing what you're thinking, reading this

Friendships, fidelities.
Things as they are.
                        Out in the Sheep Meadow
I stare at the high school lovers lying, hardly moving, their skin
shining under the gray trees; I stare
at the old people, talking together, their faces
up to the sun. As if they were talking in bed.

My hand lying open in your hand . . .

The Sunday papers   the dreamy bicycle-riders

                                        As things
                                            are
I hate, I want to embrace the man, the woman who is near you,
who hears your step.

3

not even knowing where you are

Your quick, hunched-forward walk
in this man's walk, your eyes
in that old woman's gray, restless eyes.

4

We have our lives.

The river shone white-yellow under the yellow sky; every insect
     shone,
rising and dropping. We walked back up the field to the house.

Your room there. This white room. Books, papers, letters.
Stamps, the telephone. Our lives.
We're always choosing our lives.

5

All night I thought I heard the phone, or a child
crying. Your face
turned into a snapshot of your face, one
from five years ago.

Your wife and I were sitting up late
in the kitchen, drinking coffee, talking like sisters.
A child cried; one of us went to her, held her.

Here, sitting up late, with a friend,
listening, talking, touching her hand, his hand,
I touch your hand. No one
says anything much. No one leaves anyone.

JEAN VALENTINE

3 a.m. in New York

FOR A.V.C.

I have been standing at the edge
of this green field all night.
My hand is sticky with sugar.

The village winks; it thinks it is
the muscle of the world. The heart.
The mouth.

The horse is standing across the field, near the fence.
He doesn't come any closer,
even in the dark, or run away.

Blood memory:
fixed on vacancy:
coming back and back for a sign

the flat of his coat
the shut out of his eye.

ANDREI VOZNESENSKY

New York Bird

On my windowsill,
monogrammed
                        with moonlight,
                        perches
an aluminum bird;
in place of a body,
                        a fuselage.

And on its corkscrew neck
like the tongue of flame
on a giant cigarette lighter
blazes
  a woman's
    face!

(Wound in his capitalistic sheet,
my traveling companion is asleep.)

Who are you? A cybernetic hallucination, who's
half robot, half creature of air?
A cross between a queen of the blues
and a flying saucer?

Perhaps you're the soul of America,
weary of playing, underneath?
Who are you, young Chimera,
that cigarette clenched between your teeth?

Unblinking, they stare
and steadily gleam—
the eyes like those of that girl somewhere
out in Chicago, face wreathed in cold cream,

circles under her eyes
as if by gas flames blurred—
What do you prophesy?
Don't lie to me, bird!

Will you communicate, will you report
what you know? Something strange from without
rises up in me
as in a branching retort—

The atomic age groans in this hotel room . . .

(I shout. And my companion, crying:
"You son of a bitch!" sits bolt upright in bed,
as if he'd been scalded.)

  Translated, from the Russian, by William Jay Smith

JOHN WAIN

Brooklyn Heights

This is the gay cliff of the nineteenth century,
Drenched in the hopeful ozone of a new day.

Erect and brown, like retired sea-captains,
The houses gaze vigorously at the ocean.

With the hospitable eyes of retired captains
They preside over the meeting of sea and river.

On Sunday mornings the citizens revisit their beginnings.
Whose families walk in the fresh air of the past.

Their children tricycle down the nineteenth century:
America comes smiling towards them like a neighbour.

While the past on three wheels unrolls beneath them,
They hammer in the blazing forge of the future.

Brooklyn Bridge flies through the air on feathers.
The children do not know the weight of its girders.

It is the citizens carry the bridge on their shoulders:
Its overhead lights crackle in their blood vessels.

But now it is Sunday morning, and a sky swept clean.
The citizens put down the bridge and stroll at ease.

They jingle the hopeful change in their pockets.
They forget the tripping dance of the profit motive.

The big ships glide in under the high statue,
The towers cluster like spear-grass on the famous island.

And the citizens dream themselves back in a sparkle of morning.
They ride with their children under a sky swept clean.

Dream on, citizens! Dream the true America, the healer,
Drawing the hot blood from throbbing Europe!

NEW YORK:

Dream the dark-eyed immigrants from the narrow cities:
Dream the iron steamers loaded with prayers and bundles:

Breathe the ozone older than the name of commerce:
Be the citizens of the true survival!

DEREK WALCOTT

The Bridge

Good evening, here is the news.
Tonight, here in Manhattan, on a bridge,
a matter that began

two years ago between this man
and the woman next to him, is ending.
And that concludes the news for tonight,

except the old news of the river's fairy light,
and the bridge lit up
like the postcards, the cliché views,

except that they have nothing to grip the bridge with,
and across the river all the offices are on
for safety, they are like overtyped carbon

held up to light with the tears showing.
The heart that is girded iron melts. The iron
bridge is an empty party. A man is a feather.

There are too many lights on.
It's far too fanciful; that's all;
the iron rainbow to the bright water bending.

Neither is capable of going;
they stand like still beasts in a hunter's moon,
silent like beasts, but soon,

the woman
will sense in her eyes dawn's rain beginning,
and the man

feel in his muscles the river's startled flowing.

✿

DEREK WALCOTT

The Chelsea

I

Nothing, not the hotel's beige dankness, not
the neon-flickered drifts of dirty rain,
the marigolds' drying fire from their pot
above a dead fireplace, means ruin
any more to him. The mirror's reflexes
are nerveless and indifferent as he is
to fame and money. He will find success
in the lost art of failure, so he says
to the flawless girl framed in the mirror's tarnish.
She's more than the hotel's bronze plaque of greats
who hit the bottle or the street, grew rich
or famous. Their fame curls like layers of beige
paint, just as those mirrored flowers will die.
The clear-eyed girl, letting cold tap-water
run on, watches herself watching him lie.

Between the darkening drapes of the hotel
we'd watch the lion-coloured twilight come
stalking up the sandstone, tall
bluff of the West Side Gymnasium,
the wide sky yawning as the tame light curled
around Manhattan, then felt the room fill
with a vague pity, as its objects furred
to indistinction—chair, bed, desk, turn soft
as drowsing lions. Love gives a selfish strength
if lonely lives, down the stale corridors,
still, as they turn the key, nod down the length
of their whole life at slowly closing doors.
In others' hell we made our happiness.
Across the window furnished room and loft
lamplit their intimacies. Happier lives,
settled in ruts, and great for wanting less.

DEREK WALCOTT

Piano Practice

FOR MARK STRAND

April, in another fortnight, metropolitan April.
Light rain-gauze across the museum's entrance,
like their eyes when they leave you, equivocating Spring!
The sun dries the avenue's pumice facade
delicately as a girl tamps tissues on her cheek;
this is my spring piece, can you hear me, Laforgue?
The asphalt shines like sealskin,
like the drizzle trying to bring sadness in,
as furrows part their lips to the spring rain.
But here, in mock Belle Epoque Manhattan,
its avenues hazy as Impressionist clichés,
its gargoyle cornices,
its concrete flowers on chipped pediments,
its subway stops in Byzantine mosaic—
the soul sneezes and one tries to compile
the collage of a lost vocabulary,
the epistolary pathos, the old Laforguian ache.

Deserted piazzas swept by gusts of remorse,
rain-polished cobbles where a curtained carriage
trotted around a corner of Europe for the last time,
the ending that began with Sarajevo,
when the canals were folded like accordions.
Now yellow fever flares in the trouble spots of the globe,
rain drizzles on the white iron chairs in the gardens.
Today is Thursday, Vallejo is dying,
but come, girl, get your raincoat, let's look for life
in some café behind tear-streaked windows,
let's give in to the rain, even if I catch
that touch of a fatal chill called Europe.
Perhaps the *fin-de-siècle* isn't really finished,

290

maybe there's a piano playing it somewhere,
or else they have brought the evening on too early
as the lights go on in the heart of the afternoon.
I called the Muse, she pleaded a headache,
but maybe she was just shy at being seen
with someone who has only one climate,
who knows only Manhattan's mock-malaise,
so I passed the flowers in stone, the sylvan pediments,
alone. It wasn't I who shot the archduke,
I excuse myself of all crimes of that ilk,
I accept the subway's obscene graffiti,
and I could offer her nothing but the predictable
pale head-scarf of the twilight's lurid silk.

Well, goodbye then, I'm sorry I've never gone
to the great city that gave Vallejo fever,
I can offer her nothing but the bracelet of the sun,
I know that I can never
rhyme my exile with the damp fields of Dijon,
but the place I can offer is still yours—
the north coast of an island with wind-bleached grass,
with the one season, with no history,
with stones like white sheep in its pastures
by a silver-circletted sea.

DEREK WALCOTT

Spring Street in '58

FOR FRANK O'HARA

Dirt under the fingernails of the window-ledge,
in the rococo ceiling, grime
flowering like a street opera.
Ah candles, Con Edison nights
in the packing-case district
of my Little Italy,
ah, my blown-out,
fly-blown Bohemia!

There was dirt on the peach tan
of the girls of the gold Midwest,
ou sont ces vierges?
Ah, Frank, elles sont
aux Spring Falls, Iowa,
Columbus, Tucson,
gone with coarse ponytails, gone
with autumnal reveries of Indian blankets,
birches, and the snow creek on the calendar
quivering its palomino hide
to the housefly; back
to the picket fences, Minnesota,
to the strict elms that predicted their return,
to the flowered headscarves and the supermarkets
with the Evergreen Reviews they cannot burn.

And the cheap cocktail bars
by which I homed,
their neon flickered like Mars,
then, we could still write "The moon . . ."
nostalgia was halvah and nougat
and was out of fashion, like death;

and one caught style from others like a cold,
and I could look at Mimi washing her soiled feet
as life imitating Lautrec.

In Spring Street's dirty hermitage, where I
crouched over poems, and drawings, I
knew we'd all live as long as Hokusai.

❦

ROBERT PENN WARREN

Internal Injuries

1

THE EVENT

Nigger: as if it were not
Enough to be old, and a woman, to be
Poor, having a sizeable hole (as
I can plainly see, you being flat on the ground) in
The sole of a shoe (the right one), enough to be

Alone (your daughter off in
Detroit, in three years no letter, your son
Upriver in the pen, at least now you know
Where he is, and no friends), enough to be

Fired (as you have just today
Been, and unfair to boot, for
That durn Jew-lady—there wasn't no way
To know it was you that opened that there durn
Purse, just picking on you on account of
Your complexion), enough to be

Yourself (yes, after sixty-eight
Years, just to have to be
What you are, yeah, look
In the mirror, that
Is you, and when did you
Pray last), enough to be,

Merely to be—Jesus,
Wouldn't just *being* be enough without
Having to have the pee (quite
Literally) knocked out of
You by a 1957 yellow Cadillac driven by
A spic, and him
From New Jersey?

Why couldn't it of at least been a white man?

2

THE SCREAM

The scream comes as regular
As a metronome. Twelve beats
For period of scream, twelve
For period of non-scream, there
Must be some sort of clockwork

Inside you to account for such
Perfection, perhaps you have always
And altogether been clockwork, but
Not realizing its perfection, I
Had thought you merely human.

I apologize for the error, but
It was, under the circumstances,
Only natural.

Pneumatic hammers
Are at work somewhere. In the period
Of non-scream, they seem merely a part of the silence.

3
HER HAT

They are tearing down Penn Station,
Through which joy and sorrow passed,

But against the bright blue May-sky,
In the dazzle and sun-blast,

I can see one cornice swimming
High above the boarding where

Sidewalk superintendents turn now
From their duties and at you stare,

While I, sitting in my taxi,
Watch them watching you, for I,

Ashamed of their insensitiveness,
Am no Peeping Tom with my

Own face pressed directly to the
Window of your pain to peer

Deep in your inward darkness, waiting,
With slack-jawed and spit-wet leer,

For what darkling gleam, and spasm,
Visceral and pure, like love.

Look! your hat's right under a truck wheel.
It's lucky traffic can't yet move.

Somewhere—oh, somewhere above the city—a jet is prowling
   the sky.

4
THE ONLY TROUBLE

The only trouble was, you got up
This morning on the wrong side of the bed, and of
Your life. First, you put the wrong shoe on the right
Foot, or vice versa, and next
You quarreled with your husband. No—
You merely remembered a quarrel you had with him before he
Up and died, or did he merely blow, and never
Was rightly your husband, nohow.

                    Defect of attention
Is defect of character, and now
The scream floats up, and up, like a
Soap bubble, it is enormous, it glitters
Above the city, it is as big as the city,
And on its bottom side all the city is
Accurately reflected, making allowance
For curvature, upside-down, iridescent as
A dream—and as pale!
                    If children were here now,
They would clap their hands for joy.

                    But,
No matter, for in stunning soundlessness, it
Explodes, and over the city a bright mist
Descends of—microscopically—spit.

THE JET MUST BE HUNTING FOR SOMETHING

One cop holds the spic delicately between thumb and forefinger.
It is as though he did not want to get a white glove dirty.

The jet prowls the sky and Penn Station looks bombed-out.

The spic has blood over one eye. He had tried to run away.
He will not try again, and in that knowledge, his face is as calm as
    congealing bacon grease.

Three construction workers come out from behind the hoarding.

The two cops are not even talking to each other, and in spite of
The disturbance you are so metronomically creating, ignore you.
    They are doing their duty.

The jet prowls. I do not know what it is hunting for.

The three construction workers are looking at you like a technical
Problem. I look at them. One looks at his watch. For everything
    there is a season.

How long since last I heard birdsong in the flowery hedgerows of
    France?

Just now, when I looked at you, I had the distinct impression that
    you were staring me straight in the eye, and
Who wants to be a piece of white paper filed for eternity on the
    sharp point of a filing spindle?

The orange-colored helmets of the construction workers bloom
    brilliant as zinnias.

When you were a child in Georgia, a lard-can of zinnias bloomed
    by the little cabin door.
Your mother had planted them in the lard-can. People call
    zinnias nigger-flowers.

Nobody wants to be a piece of white paper filed in the dark on the
    point of a black-enameled spindle forever.

The jet is so far off there is no sound, not even the sizzle it makes
    as it sears the utmost edges of air.
It prowls the edge of distance like the raw edge of experience.
                                 Oh, reality!

I do not know what the jet is hunting for. But it must be hunting
    for something.

   6
BE SOMETHING ELSE

Be something else, be something
    That is not what it is, for
    Being what it is, it is
    Too absolute to be.

If you insist on being
    What you are, how can we
    Ever love you, we
    Cannot love what is—

By which I mean a thing that
    Totally is and therefore
    Is absolute, for we
    Know that the absolute is

Delusion, and that Truth lives
    Only in relation—oh!
    We love you, we truly
    Do, and we love the

World, but we know
    We cannot love others unless
    We learn how to love
    Ourselves properly, and we truly

Want to love you, but
For God's sake stop that yelling!

7

THE WORLD IS A PARABLE

I must hurry, I must go somewhere
Where you are not, where you
Will never be, I
Must go somewhere where
Nothing is real, for only
Nothingness is real and is
A sea of light. The world
Is a parable and we are
The meaning. The traffic
Begins to move, and meaning
In my guts blooms like
A begonia, I dare not
Pronounce its name.—Oh, driver!
For God's sake catch that light, for

There comes a time for us all when we want to begin a new life.

All mythologies recognize that fact.

8
DRIVER, DRIVER

Driver, driver, hurry now—
Yes, driver, listen now, I
Must change the address, I want to go to

A place where nothing is the same.
My guts are full of chyme and chyle of Time and bile, my head
Of visions, I do not even know what the pancreas is for, what,

Driver, driver, is it for?
Tell me, driver, tell me true, for
The traffic begins to move, and that fool ambulance at last,

Screaming, screaming, now arrives.
Jack-hammers are trying, trying, they
Are trying to tell me something, they speak in code.

Driver, do you know the code?
Tat-tat-tat—my head is full of
The code, like Truth or a migraine, and those men in orange
        helmets,

They must know it, they must know,
For *tat-tat*, they make the hammers go, and
So must know the message, know all the slithery functions of

All those fat slick slimy things that
Are so like a tub full of those things you would find
In a vat in the back room of a butcher shop, but wouldn't eat, but

Are not that, for they are you.
Driver, do you truly, truly,
Know what flesh is, and if it is, as some people say, really sacred?

Driver, there's an awful glitter in the air. What is the weather
forecast?

ROBERT WATSON
Times Square Parade

The whores of Times Square troop to their stations.
In orange wigs and stiletto heels they march
Past porno shops, a topless bar, halt, parade rest
On 49th Street, a pimp at each flank.

It is warm. It is noon. It is June.
Muggers spy out barroom windows.
Hotel clerks await their quota of false names.
The onslaught begins. The first shot is fired.
Will love conquer all? They peel off one by one
In orange wigs and stiletto heels.
Nearby a thousand peep shows buzz and fade
With films of conquest, atrocities of flesh.
Of man and beast.

(Is it the failed who seek out the more failed
Than they? And pay for what? Loneliness
Cured for ten minutes, lust cured for a day.)

What a wonderful piece of work is man.

JOHN HALL WHEELOCK

New York
EMPIRE STATE TOWER

From this sheer tower, as from time's parapet,
  My life looks back upon the world I know—
  The desert where man's hope goes to and fro,
The iron ways in which his feet are set.
Oh, hope unquenchable—what blood, what sweat,
  Fashioned this thing! What timeless sorrows flow
  Beneath these towers and battlements that show
The heart of life indomitable yet!

Here is my world: These are the ways that knew
  My spirit in her joy, the haunts that wore
The garment of her bitterness; you, too,
  Belovèd, amid these millions in full flood,
Move somewhere, far from me—seem mine no more,
  Made one now with the nameless multitude.

❧

CLAIRE NICHOLAS WHITE

The Roses of Queens

Among the topless dancers,
warehouses, factories,
disorderly patches of weeds
and rubbish on traffic islands,
behind the endearingly dated
facades on Steinway Street,
bloom in the pocket-sized gardens
the astonishing roses of Queens.

The brick row houses with
their awnings and stoops, as neat
as paintings by Pieter De Hoogh,
line up their rival heavens
with Dutch precision, no doubt
echoing earlier settlers
who could not have foretold
the astonishing roses of Queens.

Yet here they are, as lush
as those of Ispahan,
on ramblers or on bowers,
on shrubs or trees or hedges,
as full as cabbage heads,
crimson and gold, their scent
a heady wave on the wind,
the astonishing roses of Queens.

Tied to the difficult land,
the port of immigration,
by the iron umbilical chord
of the borough's rattling bridge,
this modest array of lives
with the Babel of Europe behind,
invested its capital in
the astonishing roses of Queens.

A place to grow old in the end
when transplanting has borne its fruit,
where bread has as many shapes
as the languages grandfathers speak,
sitting on stoops in the sun
among all this blossoming wealth . . .
Their hopes have come to rest
in the radiant roses of Queens.

WALT WHITMAN

Broadway

What hurrying human tides, or day or night!
What passions, winnings, losses, ardours, swim thy waters!
What whirls of evil, bliss and sorrow, stem thee!
What curious questioning glances—glints of love!
Leer, envy, scorn, contempt, hope, aspiration!
Thou portal—thou arena—thou of the myriad long-drawn lines
and groups!
(Could but thy flagstones, curbs, facades, tell their inimitable
tales;
Thy windows rich, and huge hotels—thy side-walks wide;)
Thou of the endless sliding, mincing, shuffling feet!
Thou, like the parti-colored world itself—like infinite, teeming,
mocking life!
Thou visor'd, vast, unspeakable show and lesson!

WALT WHITMAN

A Broadway Pageant

1
Over the Western sea hither from Niphon come,
Courteous, the swart-cheek'd two-sworded envoys,
Leaning back in their open barouches, bare-headed, impassive,
Ride to-day through Manhattan.

Libertad! I do not know whether others behold what I behold,
In the procession along with the nobles of Niphon, the
    errand-bearers,
Bringing up the rear, hovering above, around, or in the ranks
    marching,
But I will sing you a song of what I behold Libertad.
When million-footed Manhattan unpent descends to her
    pavements,
When the thunder-cracking guns arouse me with the proud roar I
    love,
When the round-mouth'd guns out of the smoke and smell I love
    spit their salutes,
When the fire-flashing guns have fully alerted me and
    heaven-clouds canopy my city with a delicate thin haze,
When gorgeous the countless straight stems, the forests at the
    wharves, thicken with colors,
When every ship richly drest carries her flag at the peak,
When pennants trail and street-festoons hang from the windows,
When Broadway is entirely given up to foot-passengers and
    foot-standers, when the mass is densest,
When the facades of the houses are alive with people, when eyes
    gaze riveted tens of thousands at a time,
When the guests from the islands advance, when the pageant
    moves forward visible,
When the summons is made, when the answer that waited
    thousands of years answers,
I too arising, answering, descend to the pavements, merge with
    the crowd, and gaze with them.

2
Superb-faced Manhattan!
Comrade Americanos! to us, then at last the Orient comes.

To us, my city,
Where our tall-topt marble and iron beauties range on opposite
    sides, to walk in the space between,
To-day our Antipodes comes.

The Originatress comes,
The nest of languages, the bequeather of poems, the race of eld,
Florid with blood, pensive, rapt with musings, hot with passion,
Sultry with perfume, with ample and flowing garments,
With sunburnt visage, with intense soul and glittering eyes,
The race of Brahma comes.

See my cantabile! these and more are flashing to us from the
    procession,
As it moves changing, a kaleidoscope divine it moves changing
    before us.

For not the envoys nor the tann'd Japanee from his island only,
Lithe and silent the Hindoo appears, the Asiatic continent itself
    appears, the past, the dead,
The murky night-morning of wonder and fable inscrutable,
The envelop'd mysteries, the old and unknown hive-bees,
The north, the sweltering south, eastern Assyria, the Hebrews,
    the ancient of ancients,
Vast desolated cities, the gliding present, all of these and more
    are in the pageant-procession.

Geography, the world, is in it,
The Great Sea, the brood of islands, Polynesia, the coast beyond,
The coast you henceforth are facing—you Libertad! from your
    Western golden shores,
The countries there with their populations, the millions en-masse
    are curiously here,
The swarming market-places, the temples with idols ranged
    along the sides or at the end, bonze, brahmin, and llama,
Mandarin, farmer, merchant, mechanic, and fisherman,
The singing-girl and the dancing-girl, the ecstatic persons, the
    secluded emperors,
Confucious himself, the great poets and heroes, the warriors, the
    castes, all,
Trooping up, crowding from all directions, from the Altay
    mountains,

From Thibet, from the four winding and far-flowing rivers of
    China,
From the southern peninsulas and the demi-continental islands,
    from Malaysia,
These and whatever belongs to them palpable show forth to me,
    and are seiz'd by me,
And I am seiz'd by them, and friendlily held by them,
Till as here them all I chant, Libertad! for themselves and for
    you.

For I too raising my voice join the ranks of this pageant,
I am the chanter, I chant aloud over the pageant,
I chant the world on my Western sea,
I chant copious the islands beyond, thick as stars in the sky,
I chant the new empire grander than any before, as in a vision it
    comes to me,
I chant America the mistress, I chant a greater supremacy,
I chant projected a thousand blooming cities yet in time on those
    groups of sea-islands,
My sail-ships and steam-ships threading the archipelagoes,
My star and stripes fluttering in the wind,
Commerce opening, the sleep of ages having done its work, races
    reborn, refresh'd,
Lives, works resumed—the object I know not—but the old, the
    Asiatic renew'd as it must be,
Commencing from this day surrounded by the world.

3
And you Libertad of the world!
You shall sit in the middle well-pois'd thousands and thousands of
    years,
As to-day from one side the nobles of Asia come to you,
As to-morrow from the other side the queen of England sends
    her eldest son to you.

The sign is reversing, the orb is enclosed,
The ring is circled, the journey is done,
The box-lid is but perceptibly open'd, nevertheless the perfume
pours copiously out of the whole box.
Young Libertad! with the venerable Asia, the all-mother,
Be considerate with her now and ever hot Libertad, for you are
all,
Bend your proud neck to the long-off mother now sending
messages over the archipelagoes to you,
Bend your proud neck low for once, young Libertad.

Were the children straying westward so long? so wide the
tramping?
Were the precedent dim ages debouching westward from
Paradise so long?
Were the centuries steadily footing it that way, all the while
unknown, for you, for reasons?

They are justified, they are accomplish'd, they shall now be
turn'd the other way also, to travel toward you thence,
They shall now also march obediently eastward for your sake
Libertad.

WALT WHITMAN

City of Orgies

City of orgies, walks and joys,
City whom that I have lived and sung in your midst will one day
make you illustrious,
Not the pageants of you, not your shifting tableaus, your
spectacles, repay me,

NEW YORK:

Not the interminable rows of your houses, nor the ships at the
wharves,
Nor the processions in the streets, nor the bright windows with
goods in them,
Nor to converse with learn'd persons, or bear my share in the
soiree or feast;
Not those, but as I pass O Manhattan, your frequent and swift
flash of eyes offering me love,
Offering response to my own—these repay me,
Lovers, continual lovers, only repay me.

𝒱

WALT WHITMAN

Crossing Brooklyn Ferry

1

Flood-tide below me! I see you face to face!
Clouds of the west—sun there half an hour high—I see you also
face to face.

Crowds of men and women attired in the usual costumes, how
curious you are to me!
On the ferry-boats the hundreds and hundreds that cross,
returning home, are more curious to me than you suppose,
And you that shall cross from shore to shore years hence are more
to me, and more in my meditations, than you might
suppose.

2

The impalpable sustenance of me from all things at all hours of
the day,
The simple, compact, well-join'd scheme, myself disintegrated,
every one disintegrated yet part of the scheme,
The similitudes of the past and those of the future,
The glories strung like beads on my smallest sights and hearings,
on the walk in the street and the passage over the river,
The current rushing so swiftly and swimming with me far away,
The others that are to follow me, the ties between me and them,
The certainty of others, the life, love, sight, hearing of others.

Others will enter the gates of the ferry and cross from shore to
shore,
Others will watch the run of the flood-tide,
Others will see the shipping of Manhattan north and west, and
the heights of Brooklyn to the south and east,
Others will see the islands large and small;
Fifty years hence, others will see them as they cross, the sun half
an hour high,
A hundred years hence, or ever so many hundred years hence,
others will see them,
Will enjoy the sunset, the pouring-in of the flood-tide, the falling
back to the sea of the ebb-tide.

3

It avails not, time nor place—distance avails not,
I am with you, you men and women of a generation, or ever so
many generations hence,
Just as you feel when you look on the river and sky, so I felt,
Just as any of you is one of a living crowd, I was one of a crowd,
Just as you are refresh'd by the gladness of the river and the
bright flow, I was refresh'd,
Just as you stand and lean on the rail, yet hurry with the swift
current, I stood yet was hurried,
Just as you look on the numberless masts of ships and the
thick-stemm'd pipes of steamboats, I look'd.

I too many and many a time cross'd the river of old,
Watched the Twelfth-month sea-gulls, saw them high in the air
    floating with motionless wings, oscillating their bodies,
Saw how the glistening yellow lit up parts of their bodies and left
    the rest in strong shadow,
Saw the slow-wheeling circles and the gradual edging toward the
    south,
Saw the reflection of the summer sky in the water,
Had my eyes dazzled by the shimmering track of beams,
Look'd at the fine centrifugal spokes of light round the shape of
    my head in the sunlit water,
Look'd on the haze on the hills southward and south-westward,
Look'd on the vapor as it flew in fleeces tinged with violet,
Look'd toward the lower bay to notice the vessels arriving,
Saw their approach, saw aboard those that were near me,
Saw the white sails of schooners and sloops, saw the ships at
    anchor,
The sailors at work in the rigging or out astride the spars,
The round masts, the swinging motion of the hulls, the slender
    serpentine pennants,
The large and small steamers in motion, the pilots in their
    pilot-houses,
The white wake left by the passage, the quick tremulous whirl of
    the wheels,
The flags of all nations, the falling of them at sunset,
The scallop-edged waves in the twilight, the ladled cups, the
    frolicsome crests and glistening,
The stretch afar growing dimmer and dimmer, the gray walls of
    the granite storehouses by the docks,
On the river the shadowy group, the big steam-tug closely flank'd
    on each side by the barges, the hay-boat, the belated lighter,
On the neighboring shore the fires from the foundry chimneys
    burning high and glaringly into the night,
Casting their flicker of black contrasted with wild red and yellow
    light over the tops of houses and down into the clefts of
    streets.

4

These and all else were to me the same as they are to you,
I loved well those cities, loved well the stately and rapid river,
The men and women I saw were all near to me,
Others the same—others who look back on me because I look'd
     forward to them,
(The time will come, though I stop here to-day and to-night.)

5

What is it then between us?
What is the count of the scores or hundreds of years between us?

Whatever it is, it avails not—distance avails not, and place avails
     not,
I too lived, Brooklyn of ample hills was mine,
I too walk'd the streets of Manhattan island, and bathed in the
     waters around it,
I too felt the curious abrupt questionings stir within me,
In the day among crowds of people sometimes they came upon
     me,
In my walks home late at night or as I lay in my bed they came
     upon me,
I too had been struck from the float forever held in solution,
I too had receiv'd identity by my body,
That I was I knew was of my body, and what I should be I knew I
     should be of my body.

6

It is not upon you alone the dark patches fall,
The dark threw its patches down upon me also,
The best I had done seem'd to me blank and suspicious,
My great thoughts as I supposed them, were they not in reality
     meagre?
Nor is it you alone who know what it is to be evil,
I am he who knew what it was to be evil,
I too knitted the old knot of contrariety,
Blabb'd, blush'd, resented, lied, stole, grudg'd,

Had guile, anger, lust, hot wishes I dared not speak,
Was wayward, vain, greedy, shallow, sly, cowardly, malignant,
The wolf, the snake, the hog, not wanting in me,
The cheating look, the frivolous word, the adulterous wish, not
    wanting,
Refusals, hates, postponements, meanness, laziness, none of
    these wanting,
Was one with the rest, the days and haps of the rest,
Was call'd by my nighest name by clear loud voices of young men
    as they saw me approaching or passing,
Felt their arms on my neck as I stood, or the negligent leaning of
    their flesh against me as I sat,
Saw many I loved in the street or ferry-boat or public assembly,
    yet never told them a word,
Lived the same life with the rest, the same old laughing,
    gnawing, sleeping,
Play'd the part that still looks back on the actor or actress,
The same old role, the role that is what we make it, as great as we
    like,
Or as small as we like, or both great and small.

7
Closer yet I approach you,
What thought you have of me now, I had as much of you—I laid
    in my stores in advance,
I consider'd long and seriously of you before you were born.

Who was to know what should come home to me?
Who knows but I am enjoying this?
Who knows, for all the distance, but I am as good as looking at
    you now, for all you cannot see me?

8
Ah, what can ever be more stately and admirable to me than
    mast-hemm'd Manhattan?
River and sunset and scallop-edg'd waves of flood-tide?

The sea-gulls oscillating their bodies, the hay-boat in the twilight, and the belated lighter?

What gods can exceed these that clasp me by the hand, and with voices I love call me promptly and loudly by my nighest name as I approach?

What is more subtle than this which ties me to the woman or man that looks in my face?

Which fuses me into you now, and pours my meaning into you?

We understand then do we not?

What I promis'd without mentioning it, have you not accepted?

What the study could not teach—what the preaching could not accomplish is accomplish'd, is it not?

9

Flow on, river! flow with the flood-tide, and ebb with the ebb-tide!

Frolic on, crested and scallop-edg'd waves!

Gorgeous clouds of the sunset! drench with your splendor me, or the men and women generations after me!

Cross from shore to shore, countless crowds of passengers!

Stand up, tall masts of Mannahatta! stand up, beautiful hills of Brooklyn!

Throb, baffled and curious brain! throw out questions and answers!

Suspend here and everywhere, eternal float of solution!

Gaze, loving and thirsty eyes, in the house or street or public assembly!

Sound out, voices of young men! loudly and musically call me by my nighest name!

Live, old life! play the part that looks back on the actor or actress!

Play the old role, the role that is great or small according as one makes it!

Consider, you who peruse me, whether I may not in unknown ways be looking upon you;

Be firm, rail over the river, to support those who lean idly, yet haste with the hasting current;

Fly on, sea-birds! fly sideways, or wheel in large circles high in
the air;
Receive the summer sky, you water, and faithfully hold it till all
downcast eyes have time to take it from you!
Diverge, fine spokes of light, from the shape of my head, or any
one's head, in the sunlit water!
Come on, ships from the lower bay! pass up or down, white-sail'd
schooners, sloops, lighters!
Flaunt away, flags of all nations! be duly lower'd at sunset!
Burn high your fires, foundry chimneys! cast black shadows at
nightfall! cast red and yellow light over the tops of the
houses!
Appearances, now or henceforth, indicate what you are,
You necessary film, continue to envelop the soul,
About my body for me, and your body for you, be hung out
divinest aromas,
Thrive, cities—bring your freight, bring your shows, ample and
sufficient rivers,
Expand, being than which none else is perhaps more spiritual,
Keep your places, objects than which none else is more lasting.

You have waited, you always wait, you dumb, beautiful
ministers,
We receive you with free sense at last, and are insatiate
henceforward,
Not you any more shall be able to foil us, or withhold yourselves
from us,
We use you, and do not cast you aside—we plant you
permanently within us,
We fathom you not—we love you—there is perfection in you
also,
You furnish your parts toward eternity,
Great or small, you furnish your parts toward the soul.

𝒱

WALT WHITMAN

Give Me the Splendid Silent Sun

1

Give me the splendid silent sun with all his beams full-dazzling,
Give me juicy autumnal fruit ripe and red from the orchard,
Give me a field where the unmow'd grass grows,
Give me an arbor, give me the trellis'd grape,
Give me fresh corn and wheat, give me serene-moving animals
 teaching content,
Give me nights perfectly quiet as on high plateaus west of the
 Mississippi, and I looking up at the stars,
Give me odorous at sunrise a garden of beautiful flowers where I
 can walk undisturb'd,
Give me for marriage a sweet-breath'd woman of whom I should
 never tire,
Give me a perfect child, give me away aside from the noise of the
 world a rural domestic life,
Give me to warble spontaneous songs recluse by myself, for my
 own ears only,
Give me solitude, give me Nature, give me again O Nature your
 primal sanities!

These demanding to have them, (tired with ceaseless excitement
 and rack'd by the war-strife,)
These to procure incessantly asking, rising in cries from my
 heart,
While yet incessantly asking still I adhere to my city,
Day upon day and year upon year O city, walking your streets,
Where you hold me enchain'd a certain time refusing to give me
 up,
Yet giving to make me glutted, enrich'd of soul, you give me
 forever faces;
(O I see what I sought to escape, confronting, reversing my cries,
I see my own soul trampling down what it ask'd for.)

NEW YORK:

2

Keep your spendid silent sun,
Keep your woods O Nature, and the quiet places by the woods,
Keep your fields of clover and timothy, and your corn fields and
  orchards,
Keep the blossoming buckwheat fields where the Ninth-month
  bees hum;
Give me faces and streets—give me these phantoms incessant
  and endless along the trottoirs!
Give me interminable eyes—give me women—give me
  comrades and lovers by the thousand!
Let me see new ones every day—let me hold new ones by the
  hand every day!
Give me such shows—give me the streets of Manhattan!
Give me Broadway, with the soldiers marching—give me the
  sound of the trumpets and drums!
(The soldiers in companies or regiments—some starting away,
  flush'd and reckless,
Some, their time up, returning with thinn'd ranks, young, yet
  very old, worn, marching, noticing nothing;)
Give me the shores and wharves heavy-fringed with black ships!
O such for me! O an intense life, full to repletion and varied!
The life of the theatre, bar-room, huge hotel, for me!
The saloon of the steamer! the crowded excursion for me! the
  torchlight procession!
The dense brigade bound for the war, with high piled military
  wagons following;
People, endless, streaming, with strong voices, passions,
  pageants,
Manhattan streets with their powerful throbs, with beating
  drums as now,
The endless and noisy chorus, the rustle and clank of muskets,
  (even the sight of the wounded,)
Manhattan crowds, with their turbulent musical chorus!
Manhattan faces and eyes forever for me.

WALT WHITMAN

Mannahatta

I was asking for something specific and perfect for my city,
Whereupon lo! upsprang the aboriginal name.

Now I see what there is in a name, a word, liquid, sane, unruly,
    musical, self-sufficient,
I see that the word of my city is that word from of old,
Because I see that word nested in nests of water-bays, superb,
Rich, hemm'd thick all around with sailships and steamships, an
    island sixteen miles long, solid-founded,
Numberless crowded streets, high growths of iron, slender,
    strong, light, splendidly uprising toward clear skies,
Tides swift and ample, well-loved by me, toward sundown,
The flowing sea-currents, the little islands, larger adjoining
    islands, the heights, the villas,
The countless masts, the white shore-steamers, the lighters, the
    ferry-boats, the black sea-steamers well-model'd,
The down-town streets, the jobbers' houses of business, the
    houses of business of the ship-merchants and
    money-brokers, the river-streets,
Immigrants arriving, fifteen or twenty thousand in a week,
The carts hauling goods, the manly race of drivers of horses, the
    brown-faced sailors,
The summer air, the bright sun shining, and the sailing clouds
    aloft,
The winter snows, the sleigh-bells, the broken ice in the river,
    passing along up or down with the flood-tide or ebb-tide,
The mechanics of the city, the masters, well-form'd,
    beautiful-faced looking you straight in the eyes,
Trottoirs throng'd, vehicles, Broadway, the women, the shops
    and shows,

A million people—manners free and superb—open
    voices—hospitality—the most courageous and friendly
    young men,
City of hurried and sparkling waters! city of spires and masts!
City nested in bays! my city!

𝒱

REED WHITTEMORE

Ode to New York

Let me not be unfair Lord to New York that sink that sewer
Where the best the worst and the middle
Of our land and all others go in their days of hope to be made
    over
Into granite careerists
Let me not be unfair to that town whose residents
Not content to subside in their own stench
Drag down the heavens let me not be unfair because I have
    known
An incorruptible New Yorker (he was a saint)
Also NY has produced at least three books
Two plays
A dozen fine dresses meals shirts taxidrivers
Not to mention Jack (Steve?) Brodie
And Mayor LaGuardia why should it matter
That the rest is garbage
                    No let me be fair
And mention wonders like East 9th Street
Why should anybody care that NY is 2/3 of our country's ills
(And Washington 1/3, and Muncie Dallas Birmingham and LA
    the rest)

When it has crooks so rich and powerful that when they drive to
    town
They can park?
Let us not forget that TV is in New York and
        the worst slums
      the largest fortunes
    the most essential inhumanity
Since Nero or maybe Attila as well as
Hospitals that admit no patient without a $300 deposit
                            if I were a local
I'd take the express to Rahway but let me just say
That I don't like New York much
All that corrupt stone
All those dishonest girders decadent manholes diseased
    telephones
New York reminds me of when I had jaundice
New York is sick in the inner soul
Of its gut but we'll be dead of it
Before it is and so New York
You wonderful fun town
Who inspireth my animus
And leadeth two hundred million other Americans to wish they
    had not
        been born under the spell of free enterprise but in a
          Martian restroom
                New York
  I know that when I speak of you I speak of me
I speak of us
I speak of selves who resolved at the age of four to
      convert themselves into currency
Because at the age of four they (I, we) had already
    learned
That no food clothing housing
Existed other than currency
And no faith hope charity
Other than currency

                    good waterproof dollars
And if there were labor that could not be turned into
        currency
They (I, we) knew not to do it
And if there were thoughts that could not be turned
        into currency
They (I, we) knew not to have them

So here we are in the latter day of our wisdom
Yesterday sweetness and light reached a new low
In heavy trading
Even porn is in trouble
                        what can be done?
In a decade a dozen of our holiest ones
Will own the island
But rats will be running the island

In a decade not a minute of a working man's day will
        belong to a working man
All subway riders will pay dues to the Limousine Club

Rats will be running the island
There is no surer route to the grave than through NY
And all American routes go through NY
NY lurks in the corners of our churches paintings novels
NY infests our playing fields newspapers trade unions
There is not a square foot of American sidewalk without
        the mark of a NY entrepreneur
Wherever you drive he will cut in front of you
                        he will get there first

Rats on the island
Ravenous rats
Bred by the banks and the stock exchange
Fed by the eighteen percenters
World that will end
But when?

Lord
>you have sent us prophets

They have prattled about revolution and pocketed the
>proceeds

They have made it
>>by an infallible law of New York

In direct proportion to the extravagance and falsehood
>of their announced visions

They have built the hysteria of constant and drastic
>social change into each breakfast

They have taught our children how to stop war on
>Monday poverty on Tuesday racism on Wednesday
>sexism on Thursday and final exams on Friday

Yet nothing changes

And wherever one drives the prophets are out in front
>>they get there first

Rats on the island

Oh New York let me be fair you hell town

I was born to the north of you have lived to the west of
>you

I have sneaked up on you by land air and sea and been
>robbed in your clip joints

I have left you hundreds of times in the dream that I
>*could*

Leave you
>but always you sit there

Sinking
>my dearest my sweet

Would you buy these woids?

MILLER WILLIAMS

Of Human Bondage

In a phone booth
on 42nd Street
by secret to the death
transmogrifications
he came to be
whatever was called for

as many a night
between the click of Zippos
and the slow smoke
How do you do and
Very well thank you and you
you son of a bitch

he has brought pale women dying for love
to life
pumping into their hulls
his grand reluctance

and murdered their men

Not even Lois Lane knows for sure

WILLIAM CARLOS WILLIAMS

A Place (Any Place) to Transcend All Places

IN New York, it is said,
they *do* meet (if that is
what is wanted) talk but
nothing is exchanged
unless that guff
can be retranslated: as
to say, that is not
the end, there are channels
above that, draining
places from which New York
is dignified, created (the
deaf are not tuned in).

A church in New Hampshire
built by its pastor
from his own wood lot. One
black (of course, red)
rose; a fat old woman backing
through a screen door. Two,
from the armpits
down, contrasting in bed,
breathless; a letter from
a ship; leaves filling,
making, a tree (but
wait) not just leaves,
leaves of one design that
make a certain design,
no two alike, not like
the locust either, next in line,
nor the Rose of Sharon, in
the pod-stage, near it—a
tree! Imagine it! Pears

philosophically hard. Nor
thought that is from
branches on a root, from
an acid soil, with scant
grass about the bole
where it breaks through.

New York is built of
such grass and weeds; a modern
tuberculin-tested herd
white-faced behind a
white fence, patient and
uniform; a museum of looks
across a breakfast
table; subways of dreams;
towers of divisions
from thin pay envelopes.
What else is it? And what
else can it be? Sweatshops
and railroad yards at dusk
(puffed up by fantasy
to seem real) what else
can they be budded on
to live a little longer?
The eyes by this
far quicker than the mind.

　　—and we have
:Southern writers, foreign
writers, hugging a dis-
tinction, while perspective
behind them following
the crisis (at home)
peasant loyalties inspire
the avant-garde. Abstractly?
No: That was for something
else. "Lefutur!" grimly.
New York? That hodge-podge?

The international city
(from the Bosphorus). Poor
Hoboken. Poor sad
Eliot. Poor memory. .
        —and we have
:the memory of Elsa
von Freytag Loringhofen,
a fixation from the street
door of a Berlin
playhouse; all who "wear
their manner too obviously,"
the adopted English (white)
and many others.
        —and we have
:the script writer advising
"every line to be like
a ten word telegram" but
neglecting to add, "to a
child of twelve"—obscene
beyond belief.
                Obscene and
abstract as excrement—
that no one wants to own
except the coolie
with a garden of which
the lettuce particularly
depends on it—if you
like lettuce, but
very, very specially, heaped
about the roots for nourishment.

WILLIAM CARLOS WILLIAMS

The Last Turn

Then see it! in distressing
detail—from behind a red light
at 53d and 6th
of a November evening, with
the jazz of the cross lights
echoing the crazy weave of
the breaking mind: splash of
a half purple half naked woman's
body whose bejeweled guts
the cars drag up and down—
No house but that has its
brains blown off by the dark!
Nothing recognizable
but the whole, one jittering
direction made of all directions
spelling the inexplicable,
pigment upon flesh and flesh
the pigment the genius of a world
artless but supreme . . .

JAMES WRIGHT

Before the Cashier's Window in a Department Store

1

The beautiful cashier's white face has risen once more
Behind a young manager's shoulder.
They whisper together, and stare
Straight into my face.
I feel like grabbing a stray child
Or a skinny old woman
And diving into a cellar, crouching
Under a stone bridge, praying myself sick,
Till the troops pass.

2

Why should he care? He goes.
I slump deeper.
In my frayed coat, I am pinned down
By debt. He nods,
Commending my flesh to the pity of the daws of God.

3

Am I dead? And, if not, why not?
For she sails there, alone, looming in the heaven of the beautiful.
She knows
The bulldozers will scrape me up
After dark, behind
The officers' club.
Beneath her terrible blaze, my skeleton
Glitters out. I am the dark. I am the dark
Bone I was born to be.

4

Tu Fu woke shuddering on a battlefield
Once, in the dead of night, and made out
The mangled women, sorting
The haggard slant-eyes.
The moon was up.

5

I am hungry. In two more days
It will be Spring. So: this
Is what it feels like.

PAUL ZWEIG

Uptown

A streak of car paint;
A shopping cart dragged past the window
By a closed black face.
The worst is when the sidewalk becomes a mirror,
And the woman becomes a mirror,
With her abstract smile, her teeth like thrush eggs.

Thin child-body in November, why do you
Pass by me? Lovely freckled girl,
Naked inside those wraps of clothing,
Or maybe not. Maybe you are dressed
Underneath too, like an old armchair,
A crucifix of gray patched cloth,
But no bare touches where the secrets grow,
Soft as mushrooms underneath.

A boy hanging behind the bus wants to fly.
He squats on the rear fender, wondering
What that spread-eagled shape is grinning at him
From the scarred pavement, like Michelangelo's Prisoner.
Broken arms, yellow grin. No wings, but rising
From the mirror with the flexible haste
Of internal injuries.

In the middle of Broadway a tree strips down for winter.
It reminds me of Robinson Crusoe
Who sat on his island, winter and summer,
Moving his lips with squirrely haste,
While cars and buses grunted by him on both sides.

NEW YORK:

BIBLIOGRAPHY

CONRAD AIKEN (b. 1889, Savannah, Ga., d. 1973, Savannah, Ga.) Pulitzer Prize, Shelley Memorial Award, Bollingen Prize, Gold Medal for Poetry, American Academy of Arts and Letters. Contemporary of T. S. Eliot. Also novelist, short-story writer, and critic. *Collected Poems* (Oxford University Press, 1953, 1970). Collected criticism, *A Reviewer's ABC*.

GROVER AMEN (b. 1937, New York City) Ex-member of *The New Yorker* staff, on which he was a reporter for many years.

A. R. AMMONS (b. 1926, Whiteville, N.C.) National Book Award, Bollingen Prize. Teaches at Cornell University. *Selected Poems: 1951–1977* (W. W. Norton, 1977).

PHILIP APPLEMAN (b. 1926, Kendallville, Indiana) Professor of English at Indiana University. He has published three books of poetry—*Kites on a Windy Day* (Bryon Press, England), *Summerlove and Surf* (Vanderbilt Univ. Press), and *Open Doorways* (W. W. Norton)—and a novel, *Shame the Devil* (Crown).

JOHN ASHBERY (b. 1927, Rochester, N.Y.) Pulitzer Prize, National Book Award, National Book Critics Circle Award for *Self-Portrait in a Convex Mirror* (Viking, 1975). Art critic, editor, teacher. Lives in New York City. *As We Know* (Viking, 1979).

W. H. AUDEN (b. 1927, York, England; d. 1976, Vienna, Austria) National Book Award. After Eliot, the most influential poet of the last fifty years. Became an American citizen in 1939. *Collected Poems* (Random House, 1979): *The Dyer's Hand* (Random House, 1962); *Selected Essays* (Random House, 1964); *Secondary Worlds* (Random House, 1968); *A Certain World* (Random House, 1970); *Forewords and Afterwords* (Random House, 1973). Also opera librettist, with Chester Kallman; and playwright, with Christopher Isherwood: *The Dog Beneath the Skin* (1935) and *The Ascent of F6* (1936).

BEN BELITT (b. 1911, New York City) Poet and translator, and a teacher at Bennington College for many years. *The Double Witness* (Princeton

University Press, 1978); *Adam's Dream: A Preface to Translation* (Grove Press, 1978), essays; *Five Decades (Poems 1925–70)* (Grove Press, 1974), a translation of poems by Pablo Neruda.

JOHN BERRYMAN (b. 1914, McAlester, Ok.; d. 1972, Minneapolis, Mn.) Pulitzer Prize, Bollingen Prize. Famous for *Homage to Mistress Bradstreet* (1956) and "The Dream Songs," collected in *77 Dream Songs* (Farrar, Straus and Giroux, 1964), and *His Toy, His Dream, His Rest* (Farrar, Straus and Giroux, 1968).

ELIZABETH BISHOP (b. 1911, Worcester, Ma.; d. 1979, Boston, Ma.) Pulitzer Prize, National Book Award, *Books Abroad*/Neustadt International Prize for Literature, *Collected Poems* (Farrar, Straus and Giroux, 1955) and *Geography III* (Farrar, Straus and Giroux, 1976). Translator, *The Diary of Helena Morley* (Ecco).

MORRIS BISHOP (b. 1893; d. 1973) Professor of Romance Literature at Cornell University for many years. Humorist and light-verse writer, as well as scholar and biographer. A polymath in his field, he spoke fluent German, French, Spanish, Swedish, and Greek.

PAUL BLACKBURN (b. 1926, St. Albans, Vt.; d. 1971, New York City) Associated with the Black Mountain School; known for a diction that slipped from the poetical to the prosaic in unexpected ways. Also a translator. *Collected Poems, 1949–1961* (Grossman, 1979).

ROBERT BLY (b. 1926, Madison, Mn.) National Book Award, *The Light Around the Body* (Harper & Row, 1968). Founder, Minnesota Poets Cooperative Press; publisher, *The Fifties, The Sixties, The Seventies, The Eighties* (a magazine). Lives in Minnesota. *This Tree Will Be Here for a Thousand Years* (Harper & Row, 1972).

JOHN MALCOLM BRINNIN (b. 1916, Halifax, Nova Scotia) Taught at Boston University. *Skin-Diving in the Virgins* (Delacorte Press, 1970). Also author of prose works, *Dylan Thomas in America*, a memoir; *The Third Rose: Gertrude Stein and her World*, a critical biography; and *The Sway of the Grand Saloon*, a historical and social study of the ocean liner. He is currently working on a biography of Robert Lowell.

NICHOLAS CHRISTOPHER (b. 1951, New York City). Studied at Harvard. Regular contributor to *The New Yorker*. Working on a first book of poems and a novel. Lives in New York City.

ALFRED CORN (b. 1943, Georgia) Teaches at Yale University. *A Call in the Midst of the Crowd* (Viking, 1978).

GREGORY CORSO (b. 1930, New York City) One of the founders of the Beat Movement. *Elegiac Feelings American* (New Directions, 1970).

HART CRANE (b. 1899, Garretsville, Oh.; d. 1933, en route to New York from Mexico) Visionary poet who pursued an "ecstatic goal" in poetry and later committed suicide. *The Complete Poems and Selected Letters and Prose* (Liveright, 1966).

VICTOR HERNANDEZ CRUZ (b. 1949, Puerto Rico) Came to New York at the age of four and grew up in Spanish Harlem. *Snaps* (1968).

E. E. CUMMINGS (b. 1884, Cambridge, Ma.; d. 1962, New York City) National Book Award, Bollingen Prize. Known for poems that used unconventional syntax, punctuation and typography to achieve their (often lyrical) effects. A forerunner of Charles Olson's "composition of field" poems and "concrete" poetry. Also a novelist, playwright, photographer, and painter. *Complete Poems, 1913–1962* (Harcourt Brace Jovanovich, 1975).

MADELINE DEFREES (b. 1919, Oregon) Formerly a Catholic nun; teaches at University of Montana. *When Sky Lets Go* (Braziller, 1978).

EDWIN DENBY (b. 1903, Tientsin, China) Eminent dance critic. *Collected Poems* (Full Court Press). *Dancers Buildings and People in the Street* (Horizon Press, 1965).

REUEL DENNEY Former staff-member *Time Magazine* and *Fortune*. Co-author of *The Lonely Crowd*. Taught at The College, University of Chicago, Visiting Professor at University of Puerto Rico (1952), Salzburg (1955), the East-West Center, University of Hawaii (1961). *In Praise of Adam* (University of Chicago Press, 1961).

JAMES DICKEY (b. 1923, Atlanta, Ga.) National Book Award. Lives in Columbia, S.C. Also a novelist (*Deliverance*) and critic (*Babel to Byzantium*). *Poems 1957–1967* (Wesleyan University Press, 1967); *The Strength of Fields* (Doubleday, 1979).

ALAN DUGAN (b. Brooklyn, 1923) National Book Award and Pulitzer Prize. Lives on Cape Cod and in NYC. *Poems 4* (Yale Univ. Press, 1974).

RICHARD EBERHART (b. 1904, Austin, Mn.) Pulitzer Prize, Bollingen Prize. Member, American Academy and Institute of Arts and Letters. Poet-in-residence, Dartmouth College. *Collected Poems* (Oxford University Press, 1976).

FREDERICK FEIRSTEIN (b. 1940, New York City) *Survivors* (David Lewis, 1974). Also a playwright (*The Family Circle*, published in England).

IRVING FELDMAN (b. 1928, New York City) Teaches in Buffalo, New York. *New and Selected Poems* (Viking, 1979).

EDWARD FIELD (b. 1924, Brooklyn, N.Y.) Lives in New York City. *A Full Heart* (Sheep Meadow Press, 1977). Editor of *A Geography of Poets* (Bantam, 1979).

ROBERT FITZGERALD (b. 1910, Geneva, N.Y.) Translator (with Dudley Fitts) of the Greek playwrights. Boylston Professor of Rhetoric at Harvard since 1965. Spends part of each year at house in Perugia, Italy. *Spring Shade, Poems 1931–1970* (New Directions, 1971).

JEAN GARRIGUE (b. 1914, Indiana; d. 1972, Boston, Ma.) Awards from American Academy and Institute of Arts and Letters; Guggenheim Foundation, Rockefeller Foundation; Emily Clark Balch Prize from *Virginia Quarterly*. Educated University of Chicago, taught at University of Iowa. *Studies for an Actress and Other Poems* (Macmillan, 1973); *The Animal Hotel* (Eakins Press, 1966).

CYNTHIA KRAMAN GENSER (b. 1950, New York City) Lives in Los Angeles. *Taking on the Local Color* (Wesleyan, 1977); *Club 82* (Workingmans Press, 1979).

ALLEN GINSBERG (b. 1926, Newark, N.J.) National Book Award. Author of *Howl* (1956), a seminal work of the Beat Movement. Teaches at Naropa Institute in Colorado. Prominent spokesman for the counterculture. *The Fall of America* (City Lights, 1972).

NIKKI GIOVANNI (b. 1943, Knoxville, Tn.) Lives in New York City; works for *Encore* magazine. Taught black literature and poetry at Rutgers University. *The Women and the Men* (Morrow, 1975).

ANDREW GLAZE (b. 1920, Birmingham, Al.) National Hackney Award; Eunice Tietjens Award (*Poetry*). Press Officer, British Tourist Authority. Educated at Harvard and Stanford Universities. Author of four books of poems and several plays. *Trash Dragon of Shensi* (Copper Beech, Brown University, 1978).

PAUL GOODMAN (b. 1911, New York City; d. 1972) Influential essayist and spokesman for the counterculture. *Collected Poems* (Random House, 1970). A social critic as well as a poet.

HORACE GREGORY (b. 1898, Milwaukee, Wi.) Translator and critic as well as poet. Taught for many years at Sarah Lawrence College. *Collected Poems* (Holt, Rinehart, Winston, 1964).

BARBARA GUEST (b. 1920, Wilmington, North Carolina) Lives in Southampton and New York City. The author of two novels, *Moscow Mansions* (Viking, 1973) and *The Countess from Minneapolis* (Burning Deck, 1976). Her most recent book of poems is *Seeking Air* (Black Sparrow, 1977). Working on biography of H.D.

JORGE GUILLÉN (b. 1893, Spain) Grand Prix International de Poésie, 1961; first Joseph Bennett Award from *Hudson Review*, 1976. *Cántico*: first edition, 75 poems (1928); enlarged to 125 poems (1936), 270 poems (1945), and finally 334 poems (1950). Visiting professor at numerous American universities.

THOM GUNN (b. 1929, Gravesend, England) British expatriate; associated in the Fifties with the Movement. Lives in San Francisco. *Selected Poems* (Farrar, Straus and Giroux, 1979).

MARILYN HACKER (b. 1942, New York City) National Book Award, Lamont Award. *Presentation Piece* (Viking, 1974); *Separations* (Knopf, 1976).

DANIEL HALPERN (b. 1945, Syracuse, N.Y.) Editor, *Antaeus* magazine; publisher, Ecco Press. Teaches at Princeton University and in the writing program at Columbia University. *Life Among Others* (Viking, 1978).

ANTHONY HECHT (b. 1923, New York City) Pulitzer Prize. Teaches at University of Rochester. *The Venetian Vespers* (Atheneum, 1979). Critical pieces by Hecht have frequently appeared in *The Times Literary Supplement*.

JOHN HOLLANDER (b. 1929, New York City) Teaches at Yale University. *Spectral Emanations* (Atheneum, 1978); *Blue Wine* (Johns Hopkins, 1979). Other: *The Untuning of the Sky* (1961).

RICHARD HOWARD (b. 1929, Cleveland, Oh.) Pulitzer Prize, *Untitled Subjects* (Atheneum, 1969). Lives in New York City. Also an eminent translator from the French. *Misgivings* (Atheneum, 1979). A revised version of *Alone in America* (Atheneum, 1980).

BARBARA HOWES (b. 1914, New York City) Helped organize the Southern Tenant Farmers Union. *A Private Signal* (Wesleyan, 1978).

LANGSTON HUGHES (b. 1902, Joplin, Mo.; d. 1967, New York City) Member of the Twenties "Harlem Renaissance"; later known as the Poet Laureate of Harlem. *Selected Poems* (Knopf, 1959, 1970).

RICHARD HUGO (b. 1923, Seattle, Wa.) Director, Writing Program, University of Montana. *What Thou Loves Well Remains American* (W. W. Norton, 1975); *The Right Madness on Skye* (W.W. Norton, 1980).

DAVID IGNATOW (b. 1914, Brooklyn, N.Y.) Bollingen Prize. Poet-in-Residence, York College, City University of New York. *Selected Poems* (Wesleyan Univ. Press, 1975); *Tread the Dark* (Atlantic Monthly Press, 1978).

JOSEPHINE JACOBSEN (b. 1908, Coburg, Ontario) Has been a poetry consultant to the Library of Congress. Lives in Baltimore and New Hampshire. *The Shade Seller* (Doubleday, 1974) Also a short-story writer and co-author, with William R. Mueller, of *Genet and Ionesco: Playwrights of Silence* and *The Testament of Samuel Beckett*.

RANDALL JARRELL (b. 1914, Nashville, Tn.; d. 1965, Greensboro, N.C.) Perhaps the most prominent post-World War II critic and champion of poetry. *Complete Poems* (Farrar, Straus and Giroux, 1969); *Poetry and the Age* (criticism).

JUAN RAMON JIMÉNEZ (b. Andalusia, Spain; d. 1958) Nobel Prize for Literature, 1956. Influenced by the French symbolists in his youth, but his later work is notable for its simplicity. During the Spanish Civil War, he lived in the U.S. and Cuba, and finally settled in Puerto Rico. In English translation: *Juan Ramon Jiménez: Fifty Spanish Poems* (1951), *Platero and I* (1956), and *Selected Writings* (1957).

PATRICIA JONES (b. Arkansas) Co-editor-and-publisher, *Ordinary Women* (Ordinary Women Books, 1978). Publishes regularly in "little" magazines. Her literary reviews have appeared in *Dodeca* and *The American Book Review*.

ERICA JONG (b. 1942, New York City) Best-selling novelist (*Fear of Flying*). Lives in Connecticut. *At the Edge of the Body* (Holt, Rinehart & Winston, 1979).

JUNE JORDAN (b. Harlem, New York City) Poet, essayist, novelist, reviewer. Has taught at CCNY, Sarah Lawrence, Connecticut College, Yale University, and State University of New York at Stonybrook. Rockefeller Grant in Creative Writing, 1969. *Things That I Do In The Dark, Selected Poems* (Random House, 1977).

VICKIE KARP (b. 1953, New York City) Currently on the staff of *The New Yorker*, she has published poems in that magazine and also in *Esquire*, the *Paris Review*, and elsewhere.

WELDON KEES (b. 1914, Beatrice, Nb.; disappeared 1955) Also a painter, jazz pianist, composer, photographer, and documentary filmmaker. *Collected Poems* (University of Nebraska Press, 1962).

GALWAY KINNELL (b. 1927, Providence, R.I.) Lives in New York City. Currently teaching University of Hawaii. *The Book of Nightmares* (Houghton Mifflin, 1971).

STANLEY KUNITZ (b. 1905, Worcester, Ma.) Pulitzer Prize. Teaches at Columbia University. *The Poems of Stanley Kunitz 1928–1978* (Atlantic-Little, Brown, 1979).

SYDNEY LEA (b. 1942, Chestnut Hill, Pa.) Editor, *New England Review*. *Searching the Drowned Man* (University of Illinois Press).

AL LEE (b. 1938, Louisville, Ky.) Teaches in Newark N.J. *Time* (Ecco, 1974).

RIKA LESSER (b. 1953, Brooklyn, N.Y.) Poet and translator. Taught at Baruch and Yale University. A translation of poems by Rilke, *Holding Out* (Abbatoir Press), appeared in 1976, and her translation of *Guide to the Underworld* (University of Massachusetts Press), from the Swedish of Gunnar Ekelof, has just come out.

DENISE LEVERTOV (b. 1923, Ilford, Essex, England) Lives in Massachusetts. Also an essayist. *Life in the Forest* (New Directions, 1978); *The Poet in the World* (New Directions, 1973).

PHILIP LEVINE (b. 1928, Detroit, Mi.) National Book Award, National

Book Critics Circle Award. Lives in Fresno, California. *The Names of the Lost* (Atheneum, 1976); *Ashes* (Atheneum, 1979); *7 Years from Somewhere* (Atheneum, 1979).

FEDERICO GARCIA LORCA (b. 1899, Granada, Spain; d. 1936, Spain) One of the great modern poets and playwrights of Spain, killed by Franco's Civil Guard during the Spanish Civil War. Translated by many hands, including Ben Belitt and Robert Bly. *The Poet in New York*, from which the poems in this book are taken, is the product of Lorca's ten-month stay at Columbia University in 1928.

AUDRE LORD (b. 1934, New York City) Teaches at City University of New York. *Coal* (W. W. Norton, 1977).

ROBERT LOWELL (b. 1917, Boston, Ma.; d. 1977, Boston, Ma.) Pulitzer Prize, National Book Award. At the time of his death, considered to be the most prominent poet of his generation. Known for his (often revised) autobiographical and "historical" poems. *Selected Poems* (Farrar, Straus and Giroux, 1976); *Day by Day* (Farrar, Straus and Giroux, 1977).

VLADIMIR MAYAKOVSKY (b. 1893, Russia; d. 1930) Russia's most famous Futurist poet. In Russian: *A Cloud in Trousers* (1915); *The Mystery Bouffe* (1920, 1921). Plays: *The Bedbug* (1928); *The Bathhouse* (1930). In English: *Mayakovsky*, translated and edited by Herbert Marshall (Hill and Wang, 1965).

JANE MAYHALL (b. 1921, Louisville, Ky.) Published a novel, *Cousin to Human* (Harcourt, Brace, 1960); and a book of satires, *Ready for the Ha-Ha* (Eakins Press, 1966); and two books of poems, *Givers and Takers* 1 and 2 (Eakins Press, 1969, 1974). Lives in New York City.

CYNTHIA MACDONALD (b. 1929, New York City) Co-Chairperson of the Writing Program at the University of Houston, Texas. *(W)holes* (Knopf, 1980).

HERMAN MELVILLE (b. 1819, Boston, Ma.; d. 1891, New York City) Nineteenth-century novelist, author of *Moby Dick*.

WILLIAM MEREDITH (b. 1919, New York City) Teaches at Connecticut College. *Earth Walk: New and Selected Poems* (Knopf, 1970). Poetry consultant to the Library of Congress.

JAMES MERRILL (b. 1926, New York City) Pulitzer Prize, National Book Award, Bollingen Prize. Lives in Stonington, Connecticut and Athens,

Greece. Also a novelist and playwright. *Scripts for the Pageant* (Atheneum, 1980).

W. S. MERWIN (b. 1927, New York City) Pulitzer Prize. Divides his time between New York City and various parts of the world. Also a translator and prose fabulist. *The Compass Flower* (Atheneum 1977).

SARA MILES (b. 1952, New York City) Editor of the anthology, *Ordinary Women*, and the *NYC Poetry Calendar*. Her poems have appeared in numerous magazines, including *Ms.* and *The New Republic*.

MARIANNE MOORE (b. 1887, Kirkwood, Mo.; d. 1972, New York City) Contemporary of and admired by T. S. Eliot, Ezra Pound, Wallace Stevens, and William Carlos Williams; considered an influence by many post-World War II poets. Known for her almost scientific precision of language, attention to detail, and economy of statement. *Complete Poems* (Viking, 1967).

FREDERICK MORGAN (b. 1922, New York City) Co-founder of *The Hudson Review* in 1948. *Death Mother and Other Poems* (University of Illinois Press, 1979).

JOHN N. MORRIS (b. 1931, Oxford, England) Teaches at Washington University in Missouri. *The Life Beside This One* (Atheneum, 1975); *The Glass Houses* (Atheneum, 1980).

HOWARD MOSS (b. 1922, New York City) National Book Award, 1972. Lives in New York City. Poetry editor, *The New Yorker. Selected Poems* (Atheneum, 1972); *Notes from the Castle* (Atheneum, 1979); *The Magic Lantern of Marcel Proust* (Godine, 1979); *Two Plays* (Flying Point Press, 1980).

STANLEY MOSS (b. 1925, New York City) Art dealer; publisher, Sheep Meadow Press. Lives in New York City. *Skull of Adam* (Horizon, 1978).

HOWARD NEMEROV (b. 1920, New York City) National Book Award. Teaches at Washington University in Missouri. *Collected Poems* (University of Chicago Press, 1978).

FRANK O'HARA (b. 1926, Baltimore, Md.; d. 1966, New York City) Considered by many to be *the* poet of New York for his generation. His work became widely known only after his accidental death on Fire Island. *Collected Poems* (Knopf, 1971); *Early Poems* and *Poems Retrieved* (City Lights, 1977).

LINDA PASTAN. Lives in Potomac, Maryland. *Aspects of Eve* (Liveright, 1975).

ROBERT PHILLIPS (b. 1938, Delaware) Poet and editor. *The Pregnant Man* (Doubleday, 1978). Also admired for a short-story collection, *The Land of Lost Content* (1970). Editor, *Aspects of Alice* (1971), a collection of critical essays on *Alice in Wonderland,* and *Moonstruck: An Anthology of Lunar Poetry* (1974).

PEDRO PIETRI (b. ?) Puerto Rican poet living in New York, a member of the Nuyorican School of Poets.

MIGUEL PIÑERO (b. 1946, Gurabo, Puerto Rico) New York Drama Critics Circle Award, Obie (Off-Broadway award). Self-educated, prize-winning poet and playwright. Member of the Nuyorican School of Poets.

KENNETH PITCHFORD (b. 1931, Moorehead, Mn.) Lives in New York City. *The Contraband Poems* (Templar Press, 1976). Also a novel (*The Brothers*) and a play (*In Another Tree*).

STANLEY PLUMLY (b. 1939, Barnesville, Oh) Co-Chairperson of the Creative Writing Program at the University of Houston. His last book of poems, *Out-of-the-Body Travel* (Ecco, 1976), was nominated for a National Book Critics Circle Award.

RALPH POMEROY (b. 1926, Evanston, Il.) Art critic/curator and free-lance writer. Lives in New York City. *In the Financial District* (Macmillan, 1968).

EZRA POUND (b. 1885, Hailey, Id.; d. 1972, Italy) Bollingen Prize. Famous expatriate; leader of the Imagist Movement. Institutionalized at St. Elizabeth's Hospital in Washington, D.C. in 1946 after being found unfit to stand trial for treason for his activities during World War II; the charge was dropped in 1958 and he returned to Italy. *The Cantos* (New Directions, 1976); *Collected Early Poems* (New Directions, 1976).

ALASTAIR REID (b. 1926, Scotland) Lives in New York City and Majorca. On the staff of *The New Yorker*. *Weathering* (Dutton, 1979).

JAMES REISS (b. 1941, New York City) Teaches at Miami University in Ohio. Also a poetry critic for the *Cleveland Plain Dealer*. *The Breathers* (Ecco, 1974).

DONALD REVELL (b. 1954, Bronx, N.Y.) Lives in an old horse farm just outside of Williamsville, New York. *The Broken Juke* (Iris Press, 1975).

CHARLES REZNIKOFF (b. 1894, Brooklyn, N.Y.) Trained as a lawyer, he gave up the legal profession to become a writer. *By the Waters of Manhattan* (New Directions, 1962).

ADRIENNE RICH (b. 1929, Baltimore, Md.) National Book Award. Prominent feminist. Lives in New York City. *Poems: Selected and New, 1950–1974* (W. W. Norton, 1975); *The Dream of a Common Language* (W. W. Norton, 1978); *On Lies, Secrets, and Silence: Selected Prose 1966–1978* (W. W. Norton, 1979).

MURIEL RUKEYSER (b. 1913, New York City; d. 1980, New York City) Member, American Academy and Institute of Arts and Letters. *The Gates* (McGraw-Hill, 1976). Also author of biographical studies of Willard Gibbs, the scientist, and Wendell Wilkie, the political aspirant; as well as several short stories and a novel, *The Orgy.*

CARL SANDBURG (b. 1878; d. 1967) Pulitzer Prize for his monumental biography of Abraham Lincoln. First known for his "Chicago poems." Prided himself on writing "simple poems for simple people." *Complete Poems* (Harcourt Brace Jovanovich, 1950, 1969).

PHILIP SCHULTZ (b. Rochester, N.Y.) Nation-WMHA Discovery Award, 1976. Teaches at N.Y.U. *Like Wings* (Viking, 1978).

JAMES SCHUYLER (b. 1923, Chicago, Il.) Art critic and novelist. Lives in New York City. *The Morning of the Poem* (Farrar, Straus and Giroux, 1980).

DELMORE SCHWARTZ (b. 1913, Brooklyn, N.Y.; d. 1966, New York City) Bollingen Prize. *Selected Poems: Summer Knowledge* (New Directions, 1959).

JAMES SCULLY (b. 1937, New Haven, Ct.) Lamont Award, *The Marches* (Holt, Rinehart & Winston, 1967). *Avenue of the Americas* (University of Massachusetts Press, 1971); editor of *Modern Poetics* (1965) and *Modern Poets on Modern Poetry* (1966).

LEOPOLD SEDAR SENGHOR (b. 1906, Joal, Senegal) President of the Republic of Senegal and considered the leading poet of French-speaking

Africa. *Songs of Darkness, Black Host,* and *Ethiopics* (1965). The most recently translated of his books is *Nocturnes* (The Third Press, New York, 1971), translated by John Reed and Clive Wake, with an introduction by Paulette J. Trout.

ANNE SEXTON (b. 1928, Newton, Ma.; d. 1975, Boston, Ma.) Pulitzer Prize. Popular "confessional" poet. *The Awful Rowing Toward God* (Houghton Mifflin, 1975).

HARVEY SHAPIRO (b. 1924, Chicago, Il.) Editor of *The New York Times. Lauds and Night Sounds* (Sun, 1978).

JUDITH JOHNSON SHERWIN (b. 1936, New York City) Ex-president, Poetry Society of America. *Transparencies* (Countryman Press, 1978).

CHARLES SIEBERT (b. 1954, Brooklyn, N.Y.) Siebert grew up in Ossining, N.Y. and is currently a student in the Program in Creative Writing at the University of Houston. He is working on his first book of poems. "City Butterfly" in this anthology is his first published poem.

CHARLES SIMIC (b. 1938, Yugoslavia) Teaches at the University of New Hampshire. *Charon's Cosmology* (Braziller, 1977).

LOUIS SIMPSON (b. 1923, Jamaica, W.I.) Pulitzer Prize. Teaches at the State University of New York at Stony Brook. *Searching for the Ox* (Morrow, 1976).

L. E. SISSMAN (b. 1928, Detroit, Mi.; d. 1974, Boston, Ma.) Brilliant late-blossomer, poet and essayist. Did many book reviews for *The New Yorker*, where a great many of his poems first appeared. *Hello, Darkness* (Little, Brown, 1978); *Innocent Bystander: The Scene from the 70's* (1975), essays.

DAVE SMITH (b. 1942, Portsmouth, Va.) Creative Writing Award from American Academy and Institute of Arts and Letters, 1979. *Cumberland Station* (University of Illinois Press, 1977); *Goshawk, Antelope* (University of Illinois Press, 1979). Two books of new poems are in the works: *Homage to Edgar Allan Poe* (Louisiana State University Press, 1981) and *Crabflight* (University of Illinois Press, 1981).

GERALD STERN. Lamont Award, *Lucky Life* (Houghton Mifflin, 1977) Stern comes from Pittsburgh and has taught at numerous colleges, including Temple University. He lives with his family in Raubsville, Pa.

WALLACE STEVENS (b. 1879, Reading, Pa.; d. 1955, Hartford, Ct.) Pulitzer Prize, National Book Award, Bollingen Prize. Generally regarded as one of the leading forces in American poetry during the first part of this century. Also an executive of the Hartford Accident and Insurance Company. *Collected Poems* (Knopf, 1954); *Opus Posthumous* (Knopf, 1957).

PAMELA STEWART (b. Feb. 3, 1946, Boston, Ma.) Teaches at Arizona State University and the Women's Facility of the Arizona State Prison. *The St. Vlas Elegies* (L'Epervier Press, 1977); *Half-Tones* (Maguey Press, 1978); *Cascades* (L'Epervier Press, 1979).

TERRY STOKES (b. 1943, Flushing, N.Y.) *Boning the Dreamer* (Knopf, 1975).

MARK STRAND (b. 1934, Summerside, Prince Edward Island) Lives in New York City. *The Late Hour* (Atheneum, 1978).

JON SWAN (b. Sioux City, Ia.) Formerly on the staff of *The New Yorker*. Also a playwright (*Three Plays*), translator, free-lance writer, and editor. *Journeys and Returns* (Scribners, 1960); *A Door to the Forest* (Random House, 1979).

MAY SWENSON (b. 1919, Logan, Ut.) Lives on Long Island. *Things Taking Place: New and Selected Poems* (Atlantic-Little, Brown, 1978).

ALLEN TATE (b. 1899, Winchester, Ky.; d. 1979) Editor and critic; considered by many to have been the most influential spokesman for the Southern literary tradition. *Collected Poems, 1919–1976* (Scribners, 1977).

JEAN VALENTINE. *Dream Barker* (1965) won the Yale Series of Younger Poets Award. *Pilgrims* (Farrar, Straus and Giroux, 1969).

ANDREI VOZNESENSKY (b. 1933, Moscow) One of Russia's best-known contemporary poets. In translation: *Antiworlds* (Basic Books, 1966, with a foreword by W. H. Auden).

JOHN WAIN (b. 1925, England) Somerset Maugham Award. Author of books of poetry, criticism, short stories, five novels, and an autobiography, *Sprightly Running* (St. Martin's Press, 1962). *Weep Before God* (St. Martin's Press, 1961).

DEREK WALCOTT (b. 1930, St. Lucia, B.W.I.) Generally regarded as the finest Caribbean poet writing in English. Also a playwright. *Selected Poems* (Farrar, Straus and Giroux, 1964); *Another Life* (Farrar, Straus and Giroux, 1972); *Sea Grapes* (Farrar, Straus and Giroux, 1976); *The Star-Apple Kingdom* (Farrar, Straus and Giroux, 1979).

ROBERT PENN WARREN (b. 1905, Guthrie, Ky.) Pulitzer Prizes for fiction and for poetry. Professor Emeritus of English at Yale University. *Selected Poems: 1923–1976* (Random House, 1976).

ROBERT WATSON (b. Passaic, N.J.) Professor of English at the University of North Carolina at Greensboro. *Selected Poems* (Atheneum, 1977).

JOHN HALL WHEELOCK (b. 1886, East Hampton, N.Y.; d. 1978, New York City. A distinguished poet and man of letters whose life spanned a crucial dividing line between nineteenth-century and modern poetry. An editor for many years at Scribners, he encouraged and published the work of many young poets, including James Dickey and Louis Simpson. He may have been the last great "gentleman" editor, and a poet whose work, though traditional, continued to win him new readers throughout his long life. He is associated with "Bonac," a district on Long Island where he made his summer home in a house his father had originally built. *The Blessed Earth: New and Selected Poems, 1927–1977* (Scribners, 1979).

CLAIRE NICHOLAS WHITE (b. 1925, the Netherlands) Lives on Long Island and is a Poet-in-the-Schools. *Biography and Other Poems* will be published in 1980 by Doubleday. She is also the author of a novel, *The Death of the Orange Trees* (Harper and Row, 1963), and of several plays and libretti.

WALT WHITMAN (b. 1889, Huntington, N.Y.; d. 1892, Camden, N.J.) The author of *Leaves of Grass*.

REED WHITTEMORE (b. 1919, New Haven, Ct.) Teaches at the University of Maryland. *The Mother's Breast and the Father's House* (Houghton Mifflin, 1974).

MILLER WILLIAMS (b. 1930, Hoxie, Ark.) Teaches at the University of Arkansas and Arkansas State Penitentiary. *Why God Permits Evil* (Dutton, 1974).

WILLIAM CARLOS WILLIAMS (b. 1883, Rutherford, N.J.; d. 1963, Rutherford, N.J.) Pulitzer Prize, National Book Award, Bollingen Prize.

NEW YORK:

Author of the epic poem *Paterson* (1976); a major promoter of and influence on post-World War II poets. Also a doctor and critic. *Collected Earlier Poems* (New Directions, 1951); *Collected Later Poems* (New Directions, 1954); *Pictures from Breughel* (New Directions, 1962).

JAMES WRIGHT (b. 1927, Martin's Ferry, Oh.; d. 1980, New York City. Pulitzer Prize. Member, American Academy and Institute of Arts and Letters. Taught at Hunter College in New York City. *Collected Poems* (Wesleyan, 1971); *To a Blossoming Pear Tree* (Farrar, Straus and Giroux, 1977).

PAUL ZWEIG (b. 1941, Brooklyn, N.Y.) Teaches English at M.I.T. *Against Emptiness* (Harper and Row, 1971). Also the author of *The Heresy of Self-Love* and *Lautreaumont: The Violence of Narcissus*; and the editor of *Selected Poems of Yvon Goll*.